T0330191

Is Economics an Evolutionary Science?

EUROPEAN ASSOCIATION FOR EVOLUTIONARY POLITICAL ECONOMY

General Editor: Geoffrey M. Hodgson, *University of Hertfordshire Business School, UK*

Mixed Economies in Europe: An Evolutionary Perspective on their Emergence, Transition and Regulation
Edited by Wolfgang Blaas and John Foster

The Political Economy of Diversity: Evolutionary Perspectives on Economic Order and Disorder
Edited by Robert Delorme and Kurt Dopfer

On Economic Institutions: Theory and Applications
Edited by John Groenewegen, Christos Pitelis and Sven-Erik Sjöstrand

Rethinking Economics: Markets, Technology and Economic Evolution
Edited by Geoffrey M. Hodgson and Ernesto Screpanti

Environment, Technology and Economic Growth: The Challenge to Sustainable Development
Edited by Andrew Tylecote and Jan van der Straaten

Institutions and Economic Change: New Perspectives on Markets, Firms and Technology
Edited by Klaus Nielsen and Björn Johnson

Pluralism in Economics: New Perspectives in History and Methodology
Edited by Andrea Salanti and Ernesto Screpanti

Beyond Market and Hierarchy: Interactive Governance and Social Complexity
Edited by Ash Amin and Jerzy Hausner

Employment, Technology and Economic Needs: Theory, Evidence and Public Policy
Edited by Jonathan Michie and Angelo Reati

Institutions and the Evolution of Capitalism: Implications of Evolutionary Economics
Edited by John Groenewegen and Jack Vromen

Is Economics an Evolutionary Science?
The Legacy of Thorstein Veblen
Edited by Francisco Louçã and Mark Perlman

Technology and Knowledge: From the Firm to Innovation Systems
Edited by Pier Paolo Saviotti and Bart Nooteboom

Is Economics an Evolutionary Science?

The Legacy of Thorstein Veblen

Edited by

Francisco Louçã

*Professor of Economics,
ISEG, Technical University of Lisbon,
Portugal*

Mark Perlman

*Professor of Economics, Emeritus,
University of Pittsburgh,
USA*

European Association for Evolutionary Political Economy

Edward Elgar
Cheltenham, UK • Northampton, MA, USA

Published by
Edward Elgar Publishing Limited
Glensanda House
Montpellier Parade
Cheltenham
Glos GL50 1UA
UK

Edward Elgar Publishing, Inc.
136 West Street
Suite 202
Northampton
Massachusetts 01060
USA

A catalogue record for this book
is available from the British Library

Library of Congress Cataloguing in Publication Data

Is economics an evolutionary science? : the legacy of Thorstein Veblen / edited by Francisco Louçã and Mark Perlman.
    'In association with the European Association for Evolutionary Political Economy.'
    1. Evolutionary economics. 2. Veblen, Thorstein, 1857–1929. I. Title: Legacy of Thorstein Veblen. II. Louçã, Francisco. III. Perlman, Mark. IV. European Association for Evolutionary Political Economy.

HB97.3.18 2000
330'.092—dc21   99–089246

ISBN 1 84064 195 9

Contents

List of Figures

List of Tables

Contributors

Laure Bazzoli, University of Lumière, Lyon, France

Marco Crocco, Federal University of Minas Gerais, Brazil;
University College, UK

Alan W. Dyer, Northeastern University, Massachusetts, USA

Frank Hahn, University of Siena, Italy

Albert Jolink, Erasmus University of Rotterdam,
The Netherlands

Francisco Louçã (Editor), Technical University of Lisbon,
Portugal

Anne Mayhew, Buckwell University, Pennsylvania, USA

J.S. Metcalfe, University of Manchester, UK

Phillip A. O'Hara, Curtin University of Technology, Australia

Eyüp Özveren, Middle East Technical University, Ankara,
Turkey

Ugo Pagano, University of Siena, Italy

Mark Perlman (Editor), University of Pittsburgh, USA

James R. Stanfield, Colorado State University, USA

Jaqueline B. Stanfield, Colorado State University, USA

Introduction

1. Introduction

Francisco Louçã and Mark Perlman[1]

The 13 papers in this collection were initially presented at the 1998 meeting of the European Association for Evolutionary Political Economy, held in Lisbon between the 5th and 8th of November. They were chosen as representative of the several score papers read. The centennial of the publication of Thorstein Veblen's seminal essay, 'Why economics is not an evolutionary science', offered a chance to reconsider that essay's message and impact. But the meeting, as such things usually do, offered more. Besides the opportunity to assess how much of Veblenism is alive, it offered essays dealing with the contemporary scene, in which there is an ever-growing interest in economic dynamics.

We have divided this volume into an introduction and three parts. The eight essays in Part 1 deals with Veblen's challenge. The four essays in Part 2 reconsider that challenge in the face of work done by other seminal writers. And the final essay offers a perspective of the current scene.

One purpose of this volume is to introduce economists to the legacies of Veblen and several other institutionalists. A good point of departure is to ask what separated institutionalism from the conventional focus on abstract costs and abstract prices. There were several variations on the institutionalist side, but all of them tended to present theories derived from empirical observations. Veblen was a self-conscious institutionalist, but unlike John R. Commons he did not try to synthesise institutionalism. Nor was he like his student, Wesley Clair Mitchell, a quantitative methodologist. Rather, Veblen chose to be a continuous critic of the self-satisfaction of the abstractionists.

The latter half of the nineteenth century was an era in which the discipline of biology had made great strides. Much of the progress at the time was associated with Charles Darwin's *The Origin of Species*. Of course there was much later work done on the Darwin thesis; one question is how much of that later work was Veblen aware of. Veblen was clearly aware that most contemporary economists believed that the paradigms of solid-state physics were those that their discipline ought to emulate. In his 1898 essay he argued that until economists changed their paradigm to biology, the discipline would make little or no scientific progress.

The economics profession in the 1890s was small. Among those who wrote, everyone seemed to know everyone else. In such circumstances writing often became essentially personal. Veblen, a rebel by background, inclination, and training, came to his heterodox views in a very personal way. His college teacher was John Bates Clark (the originator of marginal product analysis) who served not only as Veblen's mentor but as the foil for Veblen's views. Veblen's views thus were antagonistic to what he had been taught. He was contemptuous of most of the leading economists of his day. He was articulate and thrust his views 'in the raw' rather than presenting them persuasively. And he cared little that he appeared ridiculous to the tradition-minded; indeed he revelled in that fact.

INSTITUTIONALISM

Our line of argument suggests that all of the first generation institutionalists seemed to prefer long term analysis. That separated them from the mainline economists, who drew their inspiration from the first five books of Alfred Marshall's 1890 and following *Principles*, that mostly emphasised short term analysis.

But the keystone of institutional economics involves something beyond studying static prices and static costs. It involves trying to understand how and why not only prices and costs change but also what are the other inputs that destabilise price and cost relationships. Static economics deals with being; evolutionary economics deals with becoming

STATIC AND DYNAMICS

In the order of things it is easier to conceptualise being than becoming. 'How does the firm or the household make the wisest decisions regarding the allocation of resources at a point in time' is what has fascinated most economists. They ask, 'what is the array of inputs, why are they chosen, how are they combined, how are they sold, and what is the expected profit.' As often happens, the earliest expositor of this approach was likely one of the best. Richard Cantillon's *Essai sur la Nature de Commerce en Général*, probably written around 1720, describes with considerable insight how an entrepreneur with known costs faces the market with uncertain prices. Cantillon, among history's most perceptive economists, wrote of a static situation, a situation in being. The great mercantilist literature of the seventeenth and eighteenth centuries reveals how merchants (or their penmen) thought public policy should be shaped in order to strengthen trading, the merchants' (or in the case of cameralists, the civil service's) public control, or even the power of the secular state. For the most part their penman wrote of possible solutions to static problems.

What about the other case, becoming, with situations continually changing? How do they change? Do they move from one static situation to another with an abrupt shift - what the mathematicians call a witch or some other kind of discontinuity? An abrupt shift from one static situation to another is not perceived as evolution; rather such analysis is comparative statics and does not explain either the 'why' or the 'how' behind the shift.

Why do they change? Can the process of evolution be explained so that observers can see the impact of new and different inputs into the process? Are there elements that are necessary but not sufficient (even elements that are catalysts); situations that are sufficient but not necessary? Is there an apt biological analogy that applies to decision-making units? Veblen thought Yes. Others have been more doubtful. What many draw from the biological analogy is no more than the realisation that equilibrium is unstable. But the reverse of that central point is what others have found so attractive. Do economies naturally move towards disequilibria or towards equilibrium?

Here there is also a methodological division. Empiricists studied specific changes in order to generalise their natures - that is to arrive at stable generalisations. What delayed success was mathematical inadequacy. But with the advent of recent breakthroughs like linear programming, turnpike theorems, and chaos theory, modelling may be possible, albeit still difficult. This development, alone (if successful) may lead the larger profession to a new era of abstract modelling, an era when models can prove to be shortcuts to full understanding.

THE ESSAYS

Veblen's Challenge

What interests Professor Perlman in his 'Mind-sets and why Veblen was Ineffectual', is why the economics profession has always turned a blind eye towards Veblen's writings. Three reasons stand out: the first is that Veblen thought that cellular biology and mutations were a better template than physics and tendencies towards equilibrium, but Alfred Marshall, also, referred to the advantages of biology and mutation over physics and equilibrium. But having done so, like Veblen, he dropped the topic. Neither he nor Veblen provided the necessary leadership, perhaps because the biology of their time was more a metaphor than a template. What the profession, conscious of its own intellectual dependence, wanted was a tight, properly closed logical, system like the first five books of Marshall's *Principles*. Veblen's writings, and particularly the 1898 essay, defied the existence of a closed system.

The second conclusion comes from the first. Veblen was a destructive critic; he offered some empirical, some theoretical, and some rhetorical criticisms but he proposed no demonstrations either through learning experiences or the testing of explicit solutions. Further, Alfred Marshall had little or no patience in distinguishing between commerce and industry, a point which was bedrock of Veblen's thinking. Marshall's game in his *Principles* was intellectually coherent; even more than that it was a closed system. And such a system was easily graspable. Veblen suggested instead that system closure was, itself, intellectually disastrous. Had Veblen been asked where the critical difference was, he would have said that closed systems were no more than intellectuals' playthings.

Perlman's third point is the problem of persuasion, properly called methodology. After identifying several different methods used to persuade most people, Perlman concludes that Veblen seemed to be indifferent to the economics profession's evaluation of his work. He scorned most of its members and did not care about having a systemic impact. Of the three early first-generation institutionalists only John R. Commons tried to synthesise his system; from the standpoint of success it was generally unsuccessful.

O'Hara's 'The Contemporary Relevance of Thorstein Veblen's Institutional-Evolutionary Economics', presents possibly an alternative or a supplementary interpretation. Addressing the question of Veblen's current relevance and quoting approvingly a 1932-33 article by Karl L. Anderson, O'Hara argues that one can find a coherent system built on instincts, institutions, and 'slow but continual change'. The essay then turns to three essential topics: (1) Instincts, habits and the individual-social nexus; (2) Invidious and non-invidious institutions; and, (3) Evolution through cumulative causation. By pursuing each of these elements O'Hara believes as with Karl J. Anderson that one can create a comprehensive theoretical system. Additionally, O'Hara finds evidence that there is a new surge of interest in Veblen's legacies, particularly if one seeks those who accept this integrated Veblenian system. O'Hara's position is that many current (1998) writers have rediscovered the system; in that sense he suggests that the Veblen legacy is still active.

'Thorstein Veblen and the Political Economy of the Ordinary: Hope and Despair', by Alan W. Dyer is an examination of the ambivalence of those who hold title in their possessions. Of particular concern is the nexus between a title to property and the culture surrounding that title. Underlying

Dyer's emphasis on the common meaning of words, he believes that Veblen's choice of words means something to those who use them freely: 'Commerce is ultimately about hunches, one-up manship, capturing markets ... Industry is ultimately about cause and effect, integrated work processes, and meeting the material needs of society' (Dyer, pp. 51). Just as the style of his clothes may make the man, so the choice of words may make the society. The essay is an integration of the Veblen legacy with the contributions of J.L. Austin, Ludwig Wittgenstein, Stanley Cavell, and others.

In her essay, 'Veblen and Theories of the "Firm"', Anne Mayhew contrasts Veblen's Gestalt with long run theories developed in more recent years by such recent comparable theories as presented by Edith Penrose, Richard R. Nelson and Sidney Winter, and Oliver Williamson. For Veblen the 'firm' was a general concept, not simply and amalgam of some empirical observations. Veblen's firm was an abstraction not limited to a single production unit; rather, it stood for a system of social organisation. The modern writers, she avers, perceive the firm within a fixed system; Veblen's firm, by way of contrast, was an appropriate abstraction for an open-ended social process. Quite apart from Veblen's wider perception of the firm as a guide to business cum social activity, is the point that Veblen's concept was too general to permit a derivative principle of agency, something requiring full specification. The author believes that with a renaissance of interest in Veblen's more open system, modern theorists of the firm may abandon their previous shackles.

Laure Bazzoli's essay, 'Institutional Economics and the Specificity of Social Evolution: About the Contribution of J.R. Commons', while admitting many similarities between Veblen and Commons, stresses *inter alia* their methodological differences. For Veblen institutions could be desirable or undesirable, but as with Hayek's more recent view, good or bad they were thrust up by the exchange system itself. Commons, fully experienced in drafting public utility and labour legislation, held something of an opposing position when he argued that institutional development could be intentionally designed, particularly by governments.

Generally Veblen, Mitchell, and Commons are identified as the first generation of Institutionalists. Who were their successors? James Ronald and Jacqueline Bloom Stanfield present a paper on Clarence Ayres as Veblen's principal intellectual heir. In a career that also involved a stint at Wisconsin (where he seems to have ignored Commons's group), Ayers landed in the autumn of 1930 at the University of Texas in Austin for a one-year professorship. The following year he became tenured. The authors date the Veblen-Ayres-Institutionalist School from 1930. He remained at Texas until 1968; he died in 1971. Just as Veblen saw the key economic distinction between commerce and industry as crucial to understanding economic development, so Ayers saw the distinction between ceremonial and technological institutional changes as the way to begin relevant analyses. So much for a hint of his intellectual product. What was equally impressive was his quality as an intellectual leader. St. Paul, we are told, popularised Jesus; Pigou was the one who made Marshall's *Principles* canon, and it is fair to state that Ayers kept Veblen's name alive in the profession. Both Mitchell and Commons - the other two first generation Institutionalists, also had their successors, but none succeeded as well as Ayers. However, it is unfair to perceive Ayers only as Veblen's heir. Far from it, Ayers offered a 'Texas exhuberance' to the biting quality of Veblen's thinking. Or to put the matter in a way mentioned earlier in this Introduction, Ayers was concerned with effective rhetoric, and he managed to persuade a great many students who might otherwise have ignored the Veblen heterodoxy, of the importance of missionary activity.

Ugo Pagano's paper, 'Bounded Rationality, Institutionalism and the Diversity of Economic Institutions', offers a retrospective view of Veblenian institutionalism. Noting that in many respects Veblen's theory and the New Institutional Economics lie at different poles, he suggests that the original Veblenian theory can be considered as an early 'strong version' of the theory of bounded rationality. The New Institutional Economics 'mild version of bounded rationality' extends economising behaviour to bounded rationality itself. Moreover, while New Institutional Analysis emphasises efficiency explanations based on the assumption of given preferences, the Veblenian explanation considers the role of inefficient path-dependent behaviour due to the endogenous formation and resilience to change of the preferences of the individual. Both approaches share an undesirable feature; the idea of 'unilinear' unfolding of a history does not allow an adequate understanding of the diversity of paths taken by different societies. In this respect the comparative analysis of institutions must go beyond both approaches.

Professor Frank Hahn uses Veblen's 1898 title, 'Is Economics an Evolutionary Science?' as a thematic question. He opens the essay by surveying several main-line writers and finds that they have wrestled over the decades with just this question - and have given different answers that suggest that some evolution has taken place. From this standpoint he finds that economics is not a science, and its development is not evolutionary. Such evolution as may be found is circumstantial, not systemic. He then turns to another query, 'Would economics be better had it focused not on profits (the maximisation of which assures one way of survival) but on other factors.' Here there is an interesting digression - biology offers an 'understanding theory', not a predictive one. Hahn believes that one difference between biologists and economists adapting an evolutionary approach is that the former have no teleological sense while evolutionary economists seem invariably to offer one. Hahn, certainly considered amongst the most sophisticated mainstream theorists of our time, believes that in the end what seems to count most is profit-maximisation as conditions change.

The Challenge Reconsidered

Albert Jolink takes up the question of market-failure and free market efficiency under wartime conditions. This analysis is part of the Calculation debate involving Pierson, Barone, Mises, Lange, and Lerner. In 1939 Friedrich Hayek had argued against a British wartime policy of a central administration of goods and services. The Hayek claim was that free markets could use pricing to do the job better. Tjalling Koopmans, writing after World War II, argued, in contrast to Hayek's pre-war position, that war tends to make markets even more imperfect than they are in peacetime. Moreover, differing from the Lange approach of comparative marginal pricing, Koopmans suggests that new electronic equipment makes full (not, as with Lange, marginal) central calculations feasible.

Francisco Louçã presents an unpublished model formulated in 1935 by Ragnar Frisch in discussion with Jan Tinbergen and Tjalling Koopmans. These authors were not part of the evolutionist tradition, neither did they discuss it in any great detail. But their model and 1935 debate is certainly part of the quest for a viable explanation of changes through time, of adjustment processes and of coordination under a capitalistic economy. The exploration of the model suggests furthermore that many different regimes were possible according to the specification of the parameters and initial conditions, i.e. according to the concrete history of the system. In other words, even in the framework of the most conventional macroeconometric approach there were, already in the thirties, hunches of the emergence of new properties and structures.

The focus in the next essay, 'An Institutionalist Foundation for Development Studies: Re-thinking Polanyi and Veblen on the *Sonderweg*', by Eyüp Özveren, is the use of evolutionary principles in the study of economic development. The question resolves around the concept of *Sonderweg*, translated as a unique route or way. In short, is there a single 'royal' road to economic development, or do underlying cultural and historical events dominate so as to deny the existence of any such pass-key? *Sonderweg* was at the heart of the German Historical School, developed by those who truly believed that the history of British industrialisation was not a template for other countries' potential transformation. Generally it has been held that the First British Industrial Revolution developed concomitantly with the political emancipation of workers. Karl Polanyi's 1944 *The Great Transformation* not only argued that the English experience of free market development was unique, but in historical terms full political emancipation was limited and the dominance of the concept of the free market lasted but a few years. Political emancipation, he believed, was not related to industrialization in any one-to-one basis. Veblen, also having been influenced by the writers of the German Historical School, saw no contradiction between the co-existence of efficient economic development and centralised imperial growth.

The task in Marco Crocco's paper, 'The Future's Unknowability: Keynes's Probability, Probable Knowledge and the Decision to Innovate', is to relate some of the best ideas of two old rivals, John Maynard Keynes and Joseph A. Schumpeter. A basic Keynesian idea, going back to his 1921 *Treatise on Probability*, involves the individual coping with uncertainty (particularly of the G.L.S. Shackle 'unknowledge' type). Keynes thought that individual decisions are made according to epistemic (essentially subjective) preferences, and that only those with the best imaginative ideas - those who forecast the future most accurately - tend to succeed. A basic 1912 Schumpeterian motif is the claim that among the greatest disequilibrating economic forces are innovations coming from the minds of imaginative individuals. Crocco implies that Polanyi has done no more than apply the Veblen theoretical formulation. And modern Schumpeterians (he calls them Neo-Schumpeterians) would do well to incorporate Keynes's idea of uncertainty into their models.

Perspectives

J.S. Metcalfe's essay, 'Institutions, Increasing Returns and Endogenous Growth', also turns to the usefulness of a theory of economic evolution to explain economic growth. His argument is that such theory offers an explanation for a varying willingness to accept innovation and the power, both positive and negative, of varying economic and political institutions. His argument, using diagrams as well as algebra, is formally developed. In this sense he offers to those schooled only in the mainline non-institutionalist rhetorical tradition a bridge to the institutional rhetoric. And this is precisely the task that Veblen ignored.

NOTES

1. We wish to thank Loes van Dijk, Sandro Mendonça and the rest of the team at ISEG (Faculty of Economics and Management), Technical University of Lisbon, whose administrative contributions made the Lisbon meeting so pleasant. We wish also to acknowledge the editorial contributions of Charles R. McCann, Jr., and the work in the preparation of the final manuscript by Sandro Mendonça.

PART I

Veblen's Challenge

2. Mind-sets, and why Veblen was Ineffectual

Mark Perlman

---

1. INTRODUCTION

During this conference, much has been said about 1998 being the centennial of the publication of Veblen's essay, 'Why Economics is not an Evolutionary Science'. His essay is said to be an indictment of our profession's ways of thought simply because he believed that economics should not be a static, but an evolutionary, science. Most of the profession, then as well as now, seems to believe that economics is fine just as it is - that it is a science but is not and should not be an 'evolutionary' one. They prefer a clear grasp of inorganic matter to an attempt to look at processes that affect our lives.[1]

Economics as a Science

The very idea of science is illusive. Some think that it is a body of investigation linked by a common denominator, namely its common Queen, mathematics. These advocates are of the Cartesian tradition, the major appeal of which is deductive logic; scientific truths are immutable - once discovered they stay firmly put. These truths can relate to state as well as to process; neither changes.

Others think that science is built on iterative periods of observation, generalisation, more observation, and more generalisation, until the nth iteration does not depart from the n-1th iteration. When this occurs the generalisation stands (for the moment). Yet, since later observations can disturb that stability, the generalisation is always tentative. Indeed, a competent scientist in his search for regularities may be the first one to discover that what once had been seen as stable may suddenly lose that quality. This is the Baconian approach to science, the tradition of the empirics; it leads not to certainty but only to a cautious confidence.

Evolution vs. Comparative Statics

Whether economics should or should not be evolutionary is clearly another leading question. What is evolutionary to some is merely comparative statics to others. Most of us here are not interested in comparative statics, and what we mean by evolutionary is something which has an organic nature - something which could be path-dependent, which adapts to known or unknown internally - or externally - imposed considerations, or to future contingencies yet to be discovered. Teleological ends, like equilibrium states, are generally shunned, if only because dealing with them in the present is not the pressing need. More important, economists interested in an evolutionary approach harbour compelling doubts about the two principal assumptions of current mainline economics, methodological individualism and informed rational choice. All of these points were made by Veblen, but in a fashion not likely to persuade the unconverted. Thus, while his ideas were sound, his rhetoric failed.

What about Biology as a Template

In my view, Veblen failed not because there were inherent flaws in the body of his ideas, but because, as I have suggested, his rhetoric, like Jonathan Swift's, was designed to shock rather than to teach.[2]

The leading question for us, who believe in an economics including a mainline evolutionary quality, is how to explain our views to audiences not accustomed, or in many cases not even open, to the kind of thinking we adopt.

Veblen's wish to use biology as a template has a recent counterpart, except that its author, Edward O. Wilson (a biologist at Harvard), is even more ambitious. He wants all science, indeed all knowledge, to come together in the form of a single vocabulary embodying all aspects of human nature (Wilson 1998). What I have to say about Veblen also applies to the Wilson proposal, a proposal that should be on the table at some future conference.

Unlike most of his contemporaries who looked to Newtonian physics as the prototypical science, Veblen looked to a modified Darwinian biology as the appropriate template for the development of an economic science. Now, few scientists see Darwinian biology as the most useful tool (cf. Hodgson 1998), and so it will do little good to repeat an old failed experiment. Yet, the line of thought found in 'Why Economics is not an Evolutionary Science' is, I believe, light-bearing in that it offers both an important facet of Veblen's thinking as well as useful insights into the failure of Veblen's message to persuade. The fact is that his essay persuaded neither the main-line economists of his day nor even very many of his few friends.

Our problem now is to succeed where Veblen failed. We are looking for something that is, again to use Bacon's felicitous phrase, fruit-bearing. I, myself, find the work of the current self-styled neo-institutionalists - Richter and Pejovich as well as North - attractive in its self-conscious effort to incorporate mainline economic thinking, but I think that they are trying to make a compound out of a mixture, and it does not work. For many reasons I am also much impressed with the merits of Oliver Williamson's work, albeit on a limited scale, but what he is doing (and what I like) is antithetical to what Coase has done. Again Williamson's and Coase's contributions are mixtures and cannot be made into a compound. The ones whose work may be the most promising are Nelson and Winter, *An Evolutionary Theory of Economic Change* (1982), but for reasons I shall shortly mention, their approach has not been developed so as to appeal to economic mainline traditionalists.

2. PROBLEMS IN THE VEBLEN LEGACY

A Lack of Synthesis

Many have written, and are still writing, about Veblen's thoughts, usually offering their interpretations of what he left. This is a never-ending quest, and the 138 selected essays in John Cunningham Wood's 1993 three-volume publication, *Thorstein Veblen: Critical Assessments*, offers a cornucopia along these lines (Wood, 1993).[3] But even amongst these essays there is no real synthesis of Veblenism. Veblen himself seemed to have no interest in providing a general synthesis of his views. Like Schumpeter, he had marvellous insights, but he did not leave a graspable theoretical system. My own surmise, one that is the cornerstone of this essay, is that such a synthesis was not possible for at least three rather obvious reasons.

An Intellectual Insularity

First, synthesis of a Veblenian evolutionary economics was premature because Veblen's views, some of which were clearly original, were mostly reactions to his wide reading and bitter social reflections rather than measured constructive and consolidative statements. He thought of himself as a modern Independent Counsel (to use a current Americanism), freely roaming the intellectual landscape looking for wickedness. Wesley Clair Mitchell, in 1936, thought him the prototypical outside observer of American culture. I do not agree. Veblen in my judgement represents no more than a repeating rip-tide washing out useless intellectual trash from American cultural beaches. Veblen was not prototypical of American culture any more than was Ida Tarbel with her crusade against Standard Oil. Both were not much more than an anti-robber baron reaction to American entrepreneurs like Carnegie, Morgan, and Rockefeller.

Second, Veblen's great period of creativity was before Max Weber's works and Vilfredo Pareto's *Trattato di Sociologia Generale* were available for general discussion (cf. Bhatty 1954; N.M. Hansen 1964).[4] It would not have been in Veblen's character to have been an easy ally of Pareto, but he too became disillusioned with any science based simply on methodological individualism and simple rationality. I do believe, however, that had Veblen had the stimulus of Weber's and Pareto's works, his own views would have been sharpened. He might even have been challenged to offer a synthesis of his own views, comparing them to Weber's and the evolution of Pareto's disgust with rational economics. Offering an examination of his own 'constellation' might have intrigued Veblen enough such that he would have tried to 'connect his stars.' For me such counter-factual history is dreamy stuff and can be indulged in only when it comes to the kind of musing Schiller offered in his fantasy about Elizabeth I and Mary Stuart. So I will drop this point – even if, in my own mind, it could have best explained Veblen's immediate and then long-term failure.

Selection of Time-limited Sides of Once Current Issues.

In his creative period, as Geoffrey Hodgson has recently pointed out (Hodgson 1998), Veblen put himself in the midst of at least two no-longer-interesting intellectual battles. The first involved nineteenth century scientific thinking (thinking exemplified by controversies between reductivist Darwinian and Lamarkian evolutionary biology concerning acquired as well as inherited human characteristics). That issue provoked endless nature vs. nurture debates and has recently been side-tracked by work suggesting that one can modify nature even if nurture fails.

The third issue involved the state of achieved knowledge. It was between, on one side, the statics of Newtonian physics, J.B. Clark's marginal analysis, Herbert Spencer's view of social organisation, and Marshall's clear geometry of partial equilibrium market price, and on the other a now largely rephrased seventeenth century view about the nature of belief and knowledge. Veblen was a true sceptic: in his disdain for revelation, he overlooked the important point that much persuasion is dependent upon understanding that the path to most people's hearts is not by dazzling them with the new, but by showing that what is new fits well with what to them is familiar. To persuade someone requires that you meet him on a common ground. I make this point because if it was the situation in the 1890s it remains the situation in the 1990s, when I find most of my professional colleagues regarding 'scientific' truths with the same lack of scepticism and true veneration that others in the past attached to God's Word. This leads me to the topic of mind-sets.

3. MIND-SETS

The term 'mind-set' is ambiguous. It differs from *Weltanschauung* (world view), in that mind-set is methodological - that is, it refers not to decisions themselves, but to the way in which decision-choices are framed. Mind-sets are the foundations of methodology - what method do I use, and why do I use it. I try to clarify my use of mind-sets by raising the question of from whence intellectual authority is derived. Why do we (and for present purposes I limit the question to economists) believe what we believe? Which mind-set recognises which authority? Who or what is our authority (or in most instances the combination of our authorities)?[5] Answering these questions is significant, for it is generally only by appealing to their appropriate authority that we can convince others. This was a topic which apparently interested Veblen not a whit, and that indifference left us all the poorer.

The Mind-set of Empiricism

I believe that Veblen failed to realise that he based his views on his sense of the superiority of his own examination of empirical evidence. Empiricism was to his mind clearly better than all other forms of acquired knowledge, but he was overconfident of his own powers of observation. Other empirics were not necessarily persuaded by the same evidence that impressed Veblen. For example, Veblen thought that there was empirically much validity to instinctive psychology - a view clearly not shared by other empirics. Even more critically, Veblen had faith, derived from his own empirical examination, that new technology, certainly physical and likely process as well, was the principal factor in explaining social change. Other empirics such as Commons (as well as no end of economic historians) thought it was the extension of the market. For them, the great achievement of economic knowledge was in explaining how product market expansion created economies of scale, and then how economies of scale led to technological innovation. I differ from both of them by arguing that, as I see the evidence, both hypotheses are stable.

But to get back to Veblen, Mitchell wrote that Veblen's empirical strength was that he was an outsider (Mitchell 1936, pp. vii-xlix), and like other outsiders (such as Jews, as Veblen discussed them in his essay, 'The Intellectual Pre-eminence of Jews in Modern Europe') Veblen's alien culture (rural Norway transported to Wisconsin) gave him an ability to see what insiders missed.[6] I think this is what impressed Mitchell early on - just as Kuznets's similar outsider's view impressed Mitchell in the 1920s. But to be an outsider taken seriously often leads to becoming stereotyped as a negative critic, and as such what the outsider has to offer is not only resented, but it is also resisted.[7] While Veblen in his own time and in his own wry way managed never to become an academic insider, his views it seems to me were stereotyped well before 1900, and he preached without much expanding his flock.[8]

Yet, if Veblen was stereotyped by 1898, his actual empirical researches were greatly broadened afterwards with his work for the United States Industrial Commission, 1898-1901 (see Perlman 1958, pp. 264-79). That experience gave him not only international insights he had previously lacked, but also a research programme involving American industrial structure, insights not anticipated in his pre-Industrial Commission work. Veblen, like all who would be good empirics, came to face new observations challenging his earlier findings. His work on Imperial Germany and his interest in European social psychology led him to new generalisations. As I reread Veblen (and what a pleasure it is), I am aware that his language remained as colourful. I do not, however, find his idea-base (his generalisations, if you will) all that improved.

One problem is the role of ideas. Veblen and Schumpeter thought in terms of the filiation of ideas. My thought is that Veblen was no Hume, because Veblen did not represent the kernel of Wisconsonian thought of the turn of the century. The signal cultural and political product of that Wisconsin 'civilisation', *La Follette Progressivism*, was an exercise in legislative pragmatism, where 'ideas' were subordinated to acts, and the latter were judged by their results, not by their pedigree. The 'Wisconsin Idea' was a great success, but it was a programme - not really an idea.

Even more significant, Veblen failed to realise that empirical generalisations mean little or nothing to many people, and among this group are most economic theorists. To me it is clear that Veblen's own mind-set was in the Francis Bacon tradition, a mind-set far more open than is today's Popperism, with its rigid rules.

The Mind-set of Logic and Immanent Criticism

Most economists in his and in our own time believe principally in the syllogism. Their test is immanent criticism (that is, the internal logic of their model), and so they are in the tradition of René Descartes and the Physiocrats. Accordingly, they are not looking for the regularities inherent in the Baconian quest; rather they are looking for logical formalism, traditionally associated with the realm of the Queen of the Sciences. In Veblen's time, there was no handle available for him to hold onto the logicians. Now, I am told, there is Chaos Theory and Complexity Analysis, which explain in a formal way many of the things that empirics have observed but which could not be explained in a logical form. Of course, there is a hitch. Few logicians and even fewer empirics currently can handle the mathematics involved in chaos or complexity studies. But time is on our side, and when our mathematically-minded colleagues progress to 21st century maths, they may discover that induction and deduction lead to the same conclusions.

But there are other mind-sets besides empiricism and logic. I believe that Veblen, in handling them carelessly, also lost part of his audience. Veblen was also aware of the impact of culture, although I think that for him culture was more firm, like clay, than it was malleable, like putty - to refer to the Cambridges controversy terminology of almost half a century ago.

Patristic Legacies and Mind-sets

I am loth to use the term 'cultural determinism' because it is an umbrella covering too many dissimilar phenomena. Rather I prefer my own term, 'patristic legacies', that for me contains immutable as well as negotiable elements. An example of a current immutable element of the British-American patristic legacy is Locke's unalienable personal 'life, liberty, and estate' 'revelation'. But, even within these immutables, there are negotiable interpretations. For example, the concept of what constitutes estate has been organic. Certain economic actions and civil rights have in our time become a major form of personal estate. So if the basic concept is clay, the interpretations of what it comprises can be putty.

The role of patristic legacies is to frame what is easily acceptable. If a new observation fits readily into our patristic system, we accept it easily. If not, acceptance can be slowed. Selig Perlman's thesis - that the right to the job was basically a property right made it easier for non-unionists to understand (if not to accept) what unionists were about.

Characteristic of patristic legacies is that they are rarely pure and almost never analysed. Isaiah Berlin's cultural pluralism is what I have in mind.

Most of us are not only the product of conflicting inherited cultures, but in practice we prioritise them when considering specific issues. Most Americans have an immutable belief in Locke's doctrine of man's right to 'life, liberty, and estate'. What is amazing is that they think it a political heritage, whereas Locke produced it as a religious revelation. If one were to ask the typical American whether he thought that his country should try to convert the People's Republic of China to a religious heritage, he would say No. But, if one were to ask the same American whether the Chinese have an individual right to 'life, liberty, and estate', the likely answer would be a resounding Yes.

Mind-sets attached to patristic legacies have similar powers to mind-sets attached to empiricism or logic. Perceiving what a person1's mind-set is may be the way to persuade him.

Let me repeat what I have said about mind-sets:

• One mind-set is a strong reliance upon cognition - much of what we believe are simple regularities coming from cognitive observations such as diminishing or increasing marginal returns.

• Another mind-set is confidence in logic - many or us are convinced by Euclidian-like presentations.

• Other mind-sets look for cultural comfortableness - if something new strikes a familiar chord it is acceptable. Within this category is what some call 'rationalism', meaning an internal order as contrasted to an absence of such order.

But also in this list must be the role of true revelation - the non-negotiable factors. One of Veblen's great failings was no appreciation of the truly revelational quality of the Lockean heritage. While understanding the magic the Lockean system had for economists, he missed the magic it held for the whole American culture. To suggest that they forgo Locke is akin to asking Roman Catholics to forego Papal leadership. Why? Because Locke's 'life, liberty, and estate', was not only religiously derived - combining his personal theological Deism with a traditional Christological individualism, but it seemed 'natural'. Lockean individualism is a Christological non-negotiable. By blurring any discussion of the Christological basis of modern western individualism, these intellectuals miss an important handhold on the minds of their time. Such was particularly the case with Veblen.

4. VEBLEN'S FAILURE

His Failure Analysed

Veblen thought that the truths of empiricism were so self-evident that there was no need to explain why they, rather than logic, should be dominantly persuasive.

Second, Veblen thought that technological change made all other elements of culture negotiable. Here I think that he made an empirical measurement-error. For those whom he might have influenced more, men like his student and friend Wesley Clair Mitchell, that error was, if not fatal, certainly very damaging. For Mitchell, like Veblen, thought changing technology was the dominant force for economic progress. But where Mitchell differed from Veblen was that he saw the speed (that is, the 'ease') of technological change being necessarily facilitated by new monetary institutions. Without a pecuniary system, the very thing upon which Veblen choked, the coming of new technology would be retarded. Veblen's mind, with its strangely misplaced impecunious Wisconsin farmers' disgust for bankers would not (or possibly could not) see Mitchell's point. Most economists, not being Wisconsin farmers, thought strongly otherwise. Accordingly, for them Veblen's seemingly blind hatred of financial intermediaries made them think him a 'primitive' - what in the American Mid-west was termed 'a hayseed'. No way to win hearts and influence people.

All three - Veblen, Mitchell, and Commons - saw institutions as the underpinnings of human decision-making. Mitchell and Veblen were fascinated by the role of technological change on institutions. Commons was more impressed with the role of market expansion than technological change. Commons, fascinated by the Magna Carta definition of property rights and by the Hobbes-Locke reconsideration of them, thought individual property rights to be the cornerstone of the British cultural legacy. So there they had it: Was it technological change or individual property rights which were the templates of the culture?

An Aside on Commons's Similar Failure

To my mind, what Commons's system lacked was an appreciation that the Lockean system, besides being an adaptation of a property rights system, was treated by most as the equivalent of a divine revelation. Commons thought, as Malcolm Rutherford has recently written (Rutherford, 1998), that institutions were eventually politically if not necessarily reasonably ordained (Rutherford, 1998). For Commons, something of a religious sceptic, the

legislative and judicial processes while certainly the omega, were likely also
the alpha of social approval. Commons clearly believed that social changes,
in his case principally extensions of the market, created pressures that
inevitably confronted going institutions. Commons, as we all know, thought
that institutions were collective (i.e. communitarian) controls that shaped
individual decisions, but how much they did so was frequently the guts of the
political process. I have written elsewhere comparing Commons' and
Hayek's views of institution-building (Perlman and McCann, 1998). We
think them much alike, although Commons's institutional approach, like
Veblen's, was Hegelian, whereas Hayek's approach was Kantian.

5. CONCLUSION

So where does all of the foregoing leave us? I have been concerned with
Veblen's failure to influence the broad spectrum of economists, including not
only the moss-backs but also those who want to break new ground.

I have tried to stress that Veblen was too intent upon asserting his own
case and insufficiently interested in what was going on in the minds of those
to whom his words were directed. It is possible that he didn't care, the fact is
that we do.

My thought is that we must understand that to persuade others we, unlike
Veblen, must explain the bases of our mind-sets, and, if possible, interest
them in that topic. I believe that most of our audience also embraces
intellectual pluralism, and if they can admit to it, half our battle is won.
Victory consists of opening minds to something that was there originally, not
full conversion to our position. Scraping some of the scales from their eyes is
victory enough - particularly because who among us has total conviction that
he or she understands it all?

It may be hard to explain to those who favour the *a priori* method that
there is virtue in the *a posteriori* method; in many instances it just cannot be
done. But if Veblen's experience shows anything, the effort must be made
lest at the next *fin de siècle*, that is, a century hence, that generation will still
be wondering why the appeal of institutionalism was so limited.

A more tolerant attitude and a realisation that more flies are caught by a
variety of honeys is what should be on our minds.

NOTES

1. Looking around, one sees the contrast between the IMF's view of handling economic
   recession with a more dynamic World Bank view. As for the IMF, *plus ça change, plus
   c'est la même chose.*

2. Irony and sarcasm are heady stuff - their appeal is more to sophisticates than it is to reformers.
3. As I read the works done by the many factions in neo-Institutionalism I am impressed by their interest in trying to synthesise their own ideas, and I am even more interested in their efforts to find parallelisms in the broad group. The recently-erected Schumpeterian tent shelters any number of evolutionary economists, even though Schumpeter, himself, paid scant heed to the American Institutionalists. Why he did so is ground for another paper. But like Veblen he was too much interested in *épater-ing les bourgeois* rather than in advancing the cause of an evolutionary economic science.
4. I have failed to find any discussion of Pareto's work in Veblen's writings, nor have I been able to discover any mention of Veblen in Pareto. However, Dorfman reports that Gustav von Schmoller was impressed with *The Theory of the Business Enterprise* and Max Weber 'thought much of *The Theory of the Leisure Class*' (Dorfman 1934, pp. 487-88), expressed generously in a footnote in *The Protestant Ethic*. Apparently Max Weber's Sozial Oeconomie did not impress Veblen enough to incorporate it in his system. As for Joseph Alois Schumpeter, according to Dorfman, the thought was that Veblen looked like 'a common poseur.' Given Schumpeter's predilections, it was the adjective where the scorn undoubtedly lay (Dorfman 1934,p. 488).
5. Mindset is often pluralistic. On some issues one authority prevails; on other issues another authority does. To complicate matters further, in adjacent bounded areas two quite different authority systems may coexist. This is Isaiah Berlin's intellectual pluralism.
6. In one of his later essays on Veblen, Mitchell compares Veblen to Hume, saying that although neither was fully accepted in their time, they nonetheless became the quintessential thinkers of their people (Mitchell, 1936). Yet, to my thinking (and both Veblen and I were raised in Wisconsin, albeit some decades apart) Veblen really did not grasp the foundations of American mid-west culture if only because that culture was grounded on something quite different from what he saw. I would go so far as to argue that both Mitchell and Commons, also products of the American Midwest, grasped what Veblen missed and that is why their legacies, never really systems of ideas, are no longer known by their names, as such, but are so incorporated into workaday America that they continue to dominate a great deal of American political and social development. They were problem-solvers: Mitchell left a legacy of data collection and artful analysis; Commons left a legacy seen in New Deal legislation.
7. There are some marked exceptions testing this generalisation. I would cite Alexander de Tocqueville as one of the greatest.
8. In his lectures, Joseph Dorfman had a bottomless well of stories about what Veblen's loneliness did not only to his manners but also to his spirit.

REFERENCES

Bhatty, I.Z. (1954), 'Some aspects of the writings of Pareto and Veblen', Reprinted in Wood (1993), *Specialized Topics*, London and New York: Routledge, vol. 3, pp. 66-73.

Hansen, N.M. (1964), 'Weber and Veblen on economic development', Reprinted in Wood (1993), *Specialized Topics*, London and New York: Routledge, vol. 3, pp. 134-53.

Hodgson, G. (1998), 'On the evolution of Thorstein Veblen's evolutionary economics. Veblen's evolutionary programme: a promise unfulfilled', *Cambridge Journal of Economics*, vol. 22, pp 415-31.

Mitchell, W. C. (1936), *What Veblen Taught: Selected Writings of Thorstein Veblen*, Edited with an Introduction by Wesley C. Mitchell, New York: Viking.

Nelson, R.R. and S.G. Winter (1982), *An Evolutionary Theory of Economic Change*, Cambridge: Belknap Press of Harvard University Press.

Perlman, M. (1958), *Labor Union Theories in America: Background and Development*, Evanston, IL: Roe, Peterson.

Perlman, M. (1998), 'Hayek, the Purposes of the Economic Market, and the Institutionalist Traditions', in Frowen, S.F. (ed.), *Hayek The Economist and Social Philosopher: A Critical Retrospect*, London: Macmillan, pp. 221-35.

Rutherford, Malcolm (1998a), 'Institutionalism as a Scientific Economics', A mimeographed paper give at the Montreal meetings of the History of Economics Society.

Rutherford, Malcolm (1998b), 'Veblen's evolutionary programme: a promise unfulfilled', *Cambridge Journal of Economics*, vol. 22, pp 463-77.

Wood, John Cunningham (ed.) (1993), *Thorstein Veblen: Critical Assessments in three volumes*, Vol. 1: *The Life of Thorstein Veblen and Perspectives on His Thought*; Volume 2: *Veblen's Political Economy*; and Volume 3: *Specialized Topics*, London and New York: Routledge.

3. How can Economics be an Institutional-Evolutionary Science?

Phillip A. O'Hara

INTRODUCTION

The centenary of the publication of Thorstein Bunde Veblen's (1857-1929) brilliant essay 'Why is Economics not an Evolutionary Science' (1898) and his best known work, *The Theory of the Leisure Class: An Economic Study of Institutions* (Veblen, 1899) is upon us. These works, 100 years on, look decidedly modern since, recently, institutional-evolutionary economics has come to the fore and postmodernist themes (which Veblen advocated 70 years before the term was coined) have been in vogue in certain quarters for a couple of decades. It could be said that Veblen was a man ahead of his time, just as (if not more) relevant to the present and next century as to the last. This theme - the relevance of Veblen for the twenty-first century - is the topic examined in this paper.

This paper argues that Veblen's major contributions to political economy that are relevant for the twenty-first century can be isolated under five headings: (1) holistic institutional economics; (2) evolutionary circular and cumulative economics; (3) social, technological and ecological capital; (4) an economic surplus approach to industry and business; and (5) an analysis of race, class, gender, nation and species. I will examine the usefulness of Veblen's method and analysis under these headings.

1. HOLISTIC INSTITUTIONAL ECONOMICS

The prime theme (or principle) of Veblen's works is that of holism, which is advanced in various ways in all his works, but most especially in *The Theory of the Leisure Class*. Three postulates are advanced under the general umbrella of holistic economics. The first is the notion that one needs to study the interplay of social, political, and environmental factors in the determination of economic processes. Economics is part of an open system, which includes values, beliefs, institutions, social behaviours and human-centred aspects of the provisioning process. Every aspect of economics, in this view, needs to be situated within a broad framework of reference in order to comprehend adequately the nature of the processes in motion. Political economy is necessarily processual, human, institutional and environmental in its scope.

This means that the processes of production, distribution and exchange need to be situated within the context of the reproduction of institutions, beliefs and behaviours. Socio-economic reproduction implies the need for a wide scope of vision when viewing the production of goods and services; the distribution of income, wealth and power between the social classes; and the exchange of money, credit and goods and services in the market. In short, the reproduction of economic processes requires that the institutional structure and motion be activated by a set of processes which transcend normal market relationships. Markets are considered to be necessarily heavily imbued with social relationships, values, and behaviours, and to abstract from these aspects is to ignore the real functioning of economies.

Furthermore, an attempt to promote market relationships - a topic of great concern as we move into the twenty-first century - devoid of complex institutions runs the risk of large-scale financial and economic crises and turmoil. Veblen would thus have agreed with Polanyi's notion that market relations need to be protected by a system of imbedded social relationships in order to reduce the potential for a significant destruction of confidence in the system. Confidence is fundamentally affected by protective measures such as lender of last resort facilities, health and safety measures, demand structures to protect the system from underconsumption, and a healthy dominance of industry over financial incentives to ensure adequate fundamentals. When people feel under threat from unemployment, workplace health and safety problems, lack of trust and/or financial wheeling and dealing, confidence in the system is eroded leading to adverse expectations of the future and hence low consumption and investment. Socio-economic uncertainty about the future is thus the main factor precipitating economic crisis and instability, a topic of great concern as we turn into the next century (a topic also emphasised by Keynes and post-Keynesian scholars).

This view of the world led Veblen to try and comprehend the institutional workings of the corporation, state, financial system, family and world economy. It is essential to Veblen's method to try and develop a realistic analysis of the workings of these institutional spheres, and especially how they change over historical time. Holistic economics thus places primary focus on the dominant institutions of capitalism as the primary motif of analysis (see Wilber 1998). However, it is important to situate these institutions in a realistic theory of how the institutions arise and how they have evolved, plus the drift of change into the future. Economics is thus primarily concerned with the real world analysis of institutions, including people's values and social behaviours, at both the macro and micro levels. At the micro level, people are often able to plan and to act according to a logical set of objectives and aims, and often they are driven by habit; at the macro level, blind drift tends to prevail due to indeterminate evolution through historical time. Hence systemic change and individual motives may be at odds with each other: what may be logical for the individual may create problems for the reproduction of the system.

A related view of holism, which Veblen adhered to, includes the notions of 'decentered totality' and 'entry point', to use post-modern terminology. Decentred totality relates to the view that there is no central institutional sphere per se that should be given privilege in economic analysis. Rather, the institutional cluster needs to be studied *in toto*, with the structure of effectivity and criticality being determined empirically on a case by case basis. Thus, while the corporation may be the central institutional cluster to many scholars, this is modified by the recognition that the corporation is heavily imbued with organisational and relationship linkages that are not unlike structures of governance activated by the state, the family and the financial systems; and that the other institutional clusters (such as the state and the family) may become more critical to analysis in certain historical situations. The message is, therefore, that the macro-institutional structure is the critical thing to be examined, including the reproduction of this totality.

The notion of 'entry point' is the other critical aspect of holism. This is the idea that it is impossible to comprehend all of the socio-economic institutions of the system, given the complexity of the formation and interaction of the totality. Therefore, all that social scientists can be expected to do - after a general view of the theory and motion of the system as a whole - is to examine the whole partially, through a series of case studies of various problems, be they inflation, unemployment, poverty, balance of payments constraint, etc. When socio-economic problems are examined, certain 'entry points' are taken into the totality in order to start analysis and make sense of aspects of the whole (see Resnick and Wolff 1987). These entry points then seek to link 'the whole' to the problems posed by the entry points, to situate the problem within the context of holistic analysis.

The problematical position of 'strong holism' - that because everything is interrelated it is necessary to comprehend the totality before one can 'know' it (an impossible position) - is replaced with 'concessive holism' (a term coined by Susan James 1984) which recognises merely that the parts are interrelated in an uneven or imperfect manner and that one is able to comprehend the system by examining important aspects of the whole and to link important parts to illustrate the workings of the whole. Such are the results of a pragmatic philosophical position (following the work of Peirce, Dewey and James, broadly speaking) and the limits of comprehension capable of the human brain.

2. EVOLUTIONARY, CIRCULAR AND CUMULATIVE ECONOMICS

Veblen was the first major economist to embrace fully a post-Darwinian evolutionary economics (see Hodgson 1998), a position which only started to redevelop in the 1960s-1990s by institutionalists, Schumpeterians and ecological economists. Without a doubt, Veblen was light years ahead of his time in this respect. By evolutionary economics Veblen meant an economics that eschewed the necessary tendency toward equilibrium in favour of one concerned with blind drift and institutional change and metamorphosis. He criticised the trend among 'classical economics' to be obsessed with the move towards equality of supply and demand, and the movement back to equilibrium, assuming *ceteris paribus* conditions, and ignoring questions of contradiction, instability, movement and crisis (See Veblen 1898).

Veblen said that the mainstream economics of his time was concerned with the 'normal [equilibrium] case', based on short-term logical time rather than longer-run questions of change and motion (Veblen 1899-1900). The equilibrium case tended to assume diminishing returns, short periods, independence of supply and demand, Say's Law, and the conformity of micro with macro laws. Veblen, by contrast, was more interested in an economic system called large scale corporate capitalism characterised by oligopoly corporations, increasing returns to scale, the long-term, and the lack of conformity of micro with the macro in many instances. Presaging Kaldor's (1972) *Economic Journal* article, Veblen believed that equilibrium economics offered no real insight into the central tendencies of the modern corporate system, and this is even more true as we move into the twenty-first century.

If one incorporates into the analysis increasing returns to scale, oligopoly, change and the interdependence of supply and demand, the analysis one develops is completely different from equilibrium economics. Interdependence of supply and demand means that an increase in demand could manifest itself in higher investment, innovation, lower prices, and expansion on the world scale, in a word a circular and cumulative influence on production and development. Rather than a once-off influence, the demand influence could not only be circular but also reinforcing or cumulative. An expansion of large scale industry without a suitable expansion of the wage goods sector or the state or the world market could promote generalised overproduction, as Veblen believed happened in the late 1800s (see Veblen 1904). He saw the process of oligopolisation as a partial panacea to this, as mark-up pricing and a higher degree of monopoly led to higher profit and hence more stability for capitalism during the early 1900s. Increasing bouts of demand (investment or consumer demand) could stimulate the capitalist process, which in turn could expand employment, which could further expand the process, and so on *ad infinitum*. This could lead to a long-term process of waves of expansion lasting decades, such as the long boom of the 1940s-1960s and the long downswing of the 1970s - 1990s in advanced capitalist economies.

This notion of circular and cumulative causation is a major innovation in political economy, currently being promoted by the post-Keynesian scholars such as McCombie and Thirwall (1994), Pini (1995) and others. The balance of payments constraint notion and Kaldor's laws challenge much of orthodox macroeconomics by showing that demand and supply are interdependent, and that long-run analysis better describes the process of systemic economic change than a static or ceteris paribus framework. Demand is shown to stimulate supply, and productivity increases as expansion proceeds (Verdoorn's Law) in a circular and cumulative fashion. This analysis supports the notion that world income is the foundation for export expansion and that proactive policy can help the process along.

The notion of circular and cumulative causation is a critical legacy left by Veblen, not only in terms of Kaldorian dynamics (influenced by Alan Young and Piero Sraffa) but also Myrdalian social analysis (influenced by Wicksell) and Schumpeterian technology studies (influenced by Schumpeter). Myrdal, the most famous institutionalist since Veblen, showed how the circular and cumulative framework works at the level of social analysis. He examined the 'negro question' in the USA (Myrdal 1944) and the 'development problem' in Asia (Myrdal 1968), in both cases arguing that poverty and lack of education can be self-reinforcing. If certain ethnic groups have relatively low levels of income, education, self-esteem, and nutrition, they all reinforce each other. Low education leads to low income; low income leads to low levels of education; low self-esteem stimulates low income and education; and low nutrition promote low self-esteem and low productivity as well as low education. They are all interrelated to varying degrees (One could also fit discrimination into the equation).

The notion of circular and cumulative motion has significance also in terms of change, metamorphosis and evolutionary analysis. Veblen was interested in the metamorphosis of capital from competitive structures to corporate capitalism to monopoly capitalism and beyond. The various phases of evolution were a critical part of his institutional analysis. This legacy is closely related to social structures of accumulation and regulation approaches to political economy, not to mention many other frameworks, such as neo-Marxism, neo-Schumpeterian and evolutionary economics. The evolution from Fordism to what may be termed 'post-Fordism' into the twenty-first century can be seen, for instance, as being very much in the mould of the sort of analysis that Veblen was undertaking, and therefore being a direct descendent of aspects of Veblen's methodology.

The other area of importance is evolutionary analysis *per se*. Veblen specifically attempted to examine economics within an evolutionary framework (see Veblen 1898). The notions of evolution, selection, adaptation and variation - at the cultural, industrial and species levels - were ones that Veblen explicitly developed. He attempted to propel an evolutionary science of economics, not of the Spencerian type but one that incorporated cumulative change and dynamics into the analysis. Specifically evolutionary terms were a part of his conceptual apparatus, including ecological concerns. Kenneth Boulding (1981) seems to have resurrected this type of framework, and the work of Geoffrey Hodgson emanates especially from Veblen's work. Schumpeter thought that such an evolutionary economics was dead in the 1950s, but more recently it has surged ahead on many fronts. A potential exists for a united evolutionary economics, perhaps from apparently disparate sources, for as Georgescu-Roegen (1971, p. 321) said: 'lessons, perhaps the only substantial ones, on how to transcend the static framework effectively have come from Marx, Veblen and Schumpeter'. Therefore, I suggest that one of the central legacies of Veblen - concerning evolution - is one shared with some other schools of political economy, and that a development of evolutionary concepts and concerns is appropriate here for the future.

The notions of path dependency, hysteresis, circular and cumulative causation, systemic blind drift, institutional and technological innovation and phases of evolution are ones that are providing a foundation for a robust evolutionary economics. Veblen's legacy, therefore, is to this extent a shared legacy, which for the development of economics needs to become activated further. Collectively the Association for Evolutionary Economics, the European Association for Evolutionary Political Economy, and the International Joseph A. Schumpeter Society illustrate some of these evolutionary legacies in the contemporary world. What we need more than anything else is further cross-fertilisation of ideas and trends between these trends.

3. ECONOMIC SURPLUS APPROACH TO INDUSTRY AND BUSINESS

Veblen utilised an economic surplus approach to political economy. For instance, he differentiated between industry that is productive of the surplus and industry that wastes the surplus, especially in *The Theory of Business Enterprise* (Veblen 1904) and *Absentee Ownership* (Veblen 1923). Industry is productive of material output (Q), which includes the historically specific subsistence wages (W), replacement cost of capital (C), and the surplus (S) over costs of the productive (p) sector:

$$Q = [W + C + S]p$$

The surplus is usually looked upon as a physical surplus over-and-above the material costs of production, including the historically specific subsistence level of workers:

$$S = [Q - C - W]p$$

According to Veblen, the surplus is dependent upon the propensity of people to engage in workmanship, technological innovation and capacity utilization in the productive areas. To the extent that these positive traits are dominated by pecuniary, exploitation and emulative interests the level of surplus declines as the surplus is transferred to the unproductive areas and cannot be invested in productive capital. Hence the surplus can be distributed to the productive sectors (p), and the reproduction of a further surplus, or it can be wasted in the unproductive areas (u) of business or warfare, generally the vested interests:

$$S = [C + K]p + [W + O + T]u$$

Thus the surplus can be used for expanding the stock of physical capital (C) or given to technologists and human capitals (K for knowledge) in the productive sector, or it can be paid to workers as wages (W), claims to ownership like property and banking (O) or paying taxes to the state (T) in the unproductive sectors. The main unproductive activities are bankers, accountants, advertisers, financiers, the state and holders of shares.

The resources of the unproductive sectors thus emanate from the surplus produced in the productive sectors. Much of Veblen's analysis comprises an analysis of the conflict between the productive and unproductive areas. He also recognised that the very nature of capitalism necessitates the distribution of surplus to the vested interests of absentee owners, bankers, monopolists, unions and rentiers. The distribution of the surplus between industry and business has limits on all sides, as the following diagram implies (see O'Hara 1993):

Figure 3.1   Veblen's limits to capitalism

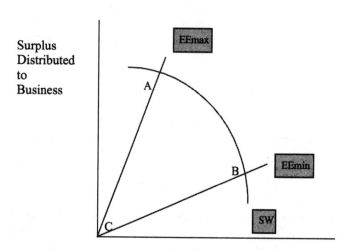

Surplus
Distributed
to
Business

Surplus Distributed to Industry

In Veblen's system there are three main limits to capitalism. The first is represented by the EE_{min} bar, which shows the very minimum ratio of surplus going to business to protect their property and distributive rights, and the minimum rate of exploitation of industry by business; without this minimum ratio of surplus, capitalism could not survive. This limit (within the EE_{min} bar) relates to the fact that competition and workmanship may be too strong, creating sustained overproduction and instability. The second limit, represented by the bar EE_{max}, is the maximum rate of exploitation bar of industry by business. If the degree of exploitation was such as to operate in the EE_{max} bar, again the system of capitalism industry would undergo sustained crisis and instability, is because a certain minimum rate of industry must be maintained for the system to survive. And lastly, the third main limit to capitalism is represented by the SW bar, showing the variable amount of social wealth available for reproducing the activities of business and industry. Thus the limits of capital - indeterminate as they are, hence the bars rather than lines - are represented by the area ABC (the areas of the 'modified triangle'). Moving into one or the other bars of exploitation usually leads to a protracted period of instability, depression and high unemployment. Capitalism can not operate outside of the limit-bounded areas (beyond the area of the 'modified triangle').

Veblen believed that during the competitive phase of capitalism (1780s-1850s) the system was in no great danger of perpetually moving near to either of the bars of exploitation. Crises were common, but they were not inherent in the very nature of capital *per se*. Rather, they related more to the weather, harvests, and some of the instabilities of speculation and the market. During the second main phase of capitalist development, the system of corporate capitalism phase one (1850s-1890s), large scale industry developed along with major process innovations and productivity improvements. During this period, the threat of overproduction started to emerge from the 1870s (in the US and the UK) when the large scale production system had reached a level commensurate with machine technology and limited effective demand. Hence the 1880s and 1890s were periods of overproduction with considerable uncertainty and instability. This represented the move into the areas of the EE_{min} bar.

Gradually increasing oligopolisation, sales expenses and the separation of ownership from control helped to stem the tide of industry and competition at around the turn of the twentieth century (1896-1904 and onwards), including mergers and collusive policies. This helped to move the economy away from the EE_{min} bar into the open area of reasonable reproducibility. Corporate oligopoly interests began to dominate the key sectors of power generation, transportation, fuel and structural materials. This paved the way for twenty years or so of growth and accumulation, without major depressions. However, as business interests began to become entrenched in the 1920s, especially with the power of speculators, bankers and oligopoly collusion (at the expense of workers' conditions), the profits of business rose at the expense of industry and productive workers. The economy then moved towards the other limit, EE_{max}, as the surplus was being increasingly shifted from industry to business. The instinct of workmanship and innovation was diminished in favour of pecuniary interests, emulation and greater exploitation (see Veblen 1914), thus leading to the Great Depression of underconsumption and overspeculation in the 1930s (which Veblen seemed to predict in *Absentee Ownership*, see Veblen 1923).

It was about this time, 1929 actually, that Veblen left his place on Earth, and after the II World War twenty or thirty years of boom eventually paved the way for the structural crises of the 1970s-1990s. Marxists and Sraffians have been at the forefront of applying surplus approach analyses to the newer phases of capitalism; institutionalists indeed were left behind in this respect for they failed to follow the footsteps of Veblen in developing the surplus approach. A critical project in political economy is to apply the surplus approach to new developments and phases of capitalism into the twenty-first

century. This problematic is again one critical dual legacy that Veblen shared
with Marxists and other political economists. However, Veblen's analysis of
the collective origin of the surplus was unique and in many ways an advance
on the other approaches to the subject. It is examined in the next section.

4. SOCIAL, HUMAN AND TECHNOLOGICAL CAPITAL

Veblen's analysis of the origins of the surplus was unique in that he
considered it to be the product of collectively generated wealth or capital. He
was the first major economist to recognise the importance of social,
technological and ecological capital in the generation of the surplus. Social
capital is the stock of human norms, mores and structures of trust and
community which bind people together. In a word, social capital comprises
the institutions upon which the economy is based. These institutions are
durable and provide a flow of services over time. Being part of an open
system, institutions are self-generating structures which are reproduced as
part of the workings of everyday life. Veblen paid special attention to the
institutions of community, peaceable coexistence, trust and knowledge. He
believed that social capital helps to generate welfare if the institutions are
influenced primarily by positive traits. In this sense, the welfare generated is
a substitute for material output, but in addition it is a necessary condition for
the long-term development of material output. Without the necessary
structures of community and trust the bonds of interaction would be fragile,
and human society would be at a low level of development. It is only in the
past 20 years or so that the notion of social capital has been actively
developed in the literature of political economy. For instance, one study
shows that in the state of Kerala, in India, social capital has provided the
foundation for a high standard of living (life expectancy, literacy and health)
with a small GDP per capita (see Heller 1996).[1] Thus, social capital can
promote growth or be a substitute for growth. Either way, it is essential to
many dimensions of the quality of life. Ignoring social capital in favour of
durable business fixed capital can lead to a lower standard of living, and so it
is critical to political economy (see O'Hara 1998; World Bank 1997).

Closely related to social capital is technological capital, which has a closer
direct link to the production process and the surplus generation process. The
knowledge, skills and arts upon which technology is based were seen by
Veblen to be collectively generated. They are the product of the past, rooted
in the way of life of the community, and the knowledge of technicians,
scholars, scientists and artists. Veblen was concerned with a spectrum that
commenced with knowledge and skills and led to machine technology and
the latest developments in scientific analysis. A small portion of this capital,

according to Veblen, is added to the stock in any particular year, and most of it cannot be linked to specific individuals, but is rather group- or system-oriented. Veblen was thus the first economist to place human capital, knowledge, and technology at the centre of his analysis of the surplus. As society and corporate structures become more complex, the surplus becomes more obviously collectively generated, by groups of workers, knowledge processes, societal bonds, and the like.

The emphasis Veblen gave to the collective generation of social, human and technological capital has the potential to revolutionise political economy. He believed that, while these forms of capital are collectively generated, they can be exploited by the vested interests for their own benefit in the form of a share of the surplus product. Corporations can exploit this wealth through degrees of monopoly. Financiers can gain a share of the surplus through interest, the lending of money and the creation of credit. Physical property owners can gain a share of the surplus by renting their premises. Unions can gain a share of the surplus through industrial action and wages over-and-above their collective contribution to workmanship. These vested interests, therefore, not only utilise a portion of the surplus, but stimulate interests which reduce the production of surplus. Thus, Veblen believed that economists need critically to analyse the power of elites and classes, with a view to sharing the surplus product in a more egalitarian manner. Since it is mainly collectively generated, it should be more equally distributed. This thesis is a critical one which needs to be more fully investigated, along with the notion of collective wealth, especially for the next century when socio-economic relationships are likely to become more complex and societal (if apparently privatised).

5. SPECIES, GENDER, CLASS AND RACE/ETHNICITY

Veblen was critical of the notion of 'homo economicus' for ignoring the institutional and specific characteristics of human beings in a social setting. 'Homo economicus' sought to reduce humanity to abstract commonalities and rational qualities, devoid of heterogeneity and 'difference'. Veblen instead sought to comprehend the historically specific social characteristics which different groups of human beings manifested, and he incorporated into his economics a notion of instincts which different societies conditioned in variable ways. While Veblen recognised that individuals may well attempt to seek specific ends and goal-directed activity, often they are said to be influenced by habit and, in any case, at the social-historical level there are no end points, since blind drift and evolutionary metamorphosis result in qualitative changes in the parameters.

Real political economies, in Veblen's view, are characterised by heterogeneous agents of varying forms, and these 'differences' are critical to the analysis of the structure and change of institutions. Examples of such heterogeneity include different species, gender, class and race/ethnicity. Much of Veblen's contribution to political economy lay in examining these differences, which link to socio-economic roles in the spheres of production, distribution, reproduction and exchange. The primary difference is based on species: Veblen centred on human beings operating in an ecological and social environment, with certain instincts and characteristics which make them different to other species. Human beings have a gene pool and social systems that influence their characteristics and behaviour fundamentally. Instincts, for Veblen, became part of the systemic processes affecting and in turn being affected by the institutional set-up of specific societies.

His analysis of instincts (see Veblen, 1899, 1914) recognised that there are certain general tendencies of humanity that manifest themselves in different ways in different social formations. The positive traits are said to be those of workmanship, parental guidance and idle curiosity. Workmanship links to the work ethic, innovation and productivity. The parental instinct is associated with the caring and loving tendencies of humanity. Idle curiosity manifests itself in 'play' and 'fundamental thinking', thus affecting new ideas and innovations. Veblen thought that these positive instincts were continually being 'infected' by negative values and tendencies that adversely affect community and sociality, namely the pecuniary, exploitative and emulative tendencies. Pecuniary traits link to the dominance of monetary rewards and incentives. Exploitative trends are associated with war, plunder and imperial pursuits. Emulative traits relate to the dominance of comparison of people on the basis of status, prestige and class. Veblen believed that these various traits or trends are interrelated and intermeshed in multifarious ways, which often makes it difficult to delineate the specific influences of each. But in general, when the positive traits dominate the negative ones, socio-economic welfare is enhanced, and when the opposite is the case, welfare is reduced (See Twomey 1998, for a discussion of the contemporary importance of instinct theory).

Historically, Veblen noted that women have been more in tune with the positive rather than negative traits. They have tended to engage in workmanship, such as the gathering of berries and fruit, handicrafts or domestic duties, and they have been inculcated more with the parental instinct of love and affection. While women have been engaged in the development of workmanship and community, men have historically precipitated warfare, military intervention and imperialistic dominance, and criminal activities such as homicide and theft. This is true while men have also had the time to engage in idle curiosity, an activity often not allowed to women who have historically been left to domesticity or limited in their social perspectives. Thus, Veblen was the first important male feminist economist, and some modern feminists have been influenced by him in this respect.

Veblen further believed that capitalism was an advance on many earlier societies, but in any case was characterised by problematical trends associated with the dominance of certain of these traits or instincts, particularly in relation to class. His great work *The Theory of the Leisure Class* recognised that capitalism in its earliest competitive phase sought workmanship over profit and pecuniary values. But as it evolved, the pecuniary instinct (business) began to infect and eventually dominate workmanship (industry). The capitalist class sought pecuniary wealth while the working and technical classes were left to work and promote industry as the foundation of their survival. The common person, Veblen realised, only had his labour power to sell, and therefore if he didn't work he would not survive. The capitalist class as well as other propertied classes, on the other hand, could benefit from the fruits of others and the collectivity not only monetarily but also in terms of status, prestige and power. Thus class, defined in terms of employment and background, was a critical factor affecting production, distribution and exchange (see Veblen 1919).

Veblen recognised that economic agents and processes were also affected by human differences on the basis of race, ethnicity and nationality, which evolve through time and space. He wanted to include this as an important part of the substantive theory and analysis. His discussion of the transition from 'peaceable savagery' (primitive communism) to 'barbarian culture' (e.g., feudalism) illustrated the importance of cultural evolution in his work. His discussion of the 'three main ethnic types - the dolichocephalic-blond, the brachyce-phalic-brunette, and the Mediterranean' (Veblen 1899, p. 146) - showed that he was conscious of ethnic differences and this impact on the economy. Veblen sought to illustrate how these cultural and ethnic differences were influenced by the balance of various instincts of humanity.

In the history of economic thought, Veblen was the only major economist who sought to integrate questions of species, class, gender and ethnicity into institutional-cultural analysis. In attempting to examine these 'differences' with a theory of heterogeneous agents in a cultural paradigm, Veblen was decades ahead of his time. This type of analysis is only now being developed within radical political economy, especially by femininsts, neo-Marxist environmentalists, institutionalists and other radicals (see Dugger 1996, for some examples). Indeed, this problematic is seen to be a central problem of modern political economy, with many challenges ahead, with Veblen's analysis being an important guiding light in the progress of political economy.

CONCLUSION

Veblen castigated orthodox economics for not being an evolutionary science, but rather being a taxonomic, formalistic analysis of abstractions. He wanted to contribute to an evolutionary analysis of institutions, with an emphasis on the dominant institutions of capitalism through historical time. To this end, he provided the foundations for a holistic method that incorporates an interdisciplinary view of business cycles, the corporation, the leisure class, the vested interests, higher education, international relations and economic anthropology. He was the first political economist to examine explicitly the cumulative forces working through the institutions, leading to amplified motion as well as blind drift. His surplus approach to political economy was egalitarian in recognising the collective nature of wealth generation, and the contradictory motion of capitalism into the twentieth century. In place of rational economic man, he provided the foundations for the first view of 'hetero-institutionalia', or the institutional foundations of gender, race, species and class.

For economics to become an institutional-evolutionary science, there is no better person to follow than Veblen. It is only recently that his method and analysis have been resurrected and found to be very relevant to modern conditions. Much of Veblen's evolutionary economics has remained undeveloped since his time, and much is consistent with other trends in political economy. Along Veblenian lines economics must necessarily be holistic (in a concessive sense), recognising the importance of cumulative processes, the surplus approach, the forces of collective social wealth, and the linkages and differences between species, gender, race and class in the social construction of reality. Much work lies ahead in developing such a perspective.

NOTES

1. The social-structures-of-accumulation school developed a notion similar to that of Veblen, that suitable institutions can provide a reproductive foundation for growth and accumulation (see O'Hara 1999).

REFERENCES

Boulding, K. (1981), *Evolutionary Economics*, Beverly Hills: Sage Publications.
Dugger, W. (ed.) (1996), *Inequality: Radical Institutionalists Views on Race, Gender, Class and Nation*, Westport, Connecticut: Greenwood Press.
Georgescu-Roegen, N. (1971), *The Entropy Law and the Economic Process*. Cambridge, Mass: Harvard University Press.

Heller, P. (1996), 'Social capital as a product of class mobilization and state intervention: industrial workers in Kerala, India', *World Development*, vol. 24, no 6, pp. 1055-71.

Hodgson, G.M. (1998), 'The approach of institutional economics', *Journal of Economic Literature*, vol. XXX, March 1998, pp. 166-92.

James, S. (1984), *The Context of Social Explanation*, Cambridge: Cambridge University Press.

Kaldor, N. (1972), 'The irrelevance of equilibrium economics', *Economic Journal*, vol. 82, pp. 1237-55.

McCombie, J.S.L. and A.P. Thirwall (1994), *Economic Growth and the Balance-of-Payments Constraint*, New York: St Martin's Press.

Myrdal, G. (1944), *An American Dilemma: The Negro Problem and Modern Democracy*, New York: Pantheon Books, 2 volumes

Myrdal, G. (1968), *Asian Drama: An Inquiry into the Poverty of Nations*, New York: Twentieth Century Fund. 3 volumes.

O'Hara, P.A. (1993), 'Veblen's analysis of business, industry and the limits of capital: an interpretation and sympathetic critique', *History of Economics Review*, No 20, Summer 1993, pp. 95-119.

O'Hara, P.A. (1997), 'Veblen's critique of Marx's philosophical preconceptions of political economy', *European Journal of the History of Economic Thought*, vol. 4, no 1, Spring 1997, pp. 65-91.

O'Hara, P.A. (1998), 'Capital, the wealth of nations and inequality in the contemporary world', in Doug Brown (ed.), *Thorstein Veblen in the Twenty-First Century*. Cheltenham: Edward Elgar Publishing.

O'Hara, P.A. (1999), 'An institutionalist review of long wave theories: Schumpeterian innovation, modes of regulation and social structures of accumulation', in Fransisco Louçã and Jan Reijnders (ed.), *The Foundations of Long Wave Theory: Models and Methodology*, Cheltenham: Edward Elgar Publishing.

Pini, P. (1995), 'Economic growth, technological change and employment: empirical evidence for a cumulative growth model with external causation for nine OECD Countries: 1960-1990', *Structural Change and Economic Dynamics*, vol. 6, pp. 185-213.

Resnick, S. and W. Richard (1987), *Knowledge and Class: A Marxian Critique of Political Economy*, Chicago: University of Chicago Press.

Twomey, P. (1998), 'Reviving eblenian economic psychology', *Cambridge Journal of Economics*, vol. 22, pp. 433-48.

Veblen, T.B. (1898), 'Why is economics not an evolutionary science?', *Quarterly Journal of Economics*, Vol XII, July; reprinted in Veblen (1961), *The Place of Science in Modern Civilization and Other Essays*, New York: Russell and Russell. Also reprinted in *Cambridge Journal of Economics*, vol. 22, pp. 403-14.

Veblen, T.B. (1899), *The Theory of the Leisure Class: An Economic Study of Institutions*, London: Unwin Books, 1970.

Veblen, T.B. (1899-1900), 'The preconceptions of economic science', *Quarterly Journal of Economics*, vol. XIII, January & July 1899 and vol. XIV, February 1990; reprinted in Veblen (1964), *What Veblen Taught: Selected Writings of Thorstein Veblen*, New York, Augustus M. Kelley.

Veblen, T.B. (1904), *The Theory of Business Enterprise*, New Brunswick, New Jersey: Transaction Books.

Veblen, T.B. (1914), *The Instinct of Workmanship and the State of the Industrial Arts*, New Brunswick, New Jersey: Transaction Books.

Veblen, T.B. (1915), *Imperial Germany and the Industrial Revolution*, New Brunswick, New Jersey: Transaction Books.

Veblen, T.B. (1919), *The Vested Interests and the Common Man ('The Modern Point of View and the New Order')*, New York: Augustus M. Kelley, (1964).

Veblen, T.B. (1921), *The Engineers and the Price System*, New Brunswick, New Jersey: Transaction Books.

Veblen, T.B. (1923), *Absentee Ownership and Business Enterprise in Recent Times: The Case of America*, New York: Augustus M. Kelley.

Wilber, C. (1998), 'Holistic Method', in P.A. O'Hara (ed.), *Encyclopedia of Political Economy*, London and New York: Routledge.

World Bank (1997), *Expanding the Measure of Wealth: Indicators of Environmentally Sustainable Development*, Washington DC: World Bank.

4. Thorstein Veblen and the Political Economy of the Ordinary: Hope and Despair

Alan W. Dyer

diction, is what puts us in bonds, that with each word we utter we emit stipulations, agreements we do not know and do not want to know we have entered, agreements we were always in . . . [W]e are subject to expression and comprehension, victims of meaning . . . [Here is] a key to our sense of our distance from our lives (Cavell 1994, p. 40)

INTRODUCTION

This paper re-examines Thorstein Veblen's argument that orthodox, neoclassical economics is estranged from the very object about which it claims a special knowledge. His criticism, I argue, reflects the novelty of his alternative approach to economics. The main parts of my paper are an exploration of his alternative to neoclassical economics. I use ordinary language philosophy in order to show that Veblen is a significant, if flawed, practitioner of (what I call) ordinary language economics. His aim is to create a closer intellectual intimacy with ordinary or everyday economic practices; his case shows that this requires diligent efforts in order to keep our language from giving in to the temptations of intellectual estrangement.

I assume that most of you, if you think about Veblen at all, think of him as instrumental to the founding of something called American institutional economics. Certainly he influenced the work of key figures in this movement, like Wesley Clair Mitchell (1937), Clarence Ayres (1946), and Marc Tool (1979).[1] These writers, among others, have made use of Veblen's ideas that the economy is dichotomised between pecuniary and industrial ways of thinking and behaving, and that the dominant commercial ethos plays an unnecessarily large and obstructive role in the economy. My aim is not to refute these interpretations of Veblen's significance and impact. Once a writer releases his thought into the public domain, it should be allowed to resonate how and where it will. But there is, I think, a deeper message in how Veblen thinks about the economy, which can be made clear by using a different set of criteria for interpreting his work, criteria that show his feelings for the spirit and the philosophical method formalised in the second half of the twentieth century as ordinary language philosophy.

My approach is influenced by Stanley Cavell, whose idiosyncratic contribution to ordinary language philosophy is drawn from the works of J.L. Austin, Ludwig Wittgenstein, Henry David Thoreau, and Edgar Allan Poe, among others. In particular, I will explore the way in which Cavell's analysis of people's yearning for and alienation from the ordinary, echoes and illuminates Veblen's analysis of why people in a commercial culture experience a similar ambivalence toward their wealth.

If you like, you may consider this paper my attempt to *place* Veblen's economic analysis. By asking how we should place Veblen, I hope to get you to think about the broader issue of the place of economics. I will show the way in which Cavell's conclusion, that each of us faces a daily threat of homelessness, implies that an intellectual discipline can face the same threat. Just because we have tenured academic jobs, contribute to journals, and attend conferences does not mean that we have built a true home for our work in the wider world. One of my objectives in reading Veblen through Cavell is to search out a home for economics in Cavell's cosmopolitan world of philosophy, psychology, and literature.

Anyone who reads the literature will find Veblen described as a master ironist, an astute linguist, a dyspeptic Marxian, a giant in cultural analysis, a technophile, a moralist, and a sociologist in economist's clothing. I am prepared to accept almost all of these descriptions. Behind his multi-faceted intellectual presence, however, is a unifying analytical theme. Veblen identifies an inherent tendency to confuse economic need with commercial expediency in business culture, which transforms ordinary economic life into a ceaseless competition for pecuniary symbols of success. Because mainstream economics distances itself from the ordinary language of business culture, it cannot provide an analytical language for comprehending this competition and its consequences. Thus, Veblen's goal is to examine our unsettled place in ordinary economic experiences by bringing our economic language back to its everyday meanings.

ORDINARY LANGUAGE PHILOSOPHY: PROBLEMS OF ESTRANGEMENT AND DESPAIR

Since my new reading of Veblen is based upon my exposure to ordinary language philosophy through Cavell, it is helpful to describe what I have learned, so far, from him. Cavell says that the promise of this way of doing philosophy is not a defence of ordinary or conventional beliefs, but is rather a method or therapy for becoming more self-conscious about how we choose to live. This method helps us to explore our everyday language in order to learn on what we stake our identities. Listen to Cavell:

> Such questions as 'What should we say if . . . ?' or 'In what circumstances would we call . . . ?' asked of someone who has mastered the language (for example, oneself) is a request for the person to say something about himself, describe what he does. So the different methods are methods for acquiring self-knowledge . . . [W]e could say that what such answers are meant to provide us with is not more knowledge of matters of fact, but the knowledge of what could count as various 'matters of fact' (Cavell 1962, pp. 87-6)

Such innocent questions, however, pose a threat to identities built on conventional meanings. An examination of our ordinary language can reveal an emptiness or despair in the person (for example, oneself) under questioning. Cavell, based on his reading of Thoreau's *Walden*, identifies the source of this threat from ordinary language philosophy in the fact that

> we do not normally avail ourselves of [the connotations of our words, which] is a comment on our lives and shows our continuing need for art. (We have yet to learn to *live* undefined in front.) . . . We have not learned in the moral life, as the scientists have in theirs, how to seek and press to the limits of experience; so we draw our limits well short of anything reason requires (Cavell 1981, pp. 104, 74)

Ordinary language philosophy, then, asserts that, in order to explore the problem of self-consciousness, we must bring 'our ordinary assertions . . . back to a context in which they are alive' (ibid., 92).

It should be clear that ordinary language philosophy is driven by a concern over the degree of self-estrangement in the modern world and locates the source of this problem, in part, in the way in which we use language. Cavell's position is that self-consciousness is real, and really enslaved. For 'what *we* know as self-consciousness is only an opinion of ourselves, and like any other opinion it comes from outside; it is hearsay, our contribution to public opinion. We must become disobedient to it, resist it, no longer listen to it' (ibid., 107). In order to disobey this imposed self-consciousness, he proposes language therapy as a way of bringing us back, or truly next, to ourselves. This work is done by locating the everyday contexts in which our words have meaning. Finally, it is a mark of ordinary language philosophy to resist professional or any other form of specialisation. It does not claim any special range of interests or language, nor does it aim at any specific truths or discoveries, which would constitute its privileged discourse.

Cavell is fascinated with scepticism as an example of how we encounter the ordinary and of its effects on us.[2] Scepticism is, for Cavell, a battle with language. He argues that too often we forget the despair we suffer as language-beings, preferring to think of this aspect of our character only as a kind of great, good luck compared to the rest of nature. But the inherited, social nature of language is a source of dissatisfaction to the sceptic whose motto, 'We can never be certain that . . .', shows an unwillingness to admit his agreement to the shared criteria for using language. Cavell puts it this way:

> How we first deprive words of their communal possession and then magically and fearfully attempt by ourselves to overcome this deprivation of ourselves by ourselves, is a way of telling the story of skepticism (Cavell 1994, p. 60)

The problem with scepticism, for Cavell, is that it mistakes the kind of relationship to the external world of objects and other people that language allows us to create. The sceptic is disappointed because ordinary language does not provide meaning or knowledge apart from that which he chooses, agrees to, enacts. The sceptic wishes for a language in which 'the connection between [his] claims of knowledge and the objects of these claims occurs without [his] intervention, apart from [his] agreement' (Cavell 1982, pp. 351-2). This wish is born of a despair of language which, Cavell insists, implies a despair of the social. Psychologist Otto Rank generalises this despair or conflict in order to describe our modern (and, even more, post-modern?) condition. Cavell's sceptic is simply the most sharply formed version of civilised man who, according to Rank:

> even if he fights the outside world, is no longer opposed to a natural enemy but at bottom to himself, to his own creation, as he finds himself mirrored, particularly in manners and customs, morality and conventions, social and cultural institutions (Rank 1978, p. 3)

Another way of describing the sceptic's disappointment with language is to say that he practices a type of misguided individualism, seeking to express

Another way of describing the sceptic's disappointment with language is to say that he practices a type of misguided individualism, seeking to express himself by denying the mutuality inherent in language. For the sceptic, the social, represented by language in this case, is a source of error and an obstacle to finally saying what I mean. The sceptic paints a self-portrait:

> which tends to soberize, or respectify, or scientize itself, claiming, for example, greater precision or accuracy or intellectual scrupulousness than, for practical purposes, we are forced to practice in our ordinary lives (Cavell, 1994, p. 59)

This is an impossible type of non-conformity that ignores the absurdity of a private language. Real non-conformity is more subtle because it remains grounded in shared commitments, aware that to do otherwise leads to insanity.

Why is language analysis so important to Cavell? He uses two of his favourite authors, Henry David Thoreau and Edgar Allan Poe, to answer this question.[3] With their help Cavell identifies an uncanniness in the ordinary that poses a threat of estrangement in the midst of our use of language to fashion a self. Language is so important because 'our words are our claims upon the objects and contexts of our world; they show how we count phenomena, what counts for us' (Cavell 1981, p. 66). Yet, words are perverse: they never lie, but they can be used to lie (to oneself as well as to others) (Cavell 1994, p. 169). Though words are our creations, we are born into them and must spend our lives becoming ourselves through a linguistic rebirth. The fact that words are familiar to us does not diminish the fact that once we begin to create a place for ourselves in the world using language, and not merely submit to public opinion, we experience these same words as unfamiliar, and must struggle to make them express our cares and concerns. As Cavell says, being present in everyday life is 'not a given but a task' (ibid., p. 171).

We can begin to understand the therapeutic role of ordinary language analysis that Cavel modestly puts forward.[4] He believes that people choose either a passive or an active stance towards the use of language. Passively, people utilise the language of their culture without evaluating whether or not it effectively advances their needs and interests. Actively, people approach language by acknowledging their 'unauthorized life as it is . . . [and] struggle for its authorship' (ibid., p. 144). Instead of the sceptic's false hope of permanently overcoming the uncanny and alienating character of the ordinary, Cavell asks us to evaluate how faithful we are to our language. We are faithless to it when we refuse 'to withhold a word, to hold ourselves before it, so that we may assess our allegiance to it, to the criteria in terms of which we apply it' (Cavell 1981, p. 66). Therefore, to use language actively means to be faithful to language. The consequences of passive, estranged language beings goes beyond the effects on language and personal identities, according to Cavell, because it 'repeats our faithlessness to all of our shared commitments' (ibid.). The point of ordinary language analysis is to help us clarify our grounds of choice and our lines of connection with others.

VEBLEN'S ORDINARY LANGUAGE CRITIQUE OF STANDARD ECONOMICS

Essentially, Veblen accuses economists of abandoning the language and behaviour of commerce, which dominate our everyday economic practices, in favour of a stylised and sterilised vocabulary based on eighteenth century metaphysics. By accepting as their criteria for naming economic experiences psychological and anthropological notions assumed in Enlightenment philosophy, economists avoid a serious and engaged intimacy with the actual economy. As he says, while they may acknowledge that a commercial mentality has seeped into our evaluations of many non-commercial aspects of our lives, economists continue to deny the commercialisation of the economy (Veblen 1919b, p. 247).

Veblen's criticism of standard economics implies that economists have constructed their doctrines out of a despair of the ordinary language of economic life in commercial society. Consequently, they estrange themselves from the real economy - the economy we are forced to practise in our ordinary lives. Like Cavell's sceptic, economists have built a special language in order to capture the essence of economic phenomena based on the mistaken belief that ordinary language always misses this essence. Veblen's message is: there is no other language available to us if we want to remain grounded in the everyday world.

In 'The limitations of marginal utility', and more fully in 'Industrial and pecuniary employments', Veblen presents an ordinary language critique of what has come to be known as neoclassical economics. He explains that the theory of value and markets serves as a screen to eliminate the everyday language of the economy and to pretend that economic outcomes are the result of minimal and static social criteria for organising economic life. Neoclassical economics assumes criteria that are more a reflection of eighteenth century metaphysical beliefs than a result of careful observation of changing institutional patterns of thought and action (Veblen 1919, pp. 279-92). Motives of private ownership, self-interest, and self-determination, he says, are accepted uncritically as the isolable motives of economic agents, with no further inquiry into these agents' psychological motivations and social constraints.

terminology, very much in the spirit of John Ralston Saul's contemporary observation that:

> The new specialized terminology amounts to a serious attack on language as a tool of common understanding . . . [and] the walls between the boxes of expertise continue to grow thicker . . . The purpose of language is communication. It has no other reason for existence. (Saul, 1993, p. 476)

Three-quarters of a century before Saul, Veblen found himself defending his unconventional definition of capital as intangible assets - made up of things such as brand loyalty, market share, and public relations - against the orthodox view of capital as a means of production. He defends his definition by arguing that it better fits the apprehension of the 'common man out of doors' who:

> commonly has no more than a slender and sliding grasp of those honorable principles of certified make-believe that distinguish the modern point of view in all that relates to property and its uses; but he has had the benefit of some exacting experience in the ways of the new order and its standards of reckoning. (Veblen 1964e, pp. 46-7)

Or, in words that emphasise the qualities of language through which economists *should* communicate to the public:

> [The] common run [of people] do not habitually formulate their aspirations and convictions in extended and grammatically defensible documentary form, and the drift of [their] impulses therefore is not masked or deflected by the illusive consistencies of set speech . . . (Veblen 1964c, p. 178)

As we know, Veblen's effort to build an economics out of the ordinary language used in the factory, boardroom, and trading floor, was unsuccessful. But we need to understand better why he thought this was so important. With Cavell's help we shall see that it was decidedly not in order to defend 'common sense' beliefs about the economy nor even, contrary to what some of his critics argue, to lower the quality of economic discussion.

VEBLEN'S HOPE: AN ORDINARY LANGUAGE ECONOMICS

Veblen's key step in crossing the boundary of conventional and, in his estimation, estranged economic discourse is to turn his back on value theory. Putting aside methodological questions about the need for real life accuracy in our assumptions and the need for testable propositions (questions indicative, perhaps, of a despair of our intellectual relationship with the world), he finds value theory such a transparent mystification of actual economic behaviour, so primitive in its psychological and sociological awareness of everyday behaviour that he can only make fun of its depiction of economic man this way:

> a lightning calculator of pleasures and pains, who oscillates like a homogeneous globule of desire of happiness under the impulse of stimuli that shift him about the area, but leave him intact. . . . When the force of the impact is spent, he comes to rest, a self-contained globule of desire as before. (Veblen 1919c, pp. 73-4)

The theory of markets is, for Veblen, documentation of the economist's estrangement from ordinary economic practices. Its origins can be found in Adam Smith's metaphysical need to discipline commercial agents. Less a statement of the rights of free agents and private enterprise, the notion of an invisible hand is more an attempt by Smith to identify a means of protecting society from the deceit and deception of business enterprise (Dyer 1997, pp. 46-7). But, to Veblen, it comes to nothing more than a metaphysical hope for social order and fails to enlighten us about everyday economic practices. Because of this repressed wishfulness in the theory of markets, we may be able to account for the way economists have resisted all attempts to 'water-down' or to expose the metaphysical foundations of this 'knowledge'.

What is Veblen's alternative interpretation of ordinary economic life? It must begin, he insists, with the frank recognition that:

> So much then of the business man's activity as is conditioned by the institution of property, is not to be classed, in economic theory, as productive or industrial activity at all. Its objective point is an alteration of the distribution of wealth. His business is, essentially, to sell and buy - sell in order to buy cheaper, buy in order to sell dearer. It may or may not, indirectly, and in a sense incidentally, result in enhanced production . . . Under existing circumstances of ownership, the discretion in economic matters, industrial or otherwise, ultimately rests in the hands of business men. It is their business to have to do with property, and property means the discretionary control of wealth . . . Industry must be conducted to suit the business man in his quest for gain; which is not the same as saying that it must be conducted to suit the needs or the convenience of the community at large. (Veblen 1919a, pp. 296-8)

That is, ordinary economic life includes commercial and industrial interests. Of these two, commerce plays the controlling interest due to laws giving the owners of industrial property ultimate discretion in the use of this property. The aim of commerce has not changed much over the centuries: private gain - not always, but if necessary - at the expense of the community. Industry, as a collection of ownable properties, will then be put to use as commercial interests see fit, not legally, morally, or intentionally to serve the needs or convenience of the community. The theory of markets was meant to iron out this wrinkle in social cohesion. Veblen observes that such deep wrinkles respond rarely to fictitious irons. The message of his *Theory of Business Enterprise* is that the economist's eighteenth century faith in markets proved too ethereal to resist the aggression of commerce (Veblen 1975). To him, the response of business to the economist's faith is, 'You keep singing the praises of the market. We will build an economy around your pretty theory.' Veblen goes into the commercial trenches to learn about the economy, abandoning value theory as if it were nothing but a blinker meant to keep the horse of economic thought from getting spooked as it carries economists through the everyday economic landscape.

Central to his alternative view of economics is Veblen's ironic sense of the way commerce and excess come to dominate our every expression of human purpose. He uses irony and satire to depict the uncanniness of our everyday experiences, suggesting that our commercial way of being estranges us from these experiences. For example, we may like to think that the choices necessary to reach a sales target at a retail store, on the one hand, and those needed to reach the academic goals of a university, on the other hand, call for dissimilar decision criteria. But, as Veblen shows, an ordinary day of academic life is much closer to an ordinary day at the office than we are in the habit of admitting. Listen to his description of the goals of academic administration:

> It is one of the unwritten, and commonly unspoken, commonplaces lying at the root of modern academic policy that the various universities are competitors for the traffic in merchantable instruction, in much the same fashion as rival establishments in the retail trade compete for custom. Indeed, the modern department store offers a felicitous analogy . . . The need of a businesslike showing is instant and imperative, particularly in a business era of large turnover and quick returns, and to meet this need the uneventful scholastic life that counts toward the higher learning in the long run is of little use; so it can wait, and it readily becomes a habit with the busy executive to let it wait. (Veblen 1965, pp 88-89)

Here he describes the organisation of instruction:

> There is a well-considered preference for semi-annual or quarterly periods of instruction, with a corresponding time limit on the courses offered . . . Such a system of accountancy acts to break the continuity and consistency of the work of instruction and to divert the interests of the students from the work in hand to the making of a passable record in terms of the academic 'miner's inch'. Typically, this miner's inch is measured in terms of standard text per time unit, and the immediate objective of the teacher and student so becomes the compassing of a given volume of prescribed text, in print or lecture form . . . [w]hich puts a

premium on mediocrity and perfunctory work, and brings academic life to revolve about the office of the Keeper of the Tape and Sealing Wax. (ibid., pp. 104-5)

One need accept only a fraction of Veblen's observations here to arrive at the unsettling conclusion that universities are in the business of producing and selling credentials. He is describing the homelessness of educators and students caused by making the everyday rhythm of learning and research obey a commercial concern for things such as the turnover of capital and the standardisation of products and production methods. His satire and irony are meant to locate the reasons for the alienating experience of education in our general habit of imagining solutions to all our aspirations through the lens of business. His reading of higher education becomes, in turn, another example of the way our wealth, which permits us to establish a large educational system, does not ensure that we feel at home in school.

Some of Veblen's most biting humour is directed at those of us whose economic lives play out as a 'struggle for respectability' (Veblen 1919c, p. 394). He makes great fun of those who choose, for example, 'to go ill-clad in order to be well dressed', whose

> unremitting demonstration of ability to pay . . . is practically the only means . . . of impressing [their] respectability on the many to whom [they] are personally unknown, but whose transient good opinion [they] would so gladly enjoy. (ibid.)

He knows, of course, that this is no laughing matter. In words that anticipate the social psychology behind our contemporary economics of consumption and politics of resentment, he knows that it 'becomes as hard to give up that part of one's habitual "standard of living" which is due to the struggle for respectability, as it is to give up many physical comforts' (ibid.). Our despair, he claims, is our inability to distinguish between necessity and luxury, which is due to our passive acceptance of the pecuniary form of our ordinary economic lives.

CONCLUSION: VEBLEN'S DESPAIR IN LIGHT OF HIS ACHIEVEMENT

What is the best way of describing the ordinary language quality of Veblen's work? The first thing is his recognition that commerce and industry represent different criteria for naming economic cares and concerns. Because of the unique way in which these two outlooks are combined in a commercial society, it is difficult to see and hear that they represent separate points of view. This confusion is due to a mingling of vocabularies and to the dominant role played by commercial interests in the allocation of industrial know-how and equipment. Commerce is ultimately about hunches, one-up manship, capturing markets (Veblen 1919a, pp. 296-308). Industry is ultimately about cause and effect, integrated work processes, and meeting the material needs of society (Veblen 1964e, ch. 3). By articulating such a sharp distinction between commerce and industry, Veblen is asking us to consider how much of what we call 'economy' in fact serves the mundane purpose of sustaining life, and how much is a grafting of non-economic goals of status, power, and authority onto the stem of industry. In other words, he is asking us to consider, in a more conscious way, what we mean when we call ourselves economical and wealthy.

A second ordinary language quality of his work is the way he highlights the *arbitrary* nature of the criteria we use to name our experiences of the world by insisting that there is an inevitable clash between commercial and industrial 'language'. By pointing out the arbitrariness of our criteria, he reminds us of the insecurity of our position as language users and of the work we are required to do in order to establish a home in the world.

Finally, his provocative way of using language is meant to stimulate us to imagine an economy different than a commercial one. His aim here is very much in the spirit of Cavell's claim that ordinary language analysis aims to free our imaginations from the prison of unpondered choices:

> We have defined our lives in front. What at first seems like a deliberate choice turns out to be a choice all right . . . but not a deliberate one, not one weighed and found good, but one taken without pondering . . . they have never preferred it. And yet this is nothing less than a choice of one's life. (Cavell 1992, p. 73)

The lesson of ordinary language philosophy is that a deliberate choice requires us to make ourselves vulnerable to misunderstanding from the guardians of conventional diction. Cavell describes why this is so this way:

> To write knowing that your words emit a breath of virtue or vice every moment, that they communicate the means by which you are expressing your desires, know them or not, is to leave your character unguarded. (Cavell 1994, p. 25)

This is only one of the ways in which Cavell explains what he means when he says that our difficulty in being faithful to our language reflects the same difficulty in all of our shared commitments.

Despite his achievements in pointing the way towards a new diction in economics, it is necessary to acknowledge Veblen's ultimate hesitation in carrying through on his ordinary language analysis of the economy. I call this his loss of faith in the ordinary. In his choice to present technology as the agent of historical change, he shrinks from the portent of the ordinary: the absence of any guarantee that people will choose to ponder sufficiently life in a commercial republic in order to redirect the unsocial and uneconomical urges behind commerce to other, non-economic, and less consequential, activities.

It is fairly easy to identify the virtues emitted through Veblen's words. As Christopher Lasch notes, he among others at the beginning of the 20th century sought to assert the dignity of labour against the increasing corporatisation of the economic landscape in America (Lasch 1991, 346). His praise of workmanship - its simple needs, fair treatment of others, and concern for community well-being - is meant to counter the view that labour is somehow old-fashioned and unheroic, a sign of missing out on the happening of the great game of commercial intrigue and self-promotion. However, throughout his writings one hears a deep pessimism towards the various attempts to give labour greater dignity or say in the nature of economic practices. So, for example, he finds that the leaders of the Army of the Commonweal are paternalistic and committed to an 'articulate hallucination' (Veblen 1964a, p. 97). Or, he describes the proponents of the arts and crafts movement as well-meaning, but nostalgic (Veblen 1964b, pp. 196-7). Finally, in the final chapter of *The Instinct of Workmanship*, he criticises the trade union movement as interested in little more than assuring their members a greater share of the income pie; little better, that is, than an infestation of commercial spirit among the ranks of labour (Veblen 1964d, p. 346). As a result, Veblen resorts to faith in technology as an historical agent of change, removing change from the will and responsibility of individual economic actors. Technology, he implies, will create the mentality needed for establishing new economic grounds of sociability. He loses faith in his words and their power to provoke a critical self-scrutiny and imaginative response in others. It is as though he succumbs to the despair of being heard and understood through ordinary language and, like so many before him, creates a salve of metaphysical certainty to cool the pain of his despair. Ultimately, he shrinks from the challenge of the everyday battle over what criteria and words we will choose to name our economic cares and concerns.

NOTES

1. For a fuller account of Veblen's influence on American institutionalists, see Allan G. Gruchy's *Modern Economic Thought* (1967) and *Contemporary Economic Thought* (1972).
2. For Cavell's most extended discussion of scepticism see, 'Skepticism and the Problem of Others', part four of his *The Claim of Reason* (1982).
3. I was tempted to write 'two of his favourite philosophers' because Cavell has nearly convinced me that Thoreau and Poe are as much philosophers as they are journal and fiction writers. But, since I am asking my readers to listen to so many strange notions anyway, it is better to leave out some of the unfamiliarity in this train of thought, especially when it is not central to my immediate purposes.
4. See (1994, p. 12) for Cavell's modest (almost reluctant) acknowledgement that ordinary language philosophy has therapeutic implications.

REFERENCES

Ayres, Clarence (1946), *The Divine Right of Capital*, Boston: Houghton-Mifflin.

Cavell, Stanley (1962), 'The availability of Wittgenstein's later philosophy', *The Philosophical Review*, 71 (January): 67-93.

Cavell, Stanley (1981), *The Senses of Walden: An Expanded Edition*, Chicago: University of Chicago Press.

Cavell, Stanley (1982), *The Claim of Reason: Wittgenstein, Skepticism, Morality, and Tragedy*, Paperback edition, Oxford: Oxford University Press.

Cavell, Stanley (1994), *In Quest of the Ordinary*, Paperback edition, Chicago: University of Chicago Press.

Dyer, Alan W. (1997), 'Prelude to a theory of Homo Absurdus: variations on themes from Thorstein Veblen and Jean Baudrillard', *Cambridge Journal of Economics*, 21 (January): 45-53.

Gruchy, Allan G. (1967), *Modern Economic Thought: The American Contribution*, Reprint, New York: Augustus M. Kelley.

Gruchy, Allan G. (1972), *Contemporary Economic Thought*, Clifton: Augustus M. Kelley.

Lasch, Christopher (1991), *The True and Only Heaven: Progress and Its Critics*, New York: Norton.

Mitchell, Wesley Claire (1937), *The Backward Art of Spending Money*, New York: McGraw-Hill.

Rank, Otto (1978), *Truth and Reality*, New York: Norton.

Saul, John Ralston (1993), *Voltaire's Bastards: The Dictatorship of Reason in the West*, New York: Vintage.

Tool, Marc (1979), *The Discretionary Economy*, Santa Monica: Goodyear.

Veblen, Thorstein (1919a), 'Industrial and pecuniary employments', in *The Place of Science in Modern Civilization*, New York: Huebsch.

Veblen, Thorstein (1919b), 'The limitations of marginal utility', in *The Place of Science in Modern Civilisation*. New York: Huebsch.

Veblen, Thorstein (1919c), 'Why is economics not an evolutionary science?', in *The Place of Science in Modern Civilisation*, New York: Huebsch.

Veblen, Thorstein (1964a), 'The army of the Commonweal', in *Essays in Our Changing Order*, Reprint, Leon Ardzrooni (ed.), New York: Augustus M. Kelley.

Veblen, Thorstein (1964b), 'Arts and crafts', in *Essays in Our Changing Order*, Reprint, Leon Ardzrooni (ed.), New York: Augustus M. Kelley.

Veblen, Thorstein (1964c), *An Inquiry Into the Nature of Peace and the Terms of Its Perpetuation*, Reprint, New York: Augustus M. Kelley.

Veblen, Thorstein (1964d), *The Instinct of Workmanship and the State of the Industrial Arts*, Reprint, New York: Augustus M. Kelley.

Veblen, Thorstein (1964e), *The Vested Interests and the Common Man*, Reprint, New York: Augustus M. Kelley.

Veblen, Thorstein (1965), *The Higher Learning in America: A Memorandum on the Conduct of Universities by Business Men*, Reprint, New York: Augustus M. Kelley.

Veblen, Thorstein (1975), *The Theory of Business Enterprise*, Reprint, New York: Augustus M. Kelley.

5. Veblen and Theories of the 'Firm'

Anne Mayhew

INTRODUCTION

The theme of these meetings: 'Why is economics not an evolutionary science?: Institutions, learning and change', honours the publication, 100 years ago, of Thorstein Veblen's famous essay. In that spirit I will draw upon one of Veblen's own applications of his evolutionary approach, in *The Theory of the Business Enterprise*, to argue (1) that analysis of organisations such as 'the firm' require a more open approach than that found in most recent 'evolutionary' theories of the firm; (2) that it is in part a desire for 'agency' that has perpetuated the anti-Veblenian and anti-evolutionary aspects of these theories of the firm; and (3) that new developments in economic sociology, cognitive anthropology and other social sciences may offer solutions to the problem of agency that are more truly Veblenian and evolutionary.

THE FIRM VERSUS OPEN THEORIES OF BUSINESS ENTERPRISE

Modern 'evolutionary' theories typically (Nelson and Winter 1982; Penrose 1959; Williamson 1985) deal with 'the firm' as part of analyses of what is assumed to be a socio-economic system populated by 'the firm', 'the state', 'consumers', and, for some analytic purposes, 'the workers'. These are discrete entities. The firm, in turn, is an abstraction from many different firms that share characteristics but whose variation in respect of 'competencies' and other traits is the subject matter of 'the theory of the firm'. Theories of the firm are said to be evolutionary in so far as they describe changes in competencies and other firm variables that emerge in a struggle for survival. In the modern theories of the firm, evolution means the process by which firms change in response to a relatively unchanging set of stresses or competitive pressures.[1] Put briefly, modern theories of the firm are concerned with common themes in the histories of firms, whereas Veblen was concerned with the history of a socio-economic system in which firms played a major role.

Modern theories are part of what I here call a fixed system. Basic socio-economic relationships are assumed to be known, defined by nature or by history or by the terms of the analysis. Firms produce and sell, consumers buy and use, states govern and regulate, workers are inputs whose labour/skills are purchased, and perhaps augmented, by firms. These relationships amount to an assumption of systemic invariance and allow analysis to begin with 'the firm', 'the state', consumers, and workers.

By contrast, Veblen's analysis in *The Theory of Business Enterprise* did not begin with an assumption of invariant socio-economic relationships.[2] Indeed, a record of systemic variance is the platform for Veblen's analyses. All of Veblen's analyses - of firms, of governments, of consumers, of workers - began with assumptions about common characteristics of human beings,[3] but with minimum assumptions about the way in which those humans are grouped in common activity at any time in history.[4] In some of his earlier efforts at evolutionary economics, Veblen borrowed very heavily from the work of the then dominant historical/evolutionary school in anthropology. He assumed the existence of a socio-economic organisation of hypothetical periods of savagery and of barbarism (Mayhew 1998). However, in *The Theory of Business Enterprise* and in almost all of his later work, Veblen began his analysis at a known place in space and time so as to give historical specificity to the human groups. From that beginning, he then described how new groups and interests formed and how interrelationships among groups changed.

How did this approach affect Veblen's analysis of business enterprise? In *The Theory of Business Enterprise*, Veblen describes a process whereby the modern firm itself comes into being. Unlike later theorists, he does not begin with the firm as a given. For Veblen, the firms that were rapidly becoming dominant in his era had emerged from a confluence of two developments in the West: the development of business enterprise and the industrial revolution. Business enterprise had begun as a way of organising trade, with little emphasis on production (Veblen 1904, pp. 21-2). The institutions that developed from the growth of trade (institutions to organise shipping, merchandising and banking) were in place when the industrial revolution of the eighteenth and nineteenth centuries began to make large-scale organisation of production a feasible target for income-seeking traders. From this confluence, the modern industrial firm - which is the firm of modern theory[5] - was born.

Veblen's story does not stop there, nor does it become a story of industrial firms competing within an unchanging system. New groups were formed through shared interests and interactions with firms. 'Workmen', as Veblen called them, became an industrial labour force (1904, pp. 307-11); consumers-as-wage-earners became dependent not so much on the vagaries of the weather as on the unfolding of a business cycle (1904, Chap. VII), and were beginning to recognise their interests in the state of the aggregate economy.[6]

Ideas of ownership and property, which had developed much earlier in respect of land and the tools of craftsmen, were modified to allow ownership of shares of future income streams. This had the rather odd consequence that

> . . . the general body of owners are necessarily reduced to the practical status of pensioners dependent on the discretion of the great holders of immaterial wealth; the general body of business men are similarly . . . disfranchised in point of business initiative and reduced to a bureaucratic hierarchy under the same guidance; and the rest, the populace, is very difficult to bring into the schedule except as raw material of industry. (1904, pp. 266-7)

Further, Veblen noted, as have many economists and economic historians,[7] that the new firms changed their own environments. Variation of output in response to price competition became a threat to survival when overhead costs became a large part of total costs, and this created a new kind of competition - cut-throat competition, in the words of the day. Veblen wrote that 'the heroic role of the captain of industry' had been to reduce the number of businessmen involved in management by virtue of consolidation: it was, he said, 'a casting out of business men by the chief of business men' (1904, p. 49).

In the last portion of *Business Enterprise*, Veblen speculated on the likely outcome of other changes underway at the time that he was writing. Consumer purchases of durable goods were increasing rapidly, advertising was becoming an important feature of the US economy, real incomes of workers were rising, and so was discretionary income. Veblen thought – rightly - that these trends were profoundly changing the nature of the economy. A new class of consumers was emerging. Within the firm itself, the engineers about whom Veblen wrote throughout his career (Knoedler and Mayhew, forthcoming) had emerged as important players in the new firms. Not even 'the state' immune from changes as business interests 'urge an aggressive national policy', even as the machine process tended to undermine patriotism among the population at large.

Veblen's speculations about the likely consequences of changes underway would repay further consideration in light of what we now know about the creation of a mass consumption society and the impact of work and consumption on families and social organisation, but that is beyond the scope of this paper.[8] What is important is that Veblen's 'theory of the firm' differs sharply from the accounts offered as part of the fixed systems of analysis of Nelson, Winter, Penrose, Williamson, and other modern theorists. Indeed, my co-panellist Nicholas Foss has recently argued that, by the standards of modern theorists, '. . .Veblen never developed a systematic theory of the firm, and even less an 'evolutionary' theory of the firm. . .' (1998, p. 479). Foss's argument in support of this conclusion is precisely relevant to the distinction I wish to make between fixed and open systems of analysis, and I will use his argument to make my point.

Foss argues that three of Veblen's concerns/preconceptions got in the way of his developing an evolutionary theory of the firm: (1) 'His views on the firm were in various ways embedded in his broader view of the capitalist, pecuniary economy in which monetary relations dominated production' (p. 479); (2) he 'was primarily interested in firms because they were necessary components in his broader arguments'; (3) like almost all economists until the mid-1970s, Veblen had little interest in the firm.[9]

In this explanation of Veblen's failure to produce a theory of the firm, Foss provides a shortcut to summarise salient features of modern theories of the firm that distinguishes between fixed and open systems. Consider each of Foss's points again, but turn them upside down. Modern theorists (1) are interested in the firm as abstracted from the socio-economic system, which is another way of saying that systemic groupings and relationships are assumed invariant; (2) assume monetary relations to be sufficiently secondary to production so that they can be set aside as belonging to a separate macroeconomic arena;[10] (3) treat the firms of neoclassical theory as entities with individual and relevant characteristics beyond those treated in the 'production function view'.

There is no doubt whatsoever that these modern 'theories of the firm' are superior to the older microtheoretic neoclassical treatments because they recognise the importance of path-dependence (history), of tacit knowledge, of group and social learning, and of other group dynamics that make firms different from each other and that cause them to change over time. However, theories that are created within a set of fixed as opposed to open socio-economic relations must always truncate analysis. One of the great strengths of Veblen's work is that he recognised the limitations imposed by such truncation. It seems likely that he recognised the importance of open analysis, at least in part, because of the role that anthropological work had played in his intellectual development and in the emphasis he placed upon cultural variation.

The dangers of truncating analysis by an assumption of invariance in basic socio-economic organisation and relationships is conventionally illustrated in anthropology with examples of the way in which how kinship varies. Within our own various societies it is easy to speak of 'the family' with a reasonable certainty that listeners will attach the same range of meaning to that term as does the speaker. 'The family unit' in most modern western societies probably means adult man and woman with biological descendants, perhaps with biologically unrelated but legally adopted offspring, and possibly with one, or at most two, parents of the adults. In a broader meaning, family includes grown offspring, their spouses, and their children. As changing relationships in recent decades have made clear, perhaps most acutely in the US, other 'family' groupings - say woman and biological children by several mates - are often viewed as unnatural and wrong. However, what anthropologists have taught us is that accurate tracing of kinship and of the rights and responsibilities of child rearing and provisioning requires that we begin with minimal assumptions. Any analysis that begins with the assumption of 'family' as a unit in which biological or legally declared 'mother' and 'father' provide care and provision would wrongly describe the many systems that have been found where mother's brother is a major provider for mother and children, or where all in a hunting/gathering band participate in provision.

Modern theories of the firm seem to be subject to these same dangers. The emphases given to technological performance and innovation, competencies, the habits and routines that are part of these competencies, and the nature of contracting with other, often financial, firms do not hide the fact that 'the firm' is still the firm of neoclassical analysis.[11] It has been given individuality and complexity and its bureaucratic nature has been recognised, but it retains 'production of goods' as its major reason for being, and it stands in the same relationships to consumers, to governments, to citizens, and to all other groups as the simpler neoclassical firm is assumed to have done. What is missed by this truncation? Among other aspects of firm interaction that have been dealt with in the more open Veblenian tradition and in economic sociology are the creation of wants, roles in taste-making, value creation, status definition through consumption, socialisation and self-definition of individuals, provision of social security through pension funds, medical care (especially in the US) and education, governance, and much more.

Most dangerous of all, however, may be the fact that 'the firm' does convey a common meaning to all who use the term. Return for a moment to the family: it is precisely the assumption that we all know what 'the family' is that makes the term so treacherous in discussions of public policy. Because the term has a ready and common meaning of mother-father-biological children, other social groupings, however common in fact, are easily thought to be aberrations. In the case of 'the firm', all of those who are involved in the conversation of modern economics also share a range of ideas that may or may not actually fit common patterns. Perhaps most strikingly to those who take Marx, Veblen, and Keynes seriously, the common assumption about what firms do seems to exclude the possibility of firms, such as the many financial service providers, that have figured out how to go directly from money to more money without the onerous step of producing goods on the way.[12] While there is nothing wrong with focusing on firms that produce goods, there is something wrong with a theory of the firm that excludes from consideration the many firms in modern economies that do not produce goods. There is also something wrong with forcing these firms into a mould created to fit goods-producing firms.

To summarise: fixed theories of 'the firm', 'the state', consumers, and workers may make accurate description of prevailing patterns difficult and, more importantly, may mask assumptions about the 'normal' state of these entities and their interrelations. Why not, then, open the analysis as Veblen did? Perhaps the failure of modern evolutionary theories of the firm to be more open simply reflects the early development of these theories. A broader range of concerns may yet develop. It is possible that the theories of the firm developed over the past 20 years or so will yet move beyond the traditional disciplinary boundaries and incorporate the broader range of firm activities that are often described in non-economic and in heterodox literature. Possible, but I suspect that there is an additional and very important barrier to openness of analysis.

THE NEED FOR AGENCY

A common criticism of the institutionalist tradition created by Veblen - if not always of Veblen himself - is that human agency was ignored, or inadequately incorporated. Similar criticisms were levied against anthropologists and sociologists who, in the first half of the 20th century, built upon the same ideas that form the core of Veblenian thought.[13] Among modern economic and other theorists, there is a deep suspicion of explanations of change that fail to recognise explicitly self-interest, a capacity for learning, and the exercise of will.

Exercise of agency, however, requires a goal, a purpose. Utility-maximising models of individual human behaviour have appealed to anthropologists, sociologists, and other social scientists as a way to incorporate agency into their models.[14] Many theorists of the firm have been aware of the tautological nature of utility-maximising models (Nelson and Winter 1982, Ch. 1) and, at the same time, have been able to avoid its traps by assuming real and common-sense goals for the firms they model. Firms do wish to survive; the commercial logic requires that they take in sufficient revenue to meet all monetary obligations, so as to enhance the likelihood of survival. This simple proposition does not necessarily lead, as Foss points out with admirable clarity, to the contractual (transactions costs) view of the firm, but can lead instead to a more revealing competencies-based approach. Nevertheless, even approaches in which firms are seen as path-determined, 'seeker[s] of (sustained) competitive advantage' who diversify, learn and innovate (Foss 1998, p. 485), still retain a great deal of the fixity of the socio-economic system.

Solutions that will allow retention of agency - that is, human purpose and intelligence–and yet recognise the openness of all aspects of socio-economic systems to redefinition and change are now emerging in several of the social sciences.[15] When, in the 1950s and 1960s, the importance of agency began to become a major basis for criticism of older social theories, the theory of rational choice seemed the only way to model it. However, over the past decade, in anthropology, psychology, political science, and sociology, there has been renewed emphasis on cognitive theory and learning. Cognitive anthropology, for example, is based upon the proposition that 'cultural meanings' indeed have force and are stable (hence, in some sense, 'culture' is real after all), yet they are not a mold into which passive humans are poured. Two modern anthropologists put it this way: "We cannot explain cultural meanings unless we see them as created and maintained in the interaction between the extraperson and intrapersonal realms' (Strauss and Quinn, 1998, p. 8).

Can this way of thinking be useful in treating firms? Yes. For example, Thomas Ford Brown (1998), an economic sociologist, describes social networks as mechanisms by which the valuations that result in demand for the products of the firms of economic theory are formed, and shows how these social networks are themselves influenced by producing firms. Goods assume value in part from their role in identifying individuals as part of a network, and through the network tastes and preferences about goods are further developed. The valuations that result from information that is created and disseminated through overlapping social networks are in part a consequence of the efforts of firms to market their goods. Though Brown's work is only a first step in interdisciplinary exploration of the interaction of firms and other social groups in demand creation, it is important as an effort to treat firms in a larger social context.

In the new and innovative social science, individuals are seen as active participants in creating complex systems that change cumulatively. How would these efforts affect current 'theories of the firm'? Much of what has been accomplished, particularly in the competencies based literature, can easily be subsumed as part of recent trends in the social sciences. The emphasis on learning, on change, on firms as cognitive communities, is entirely consistent with the work now going on elsewhere. What probably cannot be maintained is much of the formalism of many modern theories of the firm; complex goals and multiple processes of learning do not translate well into mathematical equations. What will also be required is precisely the kind of openness that Veblen used in *The Theory of Business Enterprise*. Such openness will have a number of consequences, including further erosion of the boundaries between economics and neighbouring disciplines.

An open model will also require abandonment of the search for a theory of the firm because it will be recognised that there is no such thing as the firm. Many organisations produce goods, some of which are firms (General Motors, agribusinesses); but others that produce goods are only quasi-firms (family farms). Many organisations provide various kinds of services: some are firms (banks), some are not (universities). There are organisations partially patterned as firms for reasons of law (many not-for-profit organisations), and there are groups that are not recognised as firms but which operate in part as though they were (some street gangs).

Evolutionary analyses of economic systems require recognition of a diversity of organisation within modern economies, and a lack of fixity of the lines between traditional, goods-producing firms, and other forms of social organisation. However, theories of firms as changing forms of business enterprise can flourish in the richer intellectual context that is now developing in the social sciences. They will be theories of firms that Veblen would certainly have applauded.

NOTES

1. See Hodgson 1993, Ch.3 for the best taxonomy of evolutionary approaches. Hodgson's description of the work of Nelson and Winter and others as '. . .strictly phylogenetic, but asymptotic to an ontogenetic form. . .' remains apt. All firms in the population are subject to change and their 'genes' or routines and competencies will change as a result. However, the assumption of an unchanged process - of something very like the competitive process of non-evolutionary models of firm behaviour - gives ontogenetic character to these evolutionary theories.
2. On this point, see Argyrous (1996).
3. Human beings were active, purposive in action, guided by inherited ideas (culture), inquisitive and acquisitive social beings for whom status within the social group was a major goal.
4. See *The Theory of Business Enterprise* for an analysis of firms, *Imperial Germany* as the exemplar of a state, and the chapter on 'The Cultural Incidence of the Machine Process' in *Business Enterprise* for one of Veblen's attempts to analyse workers and consumers. His writing on the last two groups was more scattered but there is a common theme. Veblen thought the relationships of both workers and of buyers of the greatly increased output of the machine process to employers and firms to be in such flux that it was difficult to describe any fixed relationship. This was a reasonable observation in early 20th century America, where modern mass consumption was in its early stages and where the relationship of wage labourers to bureaucratic firms was undergoing rapid change.

5. Penrose stresses the point that the firm of her theory is the industrial firm. See1959 pp. 19-22.
6. In light of current events, Veblen's words seem particularly appropriate: 'Before business principles came to dominate everyday life the common welfare, when it was not a question of peace and war, turned on the ease and certainty with which enough of the means of life could be supplied . . . Under the old regime of handicraft and petty trade, dearth (high prices) meant privation and might mean famine and pestilence; under the new regime low prices commonly mean privation and may on occasion mean famine' (p. 177). 'To the workmen engaged in industry, particularly, substantial benefits accrue from an era of prosperity. These benefits come, not in the way of larger returns for a given amount of work, but more work, fuller employment, at about the earlier rate of pay' (p. 211).
7. Chandler, (1977), Lamoreaux (1985), John Bates Clark and John Maurice Clark (1912).
8. For example, Veblen suggested that 'There is a visible weakening of the family ties, a disintegration of the conventions of household life, throughout large classes'. Among other things, the 'headship of the male in the household economy' is in jeopardy, Veblen. He was neither approving nor disapproving these trends, simply noting them.
9. Foss does say that, more than most economists of his time, Veblen avoided the 'standard production function view' and may be seen as a precursor of the modern competence-based approach in that he did 'not treat the firm as a completely anonymous entity in price-theoretic analysis' (1998, p. 480). Foss also says, in praise: '. . .Veblen may be reconstructed as reaching for an understanding of the firm as a distinct, historical entity, characterised among other things, by its group-based knowledge assets' (Foss 1998, p. 480). Foss is, however, bothered, as are many others, by Veblen's critical and satirical views. It is perhaps worth saying that *The Theory of Business Enterprise* contains little of the satire that, in other works of Veblen, delights many and offends many others. Indeed, both satire and criticism are muted in this book, which is in many ways Veblen's best, though not necessarily for that reason. Perhaps it remains less read than others precisely because it must be read as straightforward economic analysis.
10. Or money can be treated as simply another input, with the relationship of firm to money suppliers modelled in the same manner as relationships among other firms are modelled in the modern theories of the firm. See, for example, Thomas Marmefelt (1998).
11. Hence the greater comfort of Foss (and others) with Alfred Marshall and Frank Knight as predecessors than with Veblen (p. 482). However, I should also note that Foss levels much the same criticism against the contractual approach to the firm.
12. See Dillard (1980) for a comparison of the work of all three on the 'monetary theory of production'.
13. See Mayhew (1980) for sources.
14. See, for example, Wilk (1996).
15. Recent discussion of the relationship of 'knowledge' and of 'information' on AFEEMAIL provided a number of sources to work being done in Psychology and Philosophy. In Economic Sociology the work of Granovetter (1992) provides an excellent example

REFERENCES

Argyrous, G. and R. Sethi (1996), 'The theory of evolution and the evolution of theory: Veblen's methodology in contemporary perspective', *Cambridge Journal of Economics*, Vol. 20: 475-95.

Brown, T.F. (1998), 'Consumer demand and the social construction of industry', *Working Paper Series*, No. 22, Program in Comparative and International Development, Baltimore, MD: Department of Sociology, Johns Hopkins University.

Chandler, A.D., Jr. (1977), *The Visible Hand: The Managerial Revolution in American Business*, Cambridge, Mass: Harvard University Press.

Clark, J.B. and J.M. Clark (1912), *The Control of Trusts*, New York: Macmillan.

Dillard, D. (1980), 'A monetary theory of production', *Journal of Economic Issues*, XIV: 2 (June 1980): 255-73.

Foss, N. J. (1998), 'The competence-based approach: Veblenian ideas in the modern theory of the firm', *Cambridge Journal of Economics*, Vol. 22: 479-495.

Granovetter, M. (1992), 'Economic instituions as social constructions: A framework for Analysis', *Acta Sociologica*, 35: 3-11.

Hodgson, G. (1993), *Economics and Evolution: Bringing Life Back Into Economics*, Cambridge UK and Ann Arbor MI: Polity Press and University of Michigan Press.

Lamoreaux, N.R. (1985), *The Great Merger Movement in American Business, 1895-1904*, New York.

Marmefelt, T. (1998), 'Schumpterian banker-entrepreneur interaction and the spontaneous evolution of bank-industry networks: why institutional endowments matter', in Neilsen, K. and B. Johnson (eds), *Institutions and Economic Change: New Perspectives on Markets, Firms and Technology*, Cheltenham, UK and Northampton, MA: Edward Elgar.

Mayhew, A. (1980), 'Atomistic and cultural analyses in economic anthropology: an old argument repeated', in Adams, J. (ed.), *Institutional Economics*, Boston: Marginus Nijoff Publishing.

Mayhew, A. (1998), 'Veblen and the anthropological perspective', in Samuels, W. (ed.), *The Founding of Institutional Economics*, London: Routledge.

Nelson, R.R. and S.G. Winter (1982), *An Evolutionary Theory of Economic Change*, Cambridge MA and London: The Belknap Press of Harvard University Press.

Penrose, E. T. (1959), *The Theory of the Growth of the Firm*, Oxford: Basil Blackwell.

Strauss, C. and N. Quinn (1997), *A Cognitive Theory of Cultural Meaning*, New York: Cambridge University Press.

Veblen, T. (1904), *The Theory of Business Enterprise*, New York: Charles Scriberners Sons.

Wilk, R.R. (1996), *Economies and Cultures: Foundations of Economic Anthropology*, Bounder, CO: Westview Press.

Williamson, O. (1985), *The Economic Institutions of Capitalism: Firms, Markets, Relational Contracting*, New York: The Free Press.

6. Institutional Economics and the Specificity of Social Evolution: About the Contribution of J.R. Commons

Laure Bazzoli

INTRODUCTION

At the time of the centenary celebration of T. Veblen's famous essay on the necessity of an evolutionary approach to economic theory, it may be useful to evaluate the contribution to this project of J.R. Commons, the other major figure of Institutionalism. His conception of evolution, which is far less well-known than Veblen's, has been relatively neglected, even by the Institutionalist school of thought.

This paper examines Commons's views concerning the Institutionalist evolutionary approach. I want to argue that his conception deserves attention if one wants to consider the specificity of evolution in the area of social phenomena and that this issue is crucial for American Institutional Economics.[1] Commons differentiated himself from Veblen in order to deal with this issue of the specificity of social evolution: although he adopted Veblen's general view of the logic of an evolutionary science, he nevertheless defended the metaphor of artificial selection, and not the one of natural selection, as relevant for social sciences. Commons thereby developed a somewhat different conception of evolution and analysis of the process of institutional change, linked to an original epistemological vision of social sciences.

The point is to establish a genuinely evolutionary theory based on a conception of institutions alternative to the individualistic and the structuralist perspectives. The principle of artificial selection, I shall argue, must be put at the core of the Institutionalist research programme, because it encapsulates the complex interactions between individual action and collective action in the process of evolution. It is also the reason Commons's conception is of relevance for current debates in evolutionary theory: not only does it consitute a deep criticism of the standard natural selection metaphor adopted in mainstream economics, but it deals with a question of crucial importance today, namely the problem of the connection between the purposeful dimension of action and the non-teleological nature of evolution, a question that Veblen's conception cannot really answer (Rutherford 1998). Furthemore, Commons's conception of evolution through artificial selection considers the larger problem of the theory of social value and of the relationship between positive and normative analysis of change; social evolution can not be understood without taking into account the role of the schemes of value, their dynamics and the normative implications of institutional change. And this is a major issue for the Institutionalist theory of evolution.

I shall first consider the question as to the way in which Commons differentiated himself from Veblen. Then I will present a synthetic understanding of his analysis of social evolution. Finally, I will stress some legacy of this conception for an institutionalist evolutionary theory.

1. FROM VEBLEN TO COMMONS: THE QUESTION OF NON-TELEOLOGICAL EVOLUTION

In *Institutional Economics*, Commons considers explicitly his agreements and disagreements with the conception of Veblen. I begin with their common project.

A Common Project for the Institutionalist Evolutionary Theory

For the two authors, the issue is to build a theory of the genesis and evolution of modern institutions, that is, to understand the processes by which new forms of behaviour and rules emerge and persist. Commons in fact follows Veblen on the general meaning of Darwinian evolutionism.

Several points characterise their common understanding of the necessity to reconstruct economic theory along Darwinian lines.

Following the pragmatist philosopher C.S. Peirce, Institutionalists consider Darwinism as an epistemological and methodological break with classical thinking. Both Veblen and Commons want to build an alternative to the teleological conceptions developed by economists: the one of equilibrium or natural order of mainstream economics[2] and the one of the dialectic of class struggle in Marxist economics. The Darwinian revolution means that there is no known end state, no state of normality, no law of development ('foreordained evolution', as Commons says), no goal in evolution ; in short, an evolutionary analysis cannot be teleological. Their point is to analyse evolution as an indeterminate, cumulative and irreversible historical process. This is why Commons asserts that he starts 'as does Veblen with a cross-section, at a point of time, of a process which has no beginning and no ending, and then (proceeds) to the changing complexities of that process' (Commons [1934] 1990, p. 678).

In order to analyse the process of evolution, the category of 'institution' is taken as the crucial one: because of its stability, it is considered as the unit of selection in socio-economic evolution (cf. Hodgson 1993, 1994). In fact the reduction of evolution to institutional change is the way by which Commons and Veblen have transferred the ideas of Darwin to social phenomena (Dufourt 1993): 'It is in the changes of . . . rules . . . that we find, as does Veblen, the evolutionary theory of economics' (Commons [1934] 1990,   p. 656). Furthermore, this statement encapsulates the originality of the institutionalist research program. Hodgson expresses this point in the case of Veblen: it is because 'Veblen rejected both the individual and the society as the ultimate unit of explanation in social science . . . [that he] embraced an evolutionary framework of explanation' (Hodgson 1998, p. 416). Commons explicitly develops a methodological *via media* between individualism and holism, and it is in order to analyse the duality of action and social structure that he makes the concept of transaction the unit of his analysis (Bazzoli 1999). For this purpose, both authors put at the basis of the institutionalist theory of evolution the *articulation of a theory of action and a theory of institutions*. For them, both the free individual and the socially determined individual are obstacles to explain change, and 'it is the *social* evolution of man - as a complex of socially acquired "habits of thought" or "rules" or "social institutions" . . . that we must try to explain' (Ramstad 1994, p. 91). This leads to the thesis that both individuals and institutions are the result of a process of evolution, and interact in this process. My point shall precisely be that Commons offers a conception of social evolution that is more adequate to integrate this duality.

Finally, Veblen and Commons consider that Darwinism has to be understood as a metaphor. The point is not to explain human behaviour in terms of biological theory, but to use Darwinian concepts as guidelines of analysis. While Commons has been less explicit and more discreet on this metaphorical use of biology,[3] he aims, like Veblen, to identify the units of selection, the sources of variation in behaviour (novelty) and the nature of the selective process that leads to the disappearance of some behaviours and the persistence of others. In fact, it is precisely in regard to the last Darwinian principle that the roads taken by these two authors diverge, whereas their analysis of the other principles are very close.

Commons's Point of View

We know that Veblen defended the principle of natural selection while Commons defended the one of artificial selection - two types of selection among the variabilities analysed by Darwin himself.

Veblen wishes to analyse institutional change in terms of opaque cause and effect, as the unintented result of a blind causal process, in order to be free from teleology. Today, some authors stress that Veblen has in part failed in this project. For Rutherford (1998), the source of the problem in Veblen's thought 'is to be found in the particular interpretation and theoretical expression Veblen gave to the notion of non-teleological explanation in the social sciences' (p. 475). In fact, the point is that 'the question of agency remains problematic within [this] evolutionary framework' (Hodgson 1998, p. 423). Veblen does not consider purpose as a category distinct from mechanical causality, and so his conception does not really pay attention to the role played by choice in the evolutionary process (cf. Rutherford 1983). Finally, one can see a false association between 'the necessity to give an image of evolution lacking any overall intent, purpose or design' and 'the necessity of an analysis in terms of a causal process that does not rely on intentionality and on the role of choices'. This is precisely where the contribution of Commons lies.

Commons explicitly poses the question of the link between purposeful action and evolution, that is, the role human choice plays in social evolution. Why does he take the problem of evolution differently with regard to Veblen?

For him, 'Veblen's concept of science was the traditional concept of the physical sciences which rejected all *purpose* in the investigation of facts' (Commons [1934] 1990, p. 654), whereas the essential difference between physical science and social science lies in the fact that the latter deals with human action; this makes the category of purpose an essential one. Commons considers that social sciences are necessarily volitional sciences and he builds his social theory on the principle of Willingness, that is, voluntary action grounded on expectations of future consequences: 'Willingness, both conscious and habitual' is the 'force at work' for Commons ([1934] 1990, p. 45). Social phenomena being characterised by 'the human will in action', social processes are the results, intended or unintended, of the purposeful action of individuals and collective actors. It is because pure causal arguments cannot really take into account purpose and intentionality that mechanical and 'natural selection' analogies are not relevant and applicable. For Commons it is a mistake to follow too closely Darwin's idea of natural selection, since it leads to a false analogy between society and organism. The point is that 'after eliminating divine will, cosmic ether and all metaphysics, there remains still the human will . . . All the phenomena of the human will are "artificial", in contrast with phenomena which may be distinguished as "natural". That which is "artificial" is not thereby unnatural, but is the highly "natural" process of the human will, picking out the limiting factors of nature and human nature in order to guide certain complementary factors into the direction desired by human purpose' (Commons 1924, p. 375). So, from the standpoint of evolution, 'what clearly distinguishes "artificial" from "natural" selection is the substitution of selection via the human *will* for selection via a brute process as the central factor shaping the direction of evolution' (Ramstad 1994, p. 67). This difference was emphasised by Darwin himself, and Commons followed his principle of artificial selection, which becomes relevant 'as the will of man comes into play' (Darwin quoted by Ramstad 1994) and 'converts wolves into dogs' (Commons [1934] 1990, p. 636). Thus, natural selection describes a process of adaptation to a given environment, a process which is outside the control of organisms, whereas artificial selection describes the effects of the operation of the human will, which can alter its environment and try to control it by the use of intelligence. As Commons says, 'it is artificiality, which is merely the human will in action, that converts mechanisms into machines, living organisms into institutionalized minds, and unorganized habit into orderly transactions and [institutions]' (1934, p. 638).

One can see that the differences between Veblen and Commons about the Darwinian metaphor are linked to two crucial points.

First, these two authors place different emphasis in their analysis of change (Atkinson 1987). Veblen, who developed a narrow focus on new technology as source of change, bases his evolutionary theory on the analysis of the long term process of habituation to new material circumstances, processes in which institutions are source of inertia. For Commons, the central question is not technological change *per se* but the process of the resolution of social conflicts created by economic scarcity, which implies an evolving system of rules. In his conception, institutional rigidity has a positive role in creating social order and order is considered as a permanent process of institutional adjustment.

Second, if history has no known end state, this does not mean, for Commons, that social evolution is the result of natural selection, because the permanent process of institutional adjustment is not independent of the purposes and actions of individuals, and especially of the individuals who possess some political and economic power. We can agree with Mirowski (1987), who stresses that Veblen did not draw the conclusions from Peirce's pragmatism when he opposed sufficient reason (teleological explanation) and efficient cause (objective explanation), whereas Commons, following Peirce, rejected this dichotomy and defended that a third way is possible - a way which considers institutions as the connecting link. This way supposes we put at the core of the explanation purposeful action looking to future consequences and based on rules, that is, the interaction of intelligent action and institutions. This leads to reject the idea of opaque causality in order to stress the idea of adaptation through choices and to reverse the cause-effect time sequence. Then, social evolution cannot anymore be considered as a blind process, but rather is a volitional process of institutional adjustment.

2. COMMONS'S THEORY OF SOCIAL EVOLUTION: THE PECURIALITY OF THE PROCESSES OF EMERGENCE AND SELECTION OF RULES

In the institutionalist stream of thought, evolution is fuelled by two processes:

- A process of recurring variation in behaviours, that is, a process of innovation or the emergence of novelty. This implies a theory of how change originates.

- A process of selection of behaviours and rules of conduct, that is, a process that determines which innovation becomes institutionalized behaviour and social rule. This implies a theory of how social order is brought about in a world of change and conflicts.

On these two points, Commons develops his own ideas. We consider firstly the overall thesis linked to the artificial metaphor that concerns these two processes.

The Meaning of an 'Artificialist' Conception of Evolution

When Commons defends the idea of 'artificiality' in social sciences, he means that the 'human will in action' (individual and collective choice) has a role in the emergence and selection of rules. In other words, there are two major differences for him between the natural world and the social world (Biddle 1990): whereas variations are linked to chance in biological evolution (random or blind variations), in social evolution they are linked to the active human mind motivated by purposes, and whereas selection proceeds through differences in survival and fertility or reproduction in natural selection, it proceeds through human choices in artificial selection, that is, through a volitional process - which is stated in Darwinian terminology by the phrase 'selection through the choice of parents by the breeder' (Ramstad 1994). In Commons's terms, the analysis of the emergence and the selection of rules implies a theory of cumulative causation between individual action (individual causation) and collective action (institutional causation) (Ramstad 1990).

As it will be shown, Commons's understanding of cumulative causation has two implications which are connected to his theory of action and social order.

Variations in practices originate in the purposeful action of individuals, but individuals are always shaped by society; it is the individual as a product of society that plays a creative role in its evolution.

New rules arise from individual actions selected and modified by collective action, that is, by the present institutions of society. This artificial selection process does not mean that rules are designed through collective action, but only that they are selected among the micro variety of new practices by the officials of the institutions, that is, by the people who have, in the history of a society, obtained the right to exercise power ('authoritative figures') over the rules of the social game and in the process of conflict resolution.

Finally, the central thesis of Commons can be phrased thus: 'As in Darwin's theory, "trait variation" [alternative practices] occurs in Commons's conception of economic evolution through a process outside the control of the "breeder" (authoritative figure). However, it is the "breeder" (authoritative figure) who, by determining which trait is to survive and be nurtured, *determines* the direction of a species' (an economic system's) evolution' (Ramstad 1994, p. 110). It is because human will and power - that is, artificiality - enters at these *two levels* that social evolution cannot be either a spontaneous order or a result of natural selection, but rather is an indeterminate process of *social construction* with no overall design.

The Process of Emergence: an Analysis in Terms of Strategic Transactions

In Commons's analysis, new rules can be designed consciously by the legislature and political process. But, for him, the political process is mainly a selection process, and the major part of institutional innovation does not originate in designed variations but rather in spontaneous variations, that is, in the creative action of individuals.

This statement is accepted by all Institutionalists, and is based on the theory of action that this school of thought has developed (cf. Bazzoli and Dutraive 1996). We know that a central feature of Institutionalism is a break with the standard vision of man and rationality in adopting the pragmatist conception of mind and action proposed by Peirce and Dewey, a conception that rejects the meaningfulness of the 'free will versus determinism' dichotomy. The Darwinian principle of variation implies that we adopt a non-deterministic vision of the world and of human action, and this is why Peirce considered Darwinism as a philosophical creed (Hodgson 1998). This means that the theory of novelty is linked to the recognition of the creative dimension of the process of thought and action. So, a new conception of individual action is considered as the first condition of an evolutionary theory. Both Veblen and Commons locate novelty in the purposeful and intelligent action of individuals, that then becomes the agent of change, the operative force of the endogeneous process of innovation. Their conception of action is an alternative to methodological individualism (where human agents are atom characterised by 'free will' and pure rationality) and to methodological holism (where man is a social being determined by circumstances), because these conceptions fail to analyse change. For Institutionalists, purposeful behaviour is a result of habituation and socialisation (human rationality needs habits or rules of conduct and individual action is controlled by collective action) and at the same time expresses itself in creative and strategic activity. It is precisely because individuals rely on habits to deal with their complex environment that they can exercise their intelligence (Peirce) to engage themselves in purposeful action and to appreciate the habits they follow in what Dewey called 'problematic situations'.

In this framework, Veblen sees change as the result of pragmatic teleological behaviour and of idle curiosity (cf. Mayhew 1998). Commons focuses on pragmatic behaviour to analyse novelty, and is inclined to stress the role of pivotal individuals (*les grands hommes*), those who are able to break from existing routines and to resist the institutional status quo.

Commons uses his concept of strategic transaction to analyse the emergence of new pratices and rules. We know that, for him, the major part of transactions are routine transactions because man needs security of anticipation for acting. But this process of socialisation does not mean that individuals are passive. First, while collective rules create constraints on individuals, they also always create rights and liberties, opening a field of opportunity within which individuals pursue their own purpose and seek to expand their activities. Second, individuals face 'problematic situations', that is, situations that cannot be handled adequately with habitual patterns of behaviour and that prompt individuals to engage in a process of problem solving and attempt to modify existing rules. In these two cases, individuals use their intelligence to find a creative response to the new situation in order to adapt to, and to control, their environment. This problem solving process is thus the source of the variability of practices and transactions. What characterises the active dimension of individuals is the ability of human will to act upon little factors to bring about results intended (Commons [1934] 1990, p. 89). It is this aspect of purposeful behaviour that is captured by the notion of 'strategic transaction'. Then, strategic transactions express the active dimension of individuals and are the means by which innovation occurs as a response to new opportunities or to new obstacles to the pursuit of individuals' interests and activities; new practices designed to handle the limiting factors are strategic transactions generating an ever-changing world.

Two other points are important in Commons's conception, points that are at the core of the American institutionalist theory.

This problem solving process is a social process. This means that the creative acts are the result of 'Institutionalized Minds'; they are embedded in existing customs and rules and they are supposed to be communicated and coordinated with the behaviour of others. In other words, new practices are always linked to some existing rules, and the role of intentionality is never free from institutional influences; as Ramstad (1990) says, 'individual teleological causation' is always in part the manifestation of 'institutional causation'.[4]

Spontaneous variations generated by creative individual minds do not spontaneously lead to social order and create social rules for two major reasons: 1) new practices have to be approved by others and be consistent with existing political and judicial rules; 2) new practices create unintended consequences and new conflicts over the rules that have to be considered as legal and legitimate. The issue here is the passage from the individual level to the social level. For Commons, a diffusion process generated by the innovators is not sufficient and cannot work alone. What is essential is the selection process among the candidates for social survival.

The Artificial Selection of Rules: the Role of Authoritative Figures

So, in the chain of cumulative causation, Commons considers creative individual actions to be the engine of change. But there is still a need to understand the process by which some novelties will persist and lead to institutional change. Commons's analysis of the selection process is grounded in his conception of the source of social order, a conception that perhaps dissociates him most from mainstream theory. In fact, adopting the artificial selection metaphor is the major consequence of his vision of social order.

For Commons, the issue is to understand how order is brought about in a world in which social interactions involve both conflicts and dependence and where individuals are not equals. He rejects the classical view that spontaneous order via the invisible hand of the market is the natural tendency. For him, order implies that a coercive structure of rules to which individuals have to adhere is established and maintained. In other words, social order is the result of collective action in restraint, liberation and expansion of individual action - that is institutions - and not of an 'invisible hand process'. Collective action is the process by which rules are laid down and sanctioned in the aim of governing conflicts and maintaining the workability of society through the securing of expectations and the definition of individuals' rights, duties, liberties, exposures and powers. Thus conflicts cannot be resolved by individuals themselves: some degree of coercion is required because it is the force through which conflicts are transformed into cohesive activity; social order implies that some authoritative figures enforce rules controlling individual actions (that is, figures empowered to enforce rules). This vision leads to the view of social order as hierarchical : society is a network of interrelated rules and authoritative figures and the ultimate authority is, in modern society, the State, the institution that has taken over the physical power of coercion and that guarantees the rights and duties of citizens and others institutions (cf. Commons [1899-1900] 1965).

For Commons, it is precisely the content of the set of rules that is the result of artificial selection. Authoritative figures do not invent new practices and rules but rather select them. His theory of 'artificial' evolution can be described in this way. Novelty 'does indeed arise out the actions of individuals and concerns . . . constrained . . . by ethical and customary norms and by the political and judicial institutions that govern the process of changing other rules or institutions. [These] institutions are, however, also subject to change . . . under the pressure from the requirement of workability' (Rutherford 1983, p. 726). This pressure is produced by the process itself: indeed, the economic process always generates unintended consequences, new discoveries, new problems, new conflicts imperfectly regulated that are the sources of strategic transactions and creative actions which imply disputes over the existing institutional rule structure of society. If order is to be maintained under these new conditions, the authoritative figures have to select which of the practices and rules are to be followed in the future and accepted by all members of society (Ramstad 1994).

In so far as social order is a hierarchical articulation of public order (the sovereignty backed up by the power of the state which makes authoritative transactions) and private order (the sovereignty backed up by the power of property which makes authorised transactions), the selection process proceeds at two levels in Commons's analysis. There is a selection process in private going concerns by the authoritative figures (or officials) of those concerns: the approved practices (which are approved because they are deemed as serving the collective purpose) become working rules and lead to a redefinition of rights and liberties (Biddle 1990; Commons 1924, p. 143-52). But of course, the collective will of private going concerns is under the control of the superior collective will of the Sovereign. This means, first, that the private selection process is constrained by political and judicial rules : the selected rules have to be consistent with existing legal rules and/or have to be authorised by the Sovereign. Secondly, the process of selection at this level is what impels changes in the existing political and judicial rules. These changes are also the result of a selection process involving human choices, choices of legislatures and courts (cf. Commons [1934] 1990, pp. 72-4, 711; Chasse 1986; Gonce 1976; Rutherford 1983). Statute law evolves through the voluntary agreements between members of the legislature, by the decisions of the executive and under the pressure of interest groups. Here choices are dependent on the nature of social groups that have gained a 'voice' in the control of the sovereign power. Common law evolves through the courts deciding disputes by choosing which rule or practice is 'good' or workable and is to be given precision and legal sanction. In all cases, by equating social evolution with volitional institutional adjustment, Commons wants to show that the direction of social evolution is determined not by a brute process but by the purposes of the authoritative figures, that is, 'the breeders' (Ramstad 1994) and notably those who assume the position of the sovereign power (individually or collectivelly) and the task of resolving disputes by determining what are to be the governing rules (ibid.).

Commons (1924) then affirms that the 'invisible hand' has to be replaced by the 'visible hands' of the different authoritative figures which take decisions in the process of institutional adjustment. Thus selection is 'artificial' because the process of authoritative decisions by which it proceeds necessarily contains choices between conflicting or different interests, practices, rules. In other words, selection is artificial because it implies a social control and is not independent of the wills of authoritative figures who must determine what constitutes the 'best' adjustment of the existing rule structure in regard to the way burdens and benefits are to be shared between the participants.

In this framework, there can be neither natural imperative or tendency, nor *a priori* efficiency of the process. The artificial selection metaphor means that, in order to understand social evolution, we have to integrate the role of the social processes of valuation. Indeed, in so far as purposes and choices are the operative forces of the selection process, its results depend on the values and ends which have served as a basis of selection, that is, upon which a rule is deemed 'good'. So, when change is not determined by natural order or by natural selection, values have to be incorporated into the analysis (Atkinson 1987). And because disputes over rules involve conflicting experiences, values and customs, the decisions of authoritative figures cannot appeal to an objective value function, and the criterion of 'good' guiding the selection is based on an interpretation of the public purpose involved. Commons has shown that decisions are founded upon a standard of reasonableness, a search for reasonable degrees of efficiency and equity that can permit a workable mutuality.[5] Through this notion of 'reasonable value' (a term derived from the judiciary), Commons wants to stress that objective and absolute norms of value cannot be presumed to exist : there is no natural tendency upon which men can base determinate solutions. Reasonableness expresses the evolving public purpose as a compromise reached for the time being between conflicting interests (cf. Commons [1934] 1990, p. 680-4). What may constitute a reasonable solution is then a changing and relativistic concept. And it is precisely because values, as understood in this non-rationalistic way, play a role in artificial selection that the social process is open and unpredictable, that is, social evolution is non-teleological.

3. SOME CONCLUSIONS ABOUT THE SIGNIFICANCE OF COMMONS'S ARTIFICIAL SELECTION METAPHOR

As Rutherford (1998) notes, Commons's system of thought was so complex and so poorly expressed that his conception of social evolution has had relatively little impact, even on Institutional economics. Yet, the contribution of Commons is consistent with Veblen's agenda in his 1898 essay. Following the works of Hodgson, we can say that Veblen and Commons are in the same category of evolutionary theory, one that affirms, from an ontological point of view, the necessity of recurrent novelty, and that develops, from a methodological point of view, a non-reductionist explanation. In both cases, the issue is to elaborate a theory of the process in which the active element is the institutionalised mind and in which institutional evolution does not proceed from an original 'state of nature' but is rooted in existing institutions (cf. Hodgson, 1996).[6] But the two authors differ in the way of analysing this process. When Commons said 'Darwin had two kinds of "selection" among variabilities: Natural Selection and Artificial Selection. Ours is a theory of artificial selection. Veblen's is natural selection' (1934, p. 657), he wanted to stress an important point missing in Veblen's conception, the fact that humans can have some control over the process of institutional change: he 'understood Veblen to have described humans as being swept along in an evolutionary process over which they had no control' (Mayhew 1998, p. 455), whereas the issue is to consider seriously, on the one hand, purposeful action, and, on the other hand, institutions as selecting mechanisms. The articulation of these two elements excludes analysis of social processes in terms of blind causation.

We can stress several points in order to evaluate Commons's contribution and to underline the importance of analysing social evolution in terms of artificial selection.

Commons's Theory as a Critique of Spontaneous Order

A starting point is to affirm that one cannot understand Commons's analysis if it is read through the Hayekian dichotomy of rules and orders (like in Vanberg 1989).

As Lawson (1994) argues, 'rather than there being two, at least analytically, distinct processes resulting in order (i.e. spontaneous versus constructed or organic versus pragmatic) one being ultimately superior or preferable, these are two aspects of the same process' (p. 197). For Commons, different types of institution have the same role in that they involve 'collective action in control of individual action', and whatever their form they contain some degree of social control. On the basis of his theory of institution as collective action, he cannot agree with the invisible hand explanation because it concentrates on individual action and supposes that harmony is spontaneously created. Furthermore, Commons does not want to elaborate a general theory of evolution: his problem is not to theorise in abstract the origin of rules, but is to understand the evolution of rules in the modern society (Field 1979). Talking of 'artificiality' does not mean that social institutions are the result of a conscious design and that they are necessarily efficient. This only means that there is a process of social construction shaping the direction of evolution and that spontaneous processes are always articulated to constructed processes via selection.

Finally, Commons's theory does not fit into the Austrian distinction, and the central message of Commons is precisely to show the irrelevance of the standard idea that social evolution occurs automatically under the governance of a brute process so that institutions are naturally selected to facilitate efficiency (Ramstad 1994). There can be no sharp distinction between two types of processes by assuming that one type is totally independent from individual or collective intentions: in so far as intention always plays a role, we cannot suppose that it has no analytical consequences for the explanation.

One can think that Commons is the author who has developed the deepest criticism of the idea of natural and spontaneous order by offering an institutionalist alternative.

Commons's Conception and the Non-teleological Nature of Evolution

From the point of view of an alternative, natural selection in the sense of Veblen and artificial selection can be articulated. There is not a complete inconsistency.

First, artificial selection does not mean teleological explanation. The point is that we have to consider the role of institutions as mechanisms of selection through choice. Furthermore, artificial selection is not equivalent to a rejection of the role of unintended consequences (cf. Biddle 1990). While it stresses that we cannot consider all social results as unintended (and beneficial because unintended), it also integrates the unplanned effects of human action. In fact, for Commons, any action in a world of interdependence and scarcity has some impact on other actions. Further, because the active human mind has limits in dealing with strategic factors in problem solving (the mind concentrates on some factors and then does not deal with all the consequences of an action), purposeful action necessarily has intended *and* unintended consequences. This fact concerns as well individuals' actions as selections made by superior wills. Finally, the cumulative process consists of a never ending and ever-changing chain of actions, intended and unintended consequences, purposeful responses to these consequences from individual wills and collective wills through problem solving and selection.

Second, if for Commons natural selection can be consistent in analysing evolution on a very large scale of time, this framework needs artificial selection theory in order to analyse the continuous process of institutional adjustment which leads to long trends in the evolution of human societies. If one thinks that 'the fault with Veblen's approach is . . . that he fails to provide an adequate or convincing analysis of the decision making process, of exactly why individuals abandon some conventions and adopt others, and how a new consensus is formed and comes to find legal and political expression' (Rutherford 1983, p. 732), then Commons's analysis in terms of artificial selection becomes relevant and necessary to institutionalist evolutionary theory.

Some Implications of Commons's Conception for the Institutionalist Research Programme

We think that the artificial selection conception is implied by the search of a non-reductionist explanation which can be seen as a methodological middle way between individualism and holism. Commons's methodological convictions lead to a theory of the social process in which 'institutionalised individuals' and institutions grow up together. This conviction is expressed in his theory of action (cf. Bazzoli and Dutraive 1996) and in his theory of institutions, the articulation of which being the basis of his theory of evolution.

If Commons adopts the artificial selection metaphor, it is precisely because it permits an integration of the role of intentionality (or willingness) and of institutional determination, that is the duality of action and structure and the recursive loop between these two poles, which imply the analysis of social evolution in terms of a circular causation between individual/teleological causation and institutional causation. This metaphor stresses that social outcomes are the complex and indeterminate result of the interaction of different wills inserted in an institutional structure that gives more influence to people who possess power. For Commons, order refers to the reproduction of working rules, while conflicts and their resolution are the main dynamic for change in working rules (Lawson 1994): institutional change results from a historical process of artificial selection of reasonable rules through collective action, which is a permanent process of conflict resolution where the wills of individuals and collectives interact. This is why his system of thought articulates spontaneous and constructed processes. The relevant question relates not to dichotomies, but to the nature of dispute settlement procedures and their results in terms of institutional arrangements.

Moreover, this point of view is consistent with a system of thought that considers value as the central epistemological issue in social science (Mirowski 1987). Following pragmatist philosophers, Commons develops a conception of science that rejects the dichotomy of positive and normative analysis, of facts and values. For him, the valuations guiding action and the role of social values in shaping and securing individual valuations are the subject matter of social inquiry (Commons [1934] 1990, p. 25). He denies then the sharp distinction between positive and normative statements: since there are different values, different ways of treating interactions and conflicts in the social world, the social scientist cannot be 'value free', for he chooses facts and methods on the basis of some values, and so it is preferable to make explicit normative purposes (whereas the defenders of value-free science support implicitly some unadmitted value) (Commons [1934] 1990, p. 108, 742). In this framework, inquiry can become part of social evolution (Chasse 1986).

Commons develops this positive-normative articulation through his theory of reasonable value. This theory means that we have to negotiate solutions to social problems because there is no objective value function (Atkinson 1987). We have seen that, from the positive side, reasonable value is simply the existing public purpose (of the 'breeders') resulting from a compromise between conflicting interests attained in the existing circumstances. This interpenetration of different purposes guides selection for the better or for the worse. For Commons, public purpose is fallible, ambiguous and changing: it is contingent upon which social groups can influence or control the common understanding of what is reasonable. So, defending, from the normative side, an intervention on social process, like Commons did, is just discussing the nature of the artificial selection and trying to influence it in a way that is consistent with some explicit values; it cannot be considered as resulting in distortions of a natural efficient order. Indeed, the evolutionary view of society leads to attempts for social reform because it shows that 'humans potentially have some control over their destiny' and can move collective action in new directions through institutional change (Biddle 1990, p. 45). For Commons, authoritative figures tend to decide in favour of dominant social groups (the ruling classes). His own ethical values defend the 'common man' and deal with the social conditions of security, equality, liberty and material abundance (Gonce 1976). This is why his normative concept of reasonable value focuses on the means to extend state sovereingty to protect the transactions of the powerless through the integration of new social groups in the exercise of economic and political power. He advocates new forms of collective action (notably process of collective bargaining) which could result in working rules designed to equalise power and to provide representation of the different interests present in modern society. His evolutionary thinking leads to a pragmatic social philosophy, searching not for rational or natural rules but for reasonable adjustment of conflicting interests. Reasonable value is not, says Commons, 'what ought to be', but 'what could be'; it is 'the highest attainable idealism' ([1934] 1990, p. 741).

Finally, by adopting the evolutionary standpoint, Commons, like Veblen, rejects both the economist's idea of a natural order and the Hegelian necessity. For him, creativity and artificiality characterise the social world and its evolution. But, by stressing the fact of artificial selection, he can deal with the larger philosophical problem of the theory of social value, whereas Veblen, 'hidden behind a fictitious apathy of scientific detachment' (Harris 1934, p. 34) linked to his more classical vision of science, misses this point by analysing evolution only through efficient cause and by advocating the necessity of avoiding value judgements (although this position is not consistent with his attempt to criticise capitalism, cf. Copeland 1958). Institutional economics can find in the thought of Commons the epistemologically grounded link between the non-teleological nature of evolution, the role of purposeful actions and values, and the possibility of reformist/pragmatic intervention guided by human intelligence.

'By switching the Darwinian metaphor, by substituting for "natural selection" Darwin's concept of "artificial selection", Commons was able to remain within Darwinian preconceptions without abandoning (the) central insight' (Ramstad 1994, p. 110) of his institutional and pragmatic economics: the specificity of social evolution and the legitimacy of the attempt to manage the social process and to adjust the set of working rules in the direction of a reasonable capitalism.

NOTES

1. The aim of this paper is large and not new for the specialists of Commons. In fact, I will make a synthesis of Commons's theory and of the existing works on Commons's conception of evolution, on the basis of this issue of the specificity of social evolution.
2. At the begining of the century, this conception was expressed in 'evolutionary terms' through the doctrine of social Darwinism (natural selection of the fittest individuals). Nowadays, it is expressed through the theory of 'invisible hand process'. But the underlying logic remains the same.
3. Ramstad (1994) explains clearly that it is because the biological metaphor in general, and the artificial selection metaphor taken in the thought of Darwin in particular, seemed powerful for calling attention to the specificity of its theory of social evolution that Commons had used it. In fact, he was conscious of the lack of correspondence between biological and social evolution and would have preferred to avoid this metaphor.
4. This is a major difference from the Austrian conception which defends a purely subjectivist approach. Austrian economists consider that human knowledge is essentially subjective and, thus, that evolution relies only upon individual action without really taking into account the fact that individuals are shaped by their social environment, that is that their perceptions, their valuations and their creative acts are shaped, not only by individual experiences, but also by social experiences. It is why institutionalists can not adhere to the thesis of spontaneous order as it is stressed in my second point.
5. As Dugger (1996) summarises Commons's view, reasonable value is the value that closes 'the gap between conflicting interests that separated disputing transactors so that their mutual interests could be served and their going concerns kept going'; it lays 'somewhere within the gap between what the conflicting interests in transactions actually wanted' (p. 429).
6. This methodological standpoint is the means by which Institutional Economics seeks to break with the problem of infinite regress. Neither individuals nor institutions can have explanatory primacy; individuals can not be given as the 'institution-free' starting point; institutions have to be understood at the same time as causes and effects; it is why the idea of cumulative causation between individual action and collective action, as an alternative both to methodological individualism and methodological holism, is put at the core of the institutionalist theory of evolution (cf. Bazzoli 1999).

REFERENCES

Atkinson, G.W. (1987), 'Instrumentalism and economic policy: the quest for reasonable value', *Journal of Economic Issues*, vol. 21, n. 1, pp. 189-202.
Bazzoli, L. (1999), *L'économie politique de J.R. Commons. Essai sur l'institutionnalisme en sciences sociales*, L'Harmattan, Paris.
Bazzoli, L. and V. Dutraive (1996), 'Some legacy of J.R. Commons's conception of economics as science of behaviour', EAEPE Annual Conference, Anvers, forthcomming, Edward Elgar.
Biddle, J.E. (1990), 'Purpose and evolution in Commons's institutionalism', *History of Political Economy*, vol. 22, n. 1, pp. 19-47.
Bush, P. (1996), 'First and second order complexity in American institutional economics: an elaboration on Delorme's thesis', EAEPE Annual Conference, Anvers.
Chasse, J.D. (1986), 'John R. Commons and the democratic state', *Journal of Economic Issues*, Vol. 20, n° 3, pp. 759-84.
Clark, C.M.A. (1993), 'Spontaneous order *versus* instituted process: the market as cause and effect', *Journal of Economic Issues*, vol. 27, n. 2, pp. 373-85.

Commons, J.R. (1899-1900), 'A sociological view of sovereignty', *The American Journal of Sociology*, Augustus M.Kelley, Reprints of Economic Classics, 1965.

Commons, J.R. (1924), *Legal Foundations of Capitalism*, MacMillan.

Commons, J.R. (1934), *Institutional Economics. Its Place in Political Economy*, The Mac Millan Company, reprint 1990, Transaction Publishers, Vols. 1 & 2.

Commons J.R. (1950), *The Economics of Collective Action*, The University of Wisconsin Press, reprint 1970.

Copeland, M.A. (1936), 'Commons's institutionalism in relation to problems of social evolution and economic planing', *Quarterly Journal of Economics*, vol. 2, pp. 333-46.

Copeland, M.A. (1958), 'On the scope and method of economics', in Dowd D.F. (ed.), *T.Veblen: a Critical Appraisal*, Cornell University Press.

Dufourt, D. (1993), 'La problématique institutionnaliste de l'accumulation technologique endogène', in Abdelmalki L. (1993) (ed.), *Technologie et développement humain. Les enjeux de la maîtrise sociale de la technologie*, L'Interdisciplinaire.

Dugger, W.M. (1996), 'Sovereignty in transaction cost economics: J.R. Commons and O.E. Williamson', *Journal of Economic Issues*, vol. 30, n. 2, pp. 427-32.

Field A.J. (1979), 'On the explanation of rules using Rational Choice Models', *Journal of Economic Issues*, vol. 13, n. 1, pp. 49-72.

Gonce, R.A. (1976), 'The new property rights approach and Commons's legal foundations of capitalism', *Journal of Economic Issues*, vol. 10, n. 4, pp.765-97.

Guislain, J.J. (1996), 'Les conceptions évolutionnaires de T. Veblen et J.R. Commons', Colloque 'L'évolutionnisme', La Sorbonne Paris, September.

Harris, A.L. (1934), 'Economic evolution: dialectical and Darwinian', *Journal of Political Economy*, n. 42.

Hodgson, G.M. (1993), *Economics and Evolution. Bringing Life Back into Economics*, Polity Press.

Hodgson, G.M. (1994), 'The return of institutional economics', in Srelser N.J., R. Swedberg (1994) (eds), *The Handbook of Economic Sociology*, Princeton University Press.

Hodgson, G.M. (1996), 'The viability of institutional economics', EAEPE Annual Conference, Anvers.

Hodgson, G.M. (1998), 'On the evolution of Thorstein Veblen's evolutionary economics', *Cambridge Journal of Economics*, vol. 22, pp. 415-31.

Lawson, C. (1994), 'The transformational model of social activity and economic analysis: reinterpretation of the work of J.R. Commons', *Review of Political Economy*, vol. 6, n. 2, pp. 186-204.

Leather, C.G. (1989), 'New and old institutionalist on legal rules: Hayek and Commons', *Review of Political Economy*, vol. 1, n. 3, pp. 361-80.

Mayhew, A. (1998), 'On the difficulty of evolutionary analysis', *Cambridge Journal of Economics*, vol. 22, pp. 449-61.

Mirowski, P. (1987), 'The philosophical basis of Institutional Economics', *Journal of Economic Issues*, vol. 21, n. 3, pp. 1001-38.

Ramstad, Y. (1990), 'The Institutionalism of J.R. Commons: theoretical foundations of a volitional economics', *Research in the History of Economic Thought and Methodology*, vol. 8, pp. 53-104.

Ramstad, Y. (1994), 'On the nature of economic evolution: J.R. Commons and the metaphor of artificial selection', in L. Magnusson (1994), *Evolutionary and Neo-Schumpeterian Approaches to Economics*', Boston Kluwer.

Rutherford, M. (1983), 'J.R. Commons's institutional economics', *Journal of Economic Issues*, vol. 27, n. 3, pp. 721-44.

Rutherford, M. (1994), *Institutions in Economics. The Old and the New Institutionalism*, Cambridge University Press.

Rutherford, M. (1998), 'Veblen's evolutionary programme: a promise unfulfilled', *Cambridge Journal of Economics*, vol. 22, pp. 463-77.

Vanberg, V. (1989), 'Carl Menger's Evolutionary and J.R. Commons's Collective Action Approach to Institution: a Comparison', *Review of Political Economy*, n. 3, pp. 334-63.

Veblen, T. (1898), 'Why is economics not an evolutionary science?', *Quarterly Journal of Economics*, July, pp. 373-97.

Wolfe, A.B. (1936), 'Institutional reasonableness and value', *The Philosophical Review*, vol. XLV, n. 2, pp. 192-206.

7. The Significance of Clarence Ayres and the Texas School

James R. Stanfield and Jacqueline B. Stanfield

Clarence Ayres kept Institutionalism alive. (Geoff Hodgson 1998)

As quoted above, Geoff Hodgson remarked upon the significance of Clarence Ayres to the survival of Original Institutional Economics (OIE, as opposed to NIE, or Not-so-original Institutional Economics). While we like to poke a little fun at the NIE for their dismissive attitude to OIE, we are very impressed with the work they are doing and we look forward to powerful interaction between OIE and NIE. As Rutherford's (1996) path-breaking work indicates, there is an excellent foundation upon which to build this interaction.

We agree with Hodgson's comment and consider the point to be worthy of elaboration since there is apparently some doubt in the history of economic thought literature as to Ayres's importance (Landreth and Colander 1996). Moreover, we intend to establish a further aspect of this significance: the Ayresian view provides a unique and vitally important insight concerning the relationship between democracy and the economy. Economic value to Ayres (1962) signified the adjustment path of economic progress. Determination of economic value is the process of identifying the institutional reforms that lead to more effective use of the always expanding technological possibilities. The welfare state is first and foremost a democratic design to expand participation in the social process, and is to be admired as the result and cause of expanded participation. The rise of democracy expanded participation, and democracy creates the welfare state which further extends participation. But the welfare state is not, and never can be, perfect. Social reform is endless. In particular, popular participation needs to turn its attention to assuring that excellence and creativity are encouraged, indeed mandated, by welfare state culture (Ayres, 1967).

Since they may not be so well known outside the USA, we begin the paper with a brief discussion of Ayres and the Texas school. Then we examine the significance of the school in terms of its development of the legacy of Thorstein Veblen and John Dewey with regard to instrumental reasoning and institutional adjustment, especially the vitally important conception of the role of democracy in economic progress.

THE AYRESIAN LEGACY: AYRES AND THE TEXAS SCHOOL

Clarence Edwin Ayres (1891-1972) was the unofficial dean of the second generation of American OIE. From the 1930s to the 1960s, Ayres seems to have been the major figure, with Maurice Clark, Walton Hamilton, and a few others being prominent throughout the period as well. Early in the period, Rexford Tugwell was very prominent and later therein Kenneth Galbraith (Stanfield 1996) achieved great fame. But Ayres seems to have had a greater influence on OIE, through his work and especially through the oral tradition of the University of Texas.

Clarence E. Ayres was born in Lowell Massachusetts in 1891, the son of a baptist minister and a Christian missionary.[1] Religion, music, and reading were central family life activities. Ayres did his undergraduate work at Brown University, graduating with honours in 1912 with a major in philosophy and a minor in economics. He began graduate studies at Harvard, but returned to Brown after one year to complete his M.A. in philosophy. He then moved on to the University of Chicago, where he earned a Ph.D. in Philosophy in 1917. He then served as Instructor of Philosophy at Chicago until 1920.

While teaching Philosophy at Chicago, Ayres was likely influenced by the likes of Thorstein Veblen, Robert Hoxie, Wesley C. Mitchell, Alvin Johnson, Walton Hamilton, and J.M. Clark, who were members of the Economics department. Although he had left the Philosophy department at Chicago in 1904, John Dewey's influence may have lingered in the form of colleagues who knew him during his stay. Exposure to these heterodox economists may have been an important factor in Ayres's eventual shift into economics. It is clear that thereafter Ayres remained dedicated to Dewey's instrumental reasoning and to its introduction into economics discourse.

Ayres remained in the academic philosophy niche for several years. From Chicago he went in 1920 to Amherst College as an Associate Professor of Philosophy, and then in 1923 to Reed College in Portland, Oregon, as a

Professor of Philosophy. From Reed, Ayres travelled east to become an Associate Editor of the New Republic in 1924, staying there one year before moving to an Experimental College of the University of Wisconsin. From 1926 to 1929 Ayres took a hiatus from academic life, but in 1929 he accepted a summer job teaching economics at the Washington Square branch of New York University. Then in the fall of 1930 he accepted an offer for a one-year temporary Professor of Economics position from the University of Texas at Austin. The temporary position became a full-time tenured position the next year, and Ayres remained at Texas for almost four decades. Of his many books and papers, undoubtedly the most influential were his inquiry into the nature of economic progress (Ayres 1962) and his argument that instrumental reasoning could be the foundation of a reasonable society (Ayres 1961).

The Texas school of OIE can therefore be dated from 1930; it is a major part of the Ayresian legacy and its members continue to pursue the articulation of the instrumental philosophy of Veblen and Dewey and the commitment to the progressive modern liberal agenda in economic policy. The original Texas school also included E.E. Hale, Robert Montgomery, Ruth Allen, Alton Wiley, and Erich Zimmerman (Phillips 1989 and Phillips ed. 1995). Wendell Gordon, Carey Thompson, and H.H. Liebhafsky were eventually added to the faculty and reinforced and continued the Texas school traditions. Though certainly there were differences among them, this group shared an emphasis on the dichotomy between the technological and institutional aspects of the economic process and a commitment to the use of their professional ideas to advance social progress. They also, of course, were of one will in their view of the limitations of more conventional economics.

The Texas school oral tradition was carried away from Austin by many students and younger faculty, all of whom were greatly influenced by Ayres. Jim Reese and Nelson Peach established a major branch at the University of Oklahoma (Troub 1990). In a remarkable era from about 1960 to 1975, the Oklahoma Branch produced several doctorate students who were to go on to influence OIE, including Lewis Abernathy, Robert Brazelton, Glen Atkinson, Roger Troub, John Munkirs, Jim Sturgeon, and J.R. Stanfield.[2] The University of North Texas, although it had its OIE origins in the first generation of OIE scholars and thus antedated the Texas school to some extent, was nonetheless to become a prominent outpost (Cochran 1992). North Texas faculty included numerous students who had done graduate work at Texas, including, among others, Clarence Kulhman, Robert Conrod, Sam Barton, Hiram Friedsam, Abe Melton, Kendall Cochran, and William Dugger. Other prominent unofficial centres of the Texas school OIE were the University of Denver and the University of Missouri-Kansas City (Sturgeon

1981). At Denver, J.F. Foster influenced some of the most prominent members of OIE in recent decades, notably Marc Tool, Edy Miller, Dale Bush, and Lou Junker. At Kansas City, Walter C. Wagner, William Frederick, and John Hodges (Frederick 1998) established an unofficial centre of OIE that was to host Joe Brown, Robert Brazelton, Jim Sturgeon, and John Munkirs at various times in their careers.

Important centres of doctoral education in OIE that display the Texas school influence also developed at the University of Tennessee, the University of Nebraska, and Colorado State University. Tennessee, with Texas graduates Anne Mayhew, Hans Jensen, Bill Cole, Tony Spiva, and Roger Bowlby, and one-time Texas faculty member Terry Neale, on the faculty, have produced graduates who are currently prominent in the 'fifth generation' of OIE, including Janet Knoedler, John Harvey, and William Schaniel. Texas graduate Greg Hayden has helped establish an important OIE tradition at Nebraska, which has produced Steve Hickerson, Andy Larkin, and Janice Peterson. At Colorado State, Oklahoma graduate Stanfield and Texas graduate Ron Phillips have helped establish an OIE tradition that has turned out several graduates who are contributing to the OIE tradition, including Jim Swaney, Doug Brown, Ann Mari May, and Brent McClintock.

No doubt the Texas school network could be expanded. But enough has been noted to support the agreement with Hodgson's observation. Ayres and the Texas school network certainly did sustain OIE in a particularly bleak period of academic diaspora.

THE AYRESIAN LEGACY: DEMOCRACY AND THE ECONOMIC PROCESS

The significance of Hodgson's statement is enlarged by recognition of the vital contribution that Ayresian OIE made to political economic thinking. Much of this legacy lies in the articulation of the ideas of Veblen and Dewey with regard to the dichotomous character of culture and the process of instrumental reasoning. In so doing, the Texas school gained a unique insight with regard to the relationship between democracy and the economic process. This involves a change in the very content of economic analysis which is very often misunderstood. This is evident in the frequent lamentation of more conventional economists that OIE attacks conventional price theory but has nothing to put in its place. The misunderstanding stems from a failure to recognise that OIE defines the economy itself in an entirely different way (Ayres 1964, pp. 47, 61). The economy is not conceived as essentially a system of market exchange from which meaningful relative prices emerge. Accordingly, it is not surprising that OIE does not attempt to replace conventional price theory on its own terms because it is contended that the meaning of the economic process is not to be found in commerce but rather in the knowledge and artefacts of production in relation to the social relationships that establish power and privilege.

Viewing the economy as a process leads to an emphasis on institutional adjustment and this, in turn, establishes the vital significance of a democratic culture to the economic process. For OIE, change is the central analytic focus. The wants of individuals and the resources available for application are part of the variables to be explained. Human wants do change, and technology changes, thereby redefining and re-mixing the menu of available resources. Wants and technology do not change randomly, nor by virtue of some natural law working without human agency; they change by virtue of influences that are endogenous to the human social system. Since the human social system is fundamentally a system of power and habit, these changes emerge from the exercise of power and habit. To the extent of their power, individuals, teleological by nature, acting alone or collectively, pursue ends that refer to their habitual inclinations by use of means that are given by these same inclinations. Inventions and innovations occur as habitual ways and means are frustrated. New wants and new means flow from these innovations. As surely as some are led to innovate in order to achieve their purposes, others offer dedicated resistance to change in the pursuit of their purposes. Hence, social conflict is inherent and some instituted means for resolving conflict is required in a functional social order.

Newly emergent conflicts frequently require newly instituted means of conflict resolution. This implies that the economic problem is necessarily a matter of institutional adjustment. OIE characteristically conceives the economic problem as a continuous institutional adjustment to augment the flow of real income, i.e., to achieve economic progress. Ayres defined progress as 'finding out how to do things, finding out how to do more things, and finding out how to do all things better' (Ayres 1962, p. xiii). He went on to insist that progress thus defined is irresistible and everywhere at war with the status preoccupations and habitual sensibilities of propriety. Progress occurs through new combinations of previously unrelated technical artefacts or ideas that bear fruit in their admixture. This includes not only accretion of technical materials or tools, but more fundamentally the spread of knowledge about material progress. Hence Ayres stressed widening participation as the key to progress. The more people who have the capacity and opportunity to engage in the material process of inquiry and development, the greater the pool from whence new combinations may emerge.

Continuous institutional adjustment is necessary to expand participation and progress. Ayres insisted that the problematic of economics as a social science must be evolutionary in scope and method and dedicated to institutional reform. Technology and society are viewed as continuously in flux; the economic problem is conceived as the continuous adjustment or reconstruction of economic institutions, in light of technological and social change, more perfectly to serve human needs and development. The economic problem thus conceived is an adaptive process to secure continuity of existence as the basis for individual development. Change is seemingly irresistible, but it brings in its wake problems of maladjustment in the face of inertial ignorance or dedicated resistance from those with vested interests in potentially obsolete ways and means. Such institutional maladjustment can have dramatic consequences for the flow of real income.

Therefore, the characteristic focus of OIE economic thought with regard to the democratic capitalist societies is institutional adjustment toward the continuous reform of the regulatory complex within which the commodity production process functions. Economic policy is part of the economic problem of socially controlling economic behaviour to sustain a functioning and progressive economic order. As technological and social changes disrupt the established ways and means by which people make a living and order their existence, the key questions of the economic problem for OIE present themselves in terms of institutional failures and lacunae.

Effective economic policy lies in mandating institutional adaptations to overcome these discontinuities. Since an institution is a cluster of moral beliefs that distribute power, institutional adjustment means redistribution of power and modification of moral beliefs or judgements. Clearly this process is inherently controversial, and it is to be expected that the process of identifying and implementing progressive institutional adjustment faces severe obstacles. Hence, considerable cultural or institutional lag may be expected to be commonplace in human society so that a menu of ideological re-viewing and practical reform is a permanent feature of the social landscape.

In sum, OIE consists of the application of instrumental reasoning within the process of institutional adjustment in order to realise a fuller unfolding of the human life process. This is not, as some have alleged, a technocratic, undemocratic vision of an elite intelligentsia that operates society. Instrumental reasoning is not reserved for the intellectually advantaged segment of the population; it is the domain of all human beings and it constitutes the significance of democracy to economic progress.

Clearly, Ayres does not conceive democracy in the conventional manner. In the conventional view, democracy is merely a means of making decisions based upon values and judgements that are already given. This view, of course, mirrors the conventional economic choice theory. In this mechanistic view of democracy, the analysis is focused upon the electoral behaviour of voters and politicians and the administrative behaviour of public bureaucracies. In its most powerful articulation, that of the public choice school, this outlook suggests powerful conclusions about the intrusion of government into economic and social life. Public choice theory generally articulates the classical liberal concern for protecting liberty and free markets against democratic intrusion by means of strict constitutional constraints on political behaviour.

Ayres, following the lead of Dewey, conceived democracy differently from the common conception of majority rule. For Ayres, democracy is not a mechanism but a process. Balloting is but the tip of the democratic iceberg. Far more important is the underlying commitment to reasoned discourse on the basis of knowledge in pursuit of the public interest. Democracy is not simply or even most importantly voting to monitor preferences and to resolve preference conflicts; it is most importantly a process in which preferences are reformed with enhanced enlightenment. Individual participation in the democratic process is not simply the pursuit of one's given ends by means of political behaviour. It is rather more complex and requires that the individual make a commitment to open minded inquiry and discourse. In the process of this discourse, the individual's values and judgements are articulated and very often changed.

In other words, the critical aspect of democracy is not simply that consensus be reached, but that the process by which it is reached be one of inquiry and reasoned discourse. Clearly, then, the democratic process is kith and kin with the scientific process. The two cultures share a common commitment to inquiry. Indeed, in the instrumentalist view, the application of the process of inquiry and peer review to the social value construct implies the merger of the social scientist and social reformer in the democratic process (Tilman 1987). All who contemplate the institutional adjustment to secure improved accommodation to the tools and knowledge of the day become in effect social reformers; and all who pursue reasoned discourse on the collective action needed to accomplish this institutional adjustment become in effect applied social scientists.

Much of the significance of democracy lies in its being the best chance humanity has to institute a genuinely self-correcting social process. Democracy is applied intelligence and its practitioners must view social structures and policies experimentally or tentatively so that errors may be corrected as the test of ongoing consequences is applied. In this view, the potential for progressive social change occurs spontaneously as knowledge and information increase. Realisation of this potential requires the social will to put institutions to the test of consequences within the continuous process of institutional adjustment. In effect, the point is that human socio-economic practice is potentially self-correcting because there is systemic feedback from society and the rest of nature about the effects of technological applications

adopted or contemplated (Frederick 1995 and Tilman 1987). Since this
feedback has to be interpreted and acted upon within cultural process, the
potential for this self-correction is enhanced by the spread of democratic
participation and inhibited by the persistence of arbitrary socially constructed
inequality (Stanfield and Stanfield 1997; Dugger 1998). Ecological and
social feedback on the performance of material culture occurs via the
continuing process of natural scientific and social scientific inquiry. Within
this process, progress is therefore meaningful (Diggins 1994, pp. 457-8).

It is important to note that the emphasis on instrumental reasoning should
not lead to a neglect of culture or of psychological relativism. Instrumental
reasoning is a process of experimentation: decisions are made, consequences
are noted and interpreted (feedback), and new decisions are made. This
process necessarily occurs within a cultural context. OIEs favour a
democratic culture because the wider the participation in interpreting
feedback, the less likely a narrow frame of reference will obtain. Then also,
the less likely a bad (consequentially) decision will persist and the more
likely a good decision will be expanded and deepened. In effect, the central
conclusion of instrumental reasoning - that progress is best served by the
quest for democratic culture and ever widening participation - is based on
recognition of psychological-cultural relativism - the narrow frame of
reference mentioned above.

Clearly, then, democracy plays a fundamental role in advancing economic
progress. By extending participation, a democratic culture extends the pool
of society's skill and insight in the tinkering from which scientific and
technical advances flow and in grappling with the problems of institutional
adjustment. In this view, there is no necessary conflict between economic
security and incentive to excel (Ayres 1966). Ayres was convinced that the
democratic welfare state is the best scheme yet devised for arranging political
economic affairs because, in so doing, it draws most broadly upon the
population (Ayres, 1967). But further reform is needed. The next step is to
convert the welfare state into the creative state that celebrates and mandates
universal and diverse participation toward the greatest possible achievement
and progress. This will require the development of a welfare state culture that
emphasises solidaristic responsibility as well as solidaristic rights.

CONCLUSION: THE STATUS OF THE AYRESIAN LEGACY

We conclude with a few observations on the status of the Ayresian legacy
and its continuing, even urgent, relevance. Even apart from its obscurity and
abject dismissal by more conventional economists, the Ayresian legacy is

controversial in some regards, even on its own terms. There seems to be no doubt that Ayres went overboard in his derision of ceremony and the ritualistic fabric of human life. He seemed to regard progress in the technologic arts with an uncritical eye, and to neglect the psycho-cultural dimension of human well-being. In his elaboration of the Ayresian tradition of instrumental reasoning, Tool has indicated a key area that Ayres seems to have neglected, that being cultural continuity. This is evident in what has become the most celebrated phrase of the post-war OIE lexicon: 'that way is forward which provides for the non-invidious re-creation of community through the instrumental use of knowledge' (Tool 1979, p. 293). Modern OIE do not see the problem of institutional adjustment one-sidedly as overcoming the inertial resistance of institutions to technological change. Institutional preservation is also important because cultural continuity must not be rent by excessively rapid or ill-designed economic change (Bush 1987). The unfolding life process is shaped, defined, and interpreted by a context of patterned meanings, that is, culture. These patterned meanings inculcate the individual with respect to society's systems of communication and sanctions. Continuity is required if people are to be empowered to participate in the democratic process. Today's OIE proponents have been influenced in this regard by Polanyi's powerful lessons about social protection (Polanyi 1957; Stanfield 1986).

It must also be said that Ayres and other OIE have neglected the task of explicit development of a more systematic method or procedure for instrumental reasoning. The peer review process is critical to any scientific community, and more is needed than whether or not one agrees with the conclusions of another's instrumental reasoning. Criteria for the conduct of instrumental reasoning need to be developed and tested in the laboratory of field work. These criteria need to tested in a variety of institutional contexts in order to remain faithful to the comparative method that is the essential procedure of any institutional analysis (Stanfield 1986, ch. 2). OIE advocates must be ever mindful of the concept of culture and the need for its concrete understanding by reliance upon carefully conducted ethnographic field work. With their methodology thus underdeveloped, the OIE school has left itself open to criticism that, at best, its cause is to relax the restrictive assumptions of conventional economics and to provide a more satisfactory empirical basis for economic studies. At worst, the cause is said to be no more than destructive carping about the limitations of the conventional approach, with little or nothing by way of a programme for alternative conduct of economic investigations (Blaug 1983, pp. 708-11).

OIE needs to revitalise the procedure of participant observation, so well practised by such OIE members as Tugwell and Galbraith. To do so, OIE needs to offer a political economics which is cognisant of the political effects and objectives of economic policy, of the ways in which political processes shape economic policy and structure, of the culture of the political process, and of the effects of the economy on the polity (Hutchison 1981, ch. 2). Much can be accomplished by clarifying the ongoing political economic discourse. In any event, it would seem that there is a need for more fieldwork, more participant observation, more application of OIE talents to the issues of the day. In so doing, the procedure of instrumental reasoning must be developed; indeed, it must be revealed within the unfolding instrumental process.

If the sinews of the Ayresian legacy are not without tender areas, nonetheless, the reports of the death of the Texas school and OIE are certainly premature. While it may be less robust than we would like it to be, the Ayresian legacy is alive and well. Moreover, the Ayresian legacy is urgently relevant. The unique insight it provides with regard to the nature and means of economic progress is vitally important in this era of myopic neo-liberalism. Recent economic policy discussion is replete with the dangerously errant conviction that the policy errors of the welfare state signify the failure of the modern liberal project in general. The failures of formerly existing socialism are often cited, quite incoherently, to buttress the case for the neo-liberal programme of overturning the century of modern liberal reform. The twentieth century's widespread affluence and social acceptance of democratically managed capitalism, the great success of modern liberal reform, is cited as evidence of the failure of modern liberalism.

With this ideological new-think and double-talk, the Great Capitalist Restoration is well underway. It consists of the retrenchment of the democratic welfare states, the collapse of previously existing socialist economies and their embarkation on the transition to capitalism, and the emergence of market economies in the Third World under the aegis of neoliberal sentiment and quite often the strictures of organisational 'conditionality' imposed by the IMF or World Bank. No doubt much damage has been done to the ability of the industrial economies to deliver real income by the neglect of vital social programmes in this woefully misguided neo-liberal era. The burden of adjustment in the effort to sustain modernisation in the so-called emerging market economies has likewise fallen much too heavily upon the common people who must ultimately participate if significant economic progress is to occur (Moser 1989). In the transitional economies, there was certainly no painless way to move away from the fiasco of the centrally planned economies, but had more attention been paid to institutional analysis, the discomfort could almost certainly have been reduced (Goldman 1996).

Under such intense ideological time travel back to the nineteenth century, the critical task of designing a managed trade regime within a cooperative global governmental system is neglected. Excess capacity and financial asset inflation in a seriously unbalanced global economy may be brewing a macroeconomic disaster that will rival that of the 1930s. Even if such a cataclysm is avoided, the perennial capitalist problematic of instability, environmental and cultural destruction, and inequality will return with a vengeance. When these problems re-emerge, and when the social unrest they evoke reaches critical proportions, the compulsive shift to a political economic methodology that emphasises the place of economy in society will recur (Tool 1981). At that time, the importance of the Ayresian legacy will be more evident.

NOTES

1. For biographical information, see Breit, 1973 and 1977; Breit and Culbertson, 1976; and Eatwell, Millgate, and Newman, 1987.
2. Alas, journalistic integrity requires that we report that one Richard Armey also completed his doctoral studies at OU during this period.

REFERENCES

Ayres, C.E. (1961), *Toward a Reasonable Society*, Austin: University of Texas Press.
Ayres, C.E. (1962), *The Theory of Economic Progress*, New York: Schocken.
Ayres, C.E. (1964), 'The legacy of Thorstein Veblen', in *Institutional Economics: Veblen, Commons, and Mitchell Reconsidered*, Berkeley: University of California Press, pp. 45-62.
Ayres, C.E. (1966), 'Guaranteed income: an institutionalist view', in R. Theobald, (ed.), *The Guaranteed Income*, Garden City, NY: Doubleday, 169-82.
Ayres, C.E. (1967), 'Ideological responsibility', *Journal of Economic Issues*, vol. 1 (June): 3-11.
Blaug, M. (1983), *Economic Theory in Retrospect*, 4th edn. New York: Cambridge University Press.
Breit, W. (1973), 'The development of Clarence Ayres's theoretical Institutionalism', *Social Science Quarterly*, vol. 54, (September), 244-57.
Breit, W. (1977), 'In memoriam: Clarence Edwin Ayres', *Journal of Economic Issues*, vol. 11 (September), 475-83.
Breit, W. and W.P. Culbertson, Jr. (eds) (1976), *Science and Ceremony: The Institutional Economics of C. E. Ayres*, University of Texas Press: Austin.
Bush, P.D. (1987), 'Theory of institutional change', *Journal of Economic Issues*, vol. 21 (September), 1075-1116.
Cochran, K.P. (1992), 'A selective and sketchy history of the Department of Economics University of North Texas', Department of Economics: University of North Texas.

Diggins, J.P. (1994), *The Promise of Pragmatism*, Chicago: University of Chicago Press.

Dillard. D. (1987), 'Money as an institution of capitalism', *Journal of Economic Issues*, vol. 21(December), 1623-47.

Dugger, W.M. (1998), 'Against inequality', *Journal of Economic Issues,* vol. 32 (June).

Frederick, W.C. (1995), *Values, Nature, and Culture in the American Corporation.* New York: Oxford University Press.

Frederick, W.C. (1998), 'Camelot in Kansas City: a historical note about the Bloch school's roots in the University of Kansas city', (Unpublished ms.).

Goldman, M. (1996), *Lost Opportunity*, New York: Norton.

Hutchison, T. W. (1981), *The Politics and Philosophy of Economics*, New York: New York University Press.

Landreth, H. and D. Colander (1996), *History of Economic Thought*, Boston: Houghton-Mifflin, 3rd edn.

Moser, C. (1989), 'The impact of recession and adjustment policies at the micro-level: low income women and their households in Guayaquil, Ecuador', in UNICEF, *The Invisible Adjustment: Poor Women and the Economic Crisis*, Second rev. edn. Santiago, Chile: UNICEF.

Phillips, R.J. (1989), 'Is there a Texas School of economics?', *Journal of Economic Issues*, 23 (September): 863-72.

Phillips, R.J. (ed.) (1995), *Economic Mavericks: The Texas Institutionalists*, Greenwich, CT: JAI Press.

Polanyi, K. (1957), *The Great Transformation*, Pb. edn. Boston: Beacon.

Rutherford, M. (1996), *Institutions in Economics*, New York: Cambridge University Press.

Samuels, W.J. (1987), 'Clarence Edwin Ayres', in J.M. Eatwell, M. Millgate, and P. Newman (eds), *The New Palgrave, A Dictionary of Economics*, vol. 1. New York: Stockton Press.

Stanfield, J.R. (1986), *The Economic Thought of Karl Polanyi*, London: Macmillan and New York: St. Martin's Press.

Stanfield, J.R. (1996), *John Kenneth Galbraith*, London: MacMillan.

Stanfield, J.R. and J.B. Stanfield (1997), 'Where has love gone? Reciprocity, redistribution, and the nurturance Gap', *Journal of Socio-Economics*, (April).

Sturgeon, J. (1981), 'The history of the association for institutional thought', *Review of Institutional Thought*, vol. 1 (December), 40-53.

Tilman, R. (1987), 'The neoinstrumental theory of democracy', *Journal of Economic Issues*, 21 (September), 1379-401.

Tool, M.R. (1979), *The Discretionary Economy*, Santa Monica, CA: Goodyear Press.

Tool, M.R. (1981), 'The compulsive shift to institutional analysis', *Review of Institutional Thought*, 1 (December): 17-39.

Troub, R.M. (1990), 'Institutional economics at Oklahoma: a general perspective and a personal one', Presented at *Southwest Economics Association annual meeting*.

8. Bounded Rationality, Institutionalism and the Diversity of Economic Institutions

Ugo Pagano[1]

1. INTRODUCTION

The aim of the paper is not to consider the details of the Veblenian argument. We will rather try to evaluate the contribution that his approach can still give to economics one hundred years after the publication of his famous paper 'Why is economics not an evolutionary science?'. In particular, we will try to contrast the 'Old Institutionalist' Veblenian approach with the 'New Institutionalist' approach and point out some relative advantages of the former.

Much of New Institutional Economics has relied on some 'mild form' of bounded rationality. In turn, this has been associated with a view of evolution that allows an explanation of institutions in terms of 'transaction costs efficiency'.[2] We will try to show that this 'mild form' of bounded rationality has some serious shortcomings that are avoided in the approaches of Veblen (and Clark).

An important consequence of the approach of the 'Old Institutionalists' is that bounded rationality implies maximising behaviour only when the stress and effort associated with intentional rationality are not relevant - an observation that relates maximising behaviour to the theory of habits in a challenging and interesting way. Moreover, the Veblenian view of bounded rationality does also necessarily imply that preferences themselves are 'produced' by expending certain resources (including those related to our own bounded rationality); for this reason, they are necessarily influenced by the 'conditions of production' of preferences of a past state of society.

In the Veblenian approach, preferences are endogenous in the sense that they cannot be taken as given independently of a certain social context within which their costly formation took place. By contrast, basic human instincts are somehow exogenous to this context because they have been selected during a long period of 'natural' history. When the preferences and the associated habits do not fit a changed situation, exogenous human instincts may induce a costly revision of preferences; alternatively instincts may be repressed and a costly stagnation of society may take place.

The first section of this paper considers the transaction costs of the 'New Institutional Economics', with particular reference to bounded rationality. The second section considers how the Veblenian approach can challenge this view by proposing a theory of 'endogenous preferences' and 'exogenous instincts'. The third section considers some limitations of the Veblenian approach that are strictly associated to his Darwinian roots. It is argued that the future development of evolutionary and institutional economics should not be limited by some ambiguities of these roots.

2. BOUNDED RATIONALITY AND ECONOMISING BEHAVIOUR

According to Williamson (1985, p.45), 'Bounded rationality is the cognitive assumption on which transaction cost analysis relies'. Referring to Herbert Simon (1961, p. xxiv), Williamson defines bounded rationality as a form of rationality in which economic actors are at the same time assumed to be 'intendely rational but limited so'. Williamson emphasises that New Institutional Economics takes a sensible middle way that makes 'simultaneous references to both intended and limited rationality' (1985, p. 45). In spite of his reference to Simon, Williamson's view of 'bounded rationality' has relatively mild implications for orthodox economic theory.

From the bounded rationality assumption, Simon draws the conclusion that satisfying behaviour is more appropriate than maximisation in explaining human actions. According to him the replacement of maximisation by satisficing behaviour 'is an essential step in the application of the principle of bounded rationality' (Simon 1957, p. 198). By contrast, Williamson (1996, p. 351) argues that 'even granting that "satisficing" is a more descriptively accurate than maximising, satisficing is also a cumbersome concept and is difficult to model'. The association of bounded rationality with satisficing behaviour has, according to Williamson been a 'faithful choice'. It has not encouraged economising reasoning and it has become identified 'with aspiration level mechanics instead - which has wide appeal but it is more widely associated with psychology'.

Independently of the merits or the shortcomings of satisficing behaviour, Williamson seems to believe that a paradoxical implication of bounded rationality is some form of *'super-rationality'* by which the agents do not only rationally economise on the resources that have been the traditional object of economic theory, *but also, economise on their own bounded rationality*.

In the Williamsonian construction, the role of bounded rationality is quite marginal[3] and it is quite compatible with the fact that some agents are endowed with a rationality that does, in many respects, exceed that of the traditional neoclassical agent.

According to Williamson, the most important implication of bounded rationality is that: *'all complex contracts are unavoidably incomplete. That is the transaction cost story.'* (1996, p. 37) However, the New Property Rights approach of Grossman, Hart and Moore (that has also the aim of formalising some of the Williamsonian insights) has shown that bounded rationality is a marginally important background cause contract incompleteness (Hart 1995). In their framework, contract incompleteness is by no means due to the fact that agents cannot forecast the implications of their future actions and that they are somehow limited by their rational ability to gather all the relevant information and to compute the optimal solution. Contract incompleteness can be simply due to the 'bounded *writing and communication skills'* (Hart 1990, p. 699) that upset the relation between the contracting agents and the courts. While this particular type of bounded rationality makes third party enforcement impossible, in other respects the agents are endowed with a super-rationality well above that of the traditional neoclassical individuals. The agents not only maximise their own utility, but also fully anticipate the consequences of the maximising behaviour of the other contracting agents in the absence of third party investments. For this reason they exchange their non-human capital in such a way that the total human capital investment is maximised and a second best allocation of property of non-human assets is achieved under contractual incompleteness.

The New Property Rights approach is one example in which the agents, taking into account the constraints imposed by the bounded rationality (in this case of writing and communication skills), end up paradoxically solving a problem that is a great deal more complex than that of the traditional neo-classical agent. Perhaps this approach does really follow the Williamsonian suggestion of economising on bounded rationality; indeed it certainly ends up going in the opposite direction towards a 'common knowledge' assumption that is typical of a strategic type of 'super-rationality' in which the agents maximise by taking into account the maximising behaviour of other agents. However, the paradoxical implications of the 'New Property Rights approach' show that 'economising on bounded rationality' is a very complex form of economising behaviour which has many more dimensions (and, sometimes, contradictions) than Williamson seems willing to consider.

In this respect, one may distinguish among different types of costs associated with the different types of bounded rationality, and observe the contradictory implications that 'economising on bounded rationality' has in a traditional neoclassical framework.

Bounded Communication Skills

This is the case considered by the 'New Property Rights' approach. However, that approach considers one particular type of communication cost (that arising with third party enforcers) and assumes that the cost of transmitting this information is infinitely large. Given this assumption, the solution to the 'economising on bounded rationality problem' is trivial: zero resources will be dedicated to communicate with the third party enforcers and the agents can exclusively concentrate on the problem of allocating resources among other uses. All other types of bounded rationality are ignored. It is not surprising that the solution implies a degree of rationality that goes well beyond that which is traditionally assumed in the neoclassical framework. The 'shadows' of bounded communication skills appear only in the background and do not have any important consequence for the modelling exercise.

Bounded communication skills can, however, have a much more important and explicit role in the understanding of economic organisations. An obvious example is Hayek's criticism of central planning and his defence of the market institution. His argument relies on the same type of bounded rationality: a great deal of the information held by the agents cannot be easily transmitted to the other agents. In this context, the agents economise on communication costs by using the price system, which provides a powerful summary of information on the opportunities perceived by the individual agents. This virtue of the price system is particularly remarkable when a great deal of this information is 'tacit knowledge' that cannot be transmitted in a formal language. Unlike the Pareto optimality properties of the neoclassical model, the Hayekian virtues of the market economy can only be understood when some forms of bounded rationality are introduced into the analysis. In particular, under the assumption that prices are zero-cost communication channels and non-price information is tacit (i.e. it can only be transmitted at infinite cost), the Hayekian conclusion is rather obvious and implies a different version of 'market optimality'.[4]

Economising on communication skills becomes more interesting when one does not assume that communication channels are characterised by either zero or infinite communication costs. In this case, a combination of communication channels may, in principle, best economise on such skills. If, besides the case of communication skills, rationality is otherwise unbounded, the individual agents can easily solve this 'optimisation' problem. Even in this case there are, however, several problems. Communication channels improve because of strong 'learning by using' effects. Moreover, they are characterised by strong 'network externalities' because the utility of each channel reflects the number of agents that are using it (David 1994).

Economising on bounded communication skills would require a 'meta-channel' by which the agents could choose the most economical channels, taking into account the 'learning by using' effects and the 'network externalities' that are involved in the choice. However, this begs the very question that it is supposed to answer: how a (meta-)channel is ever chosen. A convincing story should neither exclude the possibility that agents try (sometimes, rationally) to look for better channels nor that they can be locked in to what were *a priori* inefficient channels.

Bounded Information Processing Skills

Even if communication channels are not costly and the transmission of information among agents does not involve any 'translation cost', we are still bounded by our ability to hold and to process information. Indeed, in many cases, modern society is characterised by an overflow that makes even more costly the acquisition of genuine knowledge.

Economising on this type of bounded rationality is notoriously difficult. If processing information is costly, then the agents will process additional information only when the expected marginal benefit outweighs the marginal cost. But the expected marginal benefit will depend on the *a priori* beliefs of the agents. These can be wrong because there is no way to be certain about the value of additional information before processing it (see Stigler 1961). Thus individuals can be trapped in wrong beliefs that are not changed because the acquisition of additional knowledge, which would show them to be wrong, is (wrongly) assumed to be too costly.

It is certainly reasonable to assume that individuals will try to economise on their bounded information processing capabilities. However, after years of rational expectations, we know even better that this story cannot be cast in any simple maximisation framework that does not take into account the constraints due to the history and the nature of the agents (Pagano 1992). Only if we know the beliefs, the personalities and the information that has already become part of the knowledge of the agents may we understand how they 'economise' on their limited information skills.

Bounded Calculation Skills

It is a puzzling aspect of orthodox economic theory that this cost has only rarely been considered. If optimisation is the cornerstone of the theory, the optimising costs due to the bounded calculation skills of the individuals should be relevant and individuals should try to economise a great deal on this type of bounded rationality. By contrast, while the costs of transmitting and processing information have been widely taken into account, the optimisation costs related to the individuals' bounded calculation skills have rarely been mentioned.

Economic theory has made us rather familiar with a story in which the individual optimises under constraints of communicating and processing information. One could think that bounded calculation skills could be similarly handled by adding another constraint to the optimisation problem. If the new constraint is binding, we would come to the 'usual' conclusion that a 'lower' constrained optimal result must be obtained when one takes into account the limited computational skills of the agents.

However, the parallel between computational costs and information is somehow misleading. We can immediately see that the agent does not really simplify the optimisation problem by taking into account his own optimisation costs. If he can not solve the former optimisation problem, he must find it more difficult to solve the latter problem because it involves an 'extra-constraint' on bounded rationality and an 'extra-choice' on the allocation of time devoted to computation. He is again constrained by his own computational power and faces a more complex optimisation framework.

The analogy with information costs breaks down. The agent can 'cancel' the collection and processing costs of the information that he does not consider when he optimises. By contrast, as long as she tries to optimise, she can never cancel 'optimisation costs' (Conlisk 1987 and 1996; Hodgson, 1998). Indeed, when the agent tries to optimise and chooses to allocate time between calculation and other activities, his bounded rationality implies that he has to face a new more complex calculation problem. A new optimisation problem will naturally arise because he has to decide how to distribute his time between this new 'second order' calculation and other activities; but this involves a 'third order' calculation and so on, generating an 'infinite regress'.

The 'infinite regress' problem can be somehow 'hidden' by mistaking the identity of a rationally bounded agent with that of an unbounded external observer. An external observer could easily determine the optimum solution for the agent, taking into account his own bounded calculation constraints. By contrast, this solution is impossible for the agent himself: he cannot include the bounded rationality constraints in his optimisation problem without being constrained (even more!) by his own bounded rationality. In other words, 'an external God' may easily 'calculate' what is best for us given the constraints imposed by our own human nature. By contrast, these constraints prevent ordinary human beings from engaging in this ambitious exercise without experimenting with the limitations of the human condition and allocating an increasing amount of resources in endless calculation.

Economising on bounded calculation skills must take a form different from the simple reformulation of a maximisation problem. We should accept that, while individuals may calculate among a number of limited alternatives, they can never calculate with any precision the focus of their own limited calculations. The history of the individuals must be considered in explaining which limited set of alternatives will be on the agenda. Optimisation and calculation must leave space for that mysterious concept, that some people call 'intuition'. Perhaps this vague world is one of the less unrigorous ways of referring to the mechanisms by which we economise on our own limited calculation skills.

Bounded Preference Formation Skills

We have seen how difficult it is for an agent with well-defined and complete preferences to make choices according to a more inclusive economising criterion. However, agents are also bounded by their own ability to produce and to develop preferences[5]. In some cases, the understanding of our own preferences is very difficult and requires a lot of (sometimes rather painful) introspection - a skill that we are only likely to use for the most important choices. Moreover, developing our own preferences requires other important, costly skills. Some musical skills are required to prefer Bach to Mozart, and even developing preferences for different types of wines requires some (pleasurable) investment.

If bounded rationality also implies that the 'production' of preference is costly, we should not be surprised by the fact that the agents try somehow to economise on this type of activity. However, this consideration does not only imply that the room for optimising behaviour is limited, but also involves an inversion of the traditional links between preferences and choices. When this type of bounded rationality is acknowledged, past choices have a great influence in determining the types of preferences that are going to be developed. In this sense, choices influence preferences and are not simply their outcome. In order to explain the choices of today we cannot simply rely on preferences, since the choices faced in the past explain the combinations of areas in which these preferences have been developed and in which they are underdeveloped or do not exist. Thus, an unfortunate consequence of economising on the bounded rationality associated with preference formation is that the individuals may be stuck in choice-preference self-reinforcing equilibria: because they face some choices, they developed preferences in particular areas, and because they developed preferences only within this particular range they keep making this type of choice (Pagano 1991, pp. 329-30). Economising on preference formation can only rarely be done on the basis of some 'meta-preferences' that can rationally justify the preferences that have been developed. Like preferences, these 'meta-preferences' are costly to develop and are subject to the observations we have just made.

Individual history is likely to be a highly path-dependent succession of preferences and choices. The initial choices made by parents and the community have some importance in explaining which choice-preferences paths an individual does not practice and in which areas he was an active, and often rational, player.

Bounded Emotional Skills

Even when being a rational chooser is in our best interest, our emotions can often prevent us from doing so (Screpanti 1998). In this sense, we face further constraints on our rationality. We are aware that being a rational chooser can often be stressing. For this reason, while we try to develop the emotional ability to behave in this way, we try also to economise on it. Those who do not economise on rationality and never relax may later pay for the overuse of these scarce capabilities and may have serious nervous breakdowns. In the economists' language, this is tantamount to saying that these individuals have distributed inefficiently over time their own emotional ability to behave rationally. It is again rather misleading to formulate the problem as that of finding the optimal degree of rationality and 'irrationality', because in the usual vicious circle we would take for granted unbounded emotional skills.

The emotional skill to be rational seems to be the outcome of a complicated (self)education that seems to change according to different cultures. Moreover, we do not get utility only from what we have or from what we do, but also from what (we believe) we are. Thus, it is not surprising that we are often engaged in activities of self-definition, or in the search of our own identity, and that this identity must also be emotionally satisfactory.

In principle, we would like to define ourselves as the neoclassical rational individual who is trying to maximise lifetime consumption. However, this is only one particular possibility and does not seem very appealing: when we define ourselves in this way, we immediately hit the limitations due to the shortness of life and to the relative fragility of existence.

In economic theory, 'rational individuals' should maximise taking the constraints of their life as given. Unfortunately, the constraints that are due to our own human condition do not gently bind us. Often we hit them in a very painful way, and for this reason we try to re-define ourselves in such a way that these constraints look less binding and become more acceptable. This is usually done by defining ourselves as members of something larger that does not share the same limitations. Suppose that re-defining ourselves as members of a nation relaxes these constraints and make us feel that we have overcome these limitations. In this case, utility-maximising persons may happily die for their nation and enjoy being part of something that will never die (Pagano 1995).

Again, the search for an identity could be rationally recast as an economising problem in which the net benefits of each identity are carefully compared. However, this exercise prevents the identity from satisfying the very needs it is supposed to fulfil. The point is that often people can satisfy these needs only if they believe that religion or nationality constitutes their identity, independently of their choice. An identity that is chosen by an individual would seem to share contingency and limitations. An identity that aims to satisfy the need of overcoming the fragility of individual life must be such that individuals feel that they are not choosing this identity but that they are rather 'chosen' by it.

A God or a Nation, chosen to maximise our utility, is meaningless in overcoming the fragility and the contingency of our lives. This need can be only satisfied if we believe that God or the Nation has 'chosen' us in order to realise its will. Only in this way can the individuals believe that they are now part of something bigger that survives their bodies. Somehow, the choice of these identities can be seen as another skilful way of economising on bounded emotional skills and acquiring that peace of mind that allows us to become, in other respects, rational choosers. But if any economising process is involved, it cannot be recast in any traditional orthodox framework. Moreover, nationalistic and religious wars make us wonder whether this economising process is really likely to take place. If one needs to be emotional in order to be rational, it is very unlikely that the mix of rationality and emotions that struggles in our mind is itself only the outcome of some rational economising process.

The contradictions that one encounters when one tries to economise on bounded rationality are hardly surprising. In a world of bounded rationality, the ability to economise must also be severely bounded and 'economising behaviour' cannot be mechanically extended to bounded rationality without contradicting the idea of bounded rationality itself. Bounded rationality necessarily involves some departure from the economising behaviour that is assumed in standard economic theory.

3. ENDOGENOUS PREFERENCES, EXOGENOUS INSTINCTS AND INSTITUTIONAL CHANGE

Economising behaviour cannot be easily extended to take into account the numerous forms of bounded rationality that we have just considered. The Williamsonian suggestion ends up exacerbating the weakness of a 'rational economising man'. After one hundred years, there is no better way of expressing this point than by quoting what is perhaps Veblen's most famous passage:

> The hedonistic conception of man is that of a lightning calculator of pleasures and pains, who oscillates like a homogeneous globule of desire of happiness under the impulse of stimuli that shift him about the area but live him intact. He has neither antecedent nor consequent. He is an isolated definitive human datum, in stable equilibrium except for the buffets of the impinging forces that displace him in one direction or another. Self-poised in elemental space, he spins symmetrically about his own spiritual axis until the parallelogram of forces bears down upon him where-upon he follows the line of the resultant. When the force of the impact is spent, he comes to rest a self-contained globule of desire as before. Spiritually, the hedonistic man is not a prime mover. He is not the seat of process of living, except in the sense that he is subject to a series of permutations enforced upon him by circumstances external and alien to him. (Veblen 1898, p. 390)

If we want to make sense of the ways in which individuals try to deal with their own limitations, we need a radical departure from the standard neoclassical approach. Even the simple awareness of our own limitations cannot be achieved without changing ourselves in the process. Costly communication, information and decisions, painful introspection of our own (often contradictory) 'preferences', delicate definitions of identity, complicated sentiments and emotions are all often involved when we try to understand and, possibly, do something about our own limitations. The self, that bears the full weight of our limitations, must be seen as a real person whose capabilities and shortcomings are a product of natural, social and personal history. At the same time, unlike the neoclassical individual, this same self is a 'prime mover' that does not only change the world but also oneself in the process. Again quoting from Veblen turns out to be thy the most incisive way of summarising the argument:

The economic life history of the individual is a cumulative process of adaptation of means to ends that cumulatively change as the process goes on, both the agent and his environment being at any point the outcome of the past process. His methods of life to-day are enforced upon him by his habits of life carried over from yesterday and by the circumstances left as the mechanical residue of the life of yesterday. (Veblen 1898, p. 391)

According to Veblen, when one extends the argument to the community in which the individuals live, all economic change 'is always a change in habits of thought' and 'life is an unfolding activity of a teleological kind' (p. 391). Even if changes can involve a great deal of rationality and intelligence, they are never costless and, after some time, the limited rationality of the agents switches necessarily to something else. In the meantime, the successful changes that are selected stop being outcomes of a process of rational understanding; they become rather the object of a process of habituation that allows an unconscious application that saves on bounded rationality. When this happens, the neoclassical ideal of maximisation with unbounded rationality may paradoxically take place. In this sense, as the 'Old Institutionalist' J.M. Clark pointed out in 1918, the neoclassical theory of costless maximisation could be considered as a special case of the Institutionalist approach.

In general, according to Clark, the maximisation of utility is incompatible with the hedonistic postulate of the theory:

A good hedonist would stop calculating when it seemed likely to involve more trouble that it was worth, and, as he could not in the nature of the case tell just when this point has been reached, he would make no claim to the exactness of his results. (Clark [1918] 1967, p. 25).

However, Clark points out that habits may make it reasonable to assume that in particular situations the maximisation principle is possible. According to Clark:

indeed it is only by the aid of habit that the marginal utility principle is approximated in real life, for only so it is possible to have choosing *which is both effortless and intelligent*, embodying the results of deliberation or experience, without the accompanying cost of decision, which as we have seen, must prevent the most rational hedonist from attaining hedonistic perfection. For habit is nature's machinery for handling over to the lower brain and nerve centres the carrying on of work done first by the higher apparatus of conscious deliberation. (Clark [1918] 1967, pp. 26-7).

Unfortunately the very same mechanism may imply that 'It may be one's past mistakes that grip him in spite of himself, or his unconsidered impulses that are thus hardened and set' (Clark [1918] 1967, p. 27).

Clark's particular case involves the following paradox: intentional rationality can never reach full optimality. By contrast, habits can, in principle, reach full unbounded optimality. However, in this case optimality is likely to be relative to some past situation in which the habits were formed with the possible help of some intentional rationality. For this reason, even if the habits were 'rationally' formed, we can become their slaves in the sense that they do not fit the present situation. However, it is only when individuals do not maximise that standard optimality results may somehow be achieved!

According to Veblen, the adaptive process works through both 'a selection between stable types of temperament and character' and 'an adaptation of men's habit of thought to changing circumstances' (Veblen [1899] 1953, p. 132). Or, in other words, to use contemporary terminology, adaptation has simultaneously 'Darwinian' and 'Lamarkian' characteristics. However, this is 'of less importance than the fact that, by one method or other, institutions change and develop. The development of these institutions is the development of society' (Veblen [1899] 1953, p. 132).

The evolution of institutions does not imply that they can be explained in terms of their relative efficiency at organising present economic life. In the first place, institutions are necessarily 'products of past processes, are adapted to past circumstances, and are therefore never in full accord with the requirement of the present . . . When a step in the development has been taken, this step itself constitutes a change of situation which requires a new adaptation; it becomes the point of departure for a new step in the adjustment and so interminably.' (Veblen [1899] 1953, p. 132).

In the second place, 'all change in habits of life and of thought is irksome. The difference in this respect between the wealthy and the common run of mankind lies not so much in the motive which prompts to conservatism as in the degree of exposure to the economic forces that urge a change. The members of the wealthy class do not yield to the demand for innovation as readily as other men because they are not constrained to do so. (Veblen [1899] 1953, pp. 137-8). Moreover, the members of the privileged classes have also 'a material interest in leaving things as they are' (Veblen [1899] 1953, p. 141).

In the third place, while the lower classes have an interest in the transformation of society, they lack the time and the energy to foster the change. Moreover, the lower classes are subject to the cultural hegemony of the privileged classes. Because of the 'prescriptive example of conspicuous waste and conservatism' of the wealthy classes (Veblen [1899] 1953, p. 141), the lower classes spend a lot of energy trying to imitate them instead of trying to change the prevailing habits.

Finally, 'efficient' changes of society are very difficult to achieve because of what we may today call 'institutional complementarities' that characterise each economic system. 'The code of properties, conventionalities, and usages in vogue at any given time and among any given people has more or less the character of an organic whole so that any appreciable change in one point of the scheme involves something of a change or readjustment at other points also, if not a reorganisation all along the line.' In particular, in the case of major changes, 'it is immediately felt that a serious derangement of the entire scheme would result; it is felt that a readjustment of the structure to the new form taken on by one of its chief elements would be a painful and tedious, if not a doubtful process.' (Veblen, [1899] 1953, p. 139).

The contrast between the Williamsonian and Veblenian 'rationally bounded individuals' is striking. The Williamsonian individual is striving to economise on and beyond his own bounded rationality and tends to achieve efficient behaviour and institutions. By contrast, the Veblenian individual is seriously bounded by his own rationality in the sense that it necessarily implies that the capacity to economise on bounded rationality is itself bounded. Thus, the Veblenian individual can be easily stuck in inefficient habits and institutions.

Indeed, the opposite problem seems to arise within the Veblenian framework: How can efficient institutional change ever occur? Do bounded rationality and the consequent endogenisation of preferences imply that the individual is unable to change inefficient institutions? Is not the Veblenian individual less of a 'prime mover' than the neoclassical 'lightening calculator' that Veblen had so appropriately criticised for not being 'the seat of process of leaving'? Does not the 'behaviouristic' Veblen completely overshadow the 'humanistic' criticism that he had moved against neo-classical theory?

The answer lies in the fact that, while habits and preferences are largely endogenous in the sense of being strongly influenced by the history of society, the instincts of individuals are largely exogenous in the sense that they have been selected during long periods of natural and human history.

In the Veblenian approach, instincts should not be seen as something opposed to 'rationality'. They imply that people try to analyse and to understand real situations in order to achieve some results. As Jensen (1987) points out, according to Veblen instincts are 'teleological categories' and every instinct involves 'consciousness' and intelligence (Veblen [1914] 1964, pp. 3-4). According to Jensen, in Veblen's view the 'average' human nature is dominated by six major proclivities. They are: an 'instinct of workmanship; an instinctively . . . actuated idle curiosity'; an instinctive disposition labelled 'the parental bent'; a proclivity to . . . acquisition; a 'set of self-regarding proclivities'; and 'an habitual bent' that makes instinctive 'habituation possible' on the part of human beings. (Veblen [1918] 1957, pp. 4; [1914] 1964, p. 11, 25, 26, 27, 182, 204, 285).

In this sense, there is no incompatibility between the 'humanistic Veblen' and the 'behaviouristic Veblen', or between 'intentional' and 'non-intentional' behaviour (Fiorito 1997, p. 122). They are both outcomes of the interactions between instincts and institutions - an interaction that does not necessarily entail the emergence of a spontaneous order *à la* Hayek, or of efficient institutions *à la* Williamson. Like in the Darwinian theory of natural selection, the interactions do not have *a priori* guaranteed benevolent outcomes.

Luca Fiorito (1997, p. 121) observes that the Marxian class struggle (but even more, I would add, the 'contradictions' between the relations of production and productive forces) finds its counterpart in Veblen's conflict between the positive values of technology and the existing institutions. However, the Veblenian approach does not share the deterministic teleological aspect of the Marxian view of history in which the progressive role of the development of productive forces wins necessarily against the fetters of conservative relations of production. In many cases, 'those instincts which make directly for the material welfare of the community, such as parental bent and the sense of workmanship' have prevailed over the 'bonds of custom, prescription, principles, precedent'. 'But history records more frequent and spectacular instances of the triumph of institutions over life and culture than of peoples who have by force of instinctive insight saved themselves alive out of a desperately precarious institutional situation . . .' (Veblen [1914] 1964, p. 24-5).

After one hundred years, if one takes the problem of bounded rationality seriously, the Veblenian approach has remarkable advantages with respect to the neoclassical, Marxian and New Institutional traditions. With respect to the first, it provides a more general case in which 'maximisation' can only occur as a particular case. With respect to the second and the third, it provides a framework in which efficient institutional change is possible but not necessary. Thus, unlike the case of the New Institutional Economics, in Veblen, institutions have not to be understood as efficient answers to the present situation. The role of the economist becomes rather more similar to that of geologist: the present set of institutions can be seen as a set of mutually supporting rocks that have come about in a process of cumulative growth. Somehow, they still bear the mark of the conditions under which they were generated. In this sense, 'economising behaviour' does not shape the institutions of the present day society, and even less the utilisation of 'bounded rationality' itself. Indeed, also for rationality, it turns out that 'If rational behaviour is to be assumed, then its evolution has to be explained' (Hodgson 1998, p. 189).

4. THE DARWINIAN ROOTS OF VEBLEN'S UNILINEARISM

While the Veblenian approach can allow for both indefinite stagnation and progress, it shares a 'unilinear vision of history' with the Marxian and the New Institutional schools. Anne Mayhew has convincingly explained this point as follows:

> For Veblen, as for Morgan and other members of the 'historical evolutionary school' with whom Veblen shared so much, the goal was to produce a record of mankind that would be told 'in terms of the process [of evolution] itself.' Comparisons between present societies in all their variations would allow a reconstruction of the past. The critical assumption - which Veblen shared with the anthropologists during 1880s - was that sociocultural variation could be arrayed unilinearly. *Variation was a matter of stage achieved, not a consequence of many divergent histories.* (Mayhew 1998, p. 452, my italics).

In my opinion, the 'unilinear' vision[6] that characterises the Veblenian approach can be traced to his Darwinian roots. This is somehow paradoxical. In natural history, variation is not only a matter of the 'stage achieved' by a given species, but it is also a consequence of the 'many divergent histories' that characterise the different species. The paradox is made even more striking by the fact that the title of the book, *On the Origin of Species*, stressed more the latter aspect than the former. However, as Helena Cronin points out, the title did somehow contradict the content of the book:

> The two fundamental problems that Darwin's theory was designed to solve were adaptation and diversity. The riddle of adaptation he solved superbly. As for diversity, on certain aspects he was equally successful. The patterns of geographical distribution, the fossil record, the taxonomic hierarchy, and comparative embryology all fell into place under his incisive analysis. But in the mist of such success, there was one problem that remained just outside his grasp. It was poignantly the problem of the origin of species. (Cronin 1991, p. 430)

In the *Origins*, Darwin was not only unable to explain the circumstances under which speciation (the formation of a new species) could occur, but did not even make a clear distinction between the concept of species and the concept of variety within a given species. This is very clear in the following passage:

> Laying aside the question of fertility and sterility, in all other respects there seems to be a general and close similarity in the offspring of crossed species, and of crossed varieties. If we look at species as having been specially created, and at varieties as having been produced by secondary laws, this similarity would be an astonishing fact. But it harmonises perfectly with the view that there is no essential distinction between species and varieties. (Darwin [1859] 1968, p. 288)

The confusion between species and variety is even more striking when one considers that, in his early work, Darwin was well aware of the definition of species in terms of reproductive isolation - a definition that is consistent with modern biology and implies a clear difference between varieties and species. At the same time, the passage shows how the confusion was perhaps to be found in 'a strong, even though perhaps unconscious, motivation for Darwin to demonstrate that species lack the constancy and the distinctiveness claimed by them by creationists' (Mayr 1982, p. 262). Creationists point to these characteristics of species to challenge the claim that such discontinuities could be the result of the gradual adaptation due to the working of natural selection. Thus, Darwin 'solved' the species problem by defining them by degree of difference rather than by reproductive isolation and by denying their qualitative distinctness from varieties of the same species.

In some ways, to deny the distinctness of species was a successful strategy against the creationists. 'But the switch from Darwin's species concept the 1830s to that of 1850s laid the foundation for controversies that lasted for a century' (Mayr 1982, p. 269). Perhaps another consequence of this switch was that it created some space for a view in which '*variation was a matter of stage achieved, not a consequence of many divergent histories*'.

Humankind could be seen more as *the most advanced stage* of natural history than as *one of the divergent histories* that characterises living species. The discontinuity of speciation and the comparative understanding of the diverging histories of the different species were sacrificed to a vision in which evolution could even been seen as unfolding along a single line. When the vision was transposed from natural to human history, it implied something similar to what Veblen (like Marx) believed to be true: while progress and stagnation were both possible, they were only occurring along a single line (Pagano 1999). The vision also had an attractive implication: the synchronic analysis of different societies existing at the same point of time allowed the diachronic reconstruction of the different stages that defined the single line of development of each society. Or, in other words, the comparisons between present societies in all their variations would have allowed a reconstruction of the past. When anthropological and historical evidence disclaimed this unilinear vision of history, 'the convergence of many disciplines on a 'single natural-historical model of the world' ceased and, with it, the evolutionary vision faded' (Mayhew 1998, p. 452).

5. CONCLUSION

After one hundred years, the Veblenian appeal for an evolutionary approach to economics is surprisingly appealing and one must proceed by some Veblenian type of study of the evolution of economic theories to understand why this is the case (Argyrous and Sethi 1996).

If we take seriously bounded rationality, we can make very little use of the New Institutional approach in which rational economising behaviour is extended to bounded rationality itself. Preferences cannot be taken as exogenous to a given institutional context (see Bowles 1988), while important aspects of human nature (like Veblen instincts) can. Stagnation and progress both must be possible outcomes when institutions are seen as the outcome of habits that have developed in the past and are only seldom going to be revised.

At the same time, it is necessary to go beyond Veblen's unilinearism and understand the process of cumulative growth which distinguishes the many lines along which the different histories of the different societies flow (Pagano and Rowthorn 1996). After one hundred years, with the advantage of the 'speciation debates' in modern biology (Pagano 1999), we cannot afford to be grounded in the unilinear roots of Charles Darwin.

NOTES

1. I am very grateful to Frank Hahn, Luca Fiorito, Ernesto Screpanti, Francisco Louçã, Sandro Mendonça, the participants in the EAEPE seminar in Lisbon and the participants to General Forum seminar at CEU-Budapest for useful comments and suggestions. This paper is part of a Project of National Interest (P.I.N.) on 'Incomplete Contracts and Analysis of Institutions' financed by M.U.R.S.T.
2. For a criticism of this view and how it relates to certain types of evolutionary theories see Hodgson (1996).
3. The fundamental blocks of the Williamsonian construction are the concept of asset-specificity, the concept of 'private governance' and the related fruitful 'unification' of the fields of law, economics and organization theory.
4. The Hayekian version of the optimality of markets is at the same time stronger and weaker than the traditional 'Pareto optimality'. While the Hayekian market is far from the 'first best' condition that characterises Pareto optimality, it is optimal in the strong sense that it is not

only the best but even the only feasible system by which the information dispersed among the agents can be communicated to the other agents. On this issue see Pagano (1992).

5. It is even more costly to produce preferences that are consistent. Our multiple self can involve an aggregation problem that replicates Arrow's problem of social choice at the individual level. If facing these contradictions is costly, the production of preferences would then run against the limits of bounded emotional skills (see point on Bounded emotional skills). Screpanti (1998 Ch. 2) points out how, according to the characteristics of our personality, we could either suppress or face our own internal pluralism. In both cases, because of our multiple self, the 'production costs' of preferences would increase in a rather dramatic way. One of the many possible roles of ideology and socialization could lie in the creation of some 'economies of scope and scale', especially in the processes of repression of some of the multiple aspects of our personality. If we want to push even further this 'economic' analogy, intolerance and conformism may be due to the fact that, because of the economies of scope and of scale, the absence of 'internal' repression by an individual increases the repression costs of other individuals. Of course, the increase in costs may or may not increase welfare (that is, in this case, particularly hard to measure).

6. This unilinear view of history is, in fact, perhaps close to what Popper (1957) called 'historicism' and criticised for the fact that it denies the existence of historical change in a strong sense: 'It almost looks as if historicists were trying to compensate themselves for the loss of an unchanging world by clinging to the faith that change can be foreseen because it is ruled by an unchanging law' (Popper 1957, p. 161). Even if Popper does not use this terminology, unilinearism is, perhaps, the best way to explain what he calls the 'unholy' alliance between historicism and utopianism: since history runs along a single line, the advent of a given utopia can be 'scientifically' predicted.

REFERENCES

Argyrous, G. Sethi R. (1996), 'The theory of evolution and the evolution of theories: Veblen's methodology in contemporary perspective', *Cambridge Journal of Economics*, No. 20, pp. 475-95.

Bowles, S. (1988), 'Endogenous preferences: the cultural consequences of markets and other economic institutions', *Journal of Economic Literature*, Vol. XXXVI, pp. 75-111.

Clark, J.M. (1918), 'Economics and modern psychology', reprinted in *Preface to Social Economics*, New York: Augustus M. Kelley, pp. 92-169 (1967).

Conlisk, J. (1987), 'Optimisation cost', *Journal of Economic Behaviour and Organization*, N. 9, pp. 213-28.

Coslink, J. (1996), 'Why bounded rationality?', *Journal of Economic Literature*, Vol. XXXIV, pp. 669-700.

Cronin, H. (1991), *The Ant and the Peacock*, Cambridge: Cambridge University Press.

Darwin, C. (1859), *The Origin of Species*, edited by J. W. Burrow, Harmondsworth. Penguin Books (1968).

Fiorito, L. (1997), 'Sul declino dell'istituzionalismo americano. Una tesi alternativa', *Studi e Note di Economia*, N. 3, pp. 113-39.

Hart, O. (1990), 'Is bounded rationality an important element of a theory of institutions?', *Journal of Institutional and Theoretical Economics*, N. 146, pp. 696-702.

Hart, O. (1995), *Firms, Contracts, and Financial Structure*, Oxford: Clarendon Press.

Hodgson, G.M. (1996), 'Organizational form and economic evolution: a critique of the Williamsonian hypothesis', in U. Pagano and R. Rowthorn (eds), *Democracy and Efficiency in the Economic Enterprise*, Routledge, London, pp. 98-116.

Hodgson, G.M. (1998), 'The approach of institutional economics', *Journal of Economic Literature*, Vol. XXXVI, pp. 166-92.

Jensen, H. J. (1987), 'The theory of human nature', *Journal of Economic Issues*, Vol. XXI, pp. 1039-73.

Mayhew, A. (1998), 'On the difficulty of evolutionary analysis', *Cambridge Journal of Economics*, Vol. 22, No. 4, pp. 449-61.

Mayr, E. (1982), *The Growth of Biological Thought*, Massachusetts: Harvard University Press.

Pagano, U. (1991), 'Property rights, asset specificity, and the division of labour under alternative capitalist relations', *Cambridge Journal of Economics*, Vol. 15, N. 3, reprinted in G. Hodgson (1993), *The Economics of Institutions,* a volume of Mark Blaug (ed.), *The International Library of Critical Writings in Economics*, Cheltenham, UK and Northampton, MA, USA: Edward Elgar, pp. 315-42.

Pagano, U. (1992), 'Authority, co-ordination and disequilibrium: an explanation of the co-existence of markets and firms', *Economic Dynamics and Structural Change*, June 1992, reprinted in G. Hodgson (1993), *The Economics of Institutions,* a volume of Mark Blaug (ed.), *The International Library of Critical Writings in Economics*, Cheltenham, UK and Northampton, MA, USA: Edward Elgar.

Pagano, U. (1995), 'Can economics explain nationalism?', in A. Breton et al. (eds) *Nationalism and Rationality*, New York: Cambridge University Press.

Pagano, U. and R. Rowthorn (1996), 'The competitive selection of democratic firms in a world of self-sustaining institutions', in U. Pagano and R. Rowthorn (eds.), *Democracy and Efficiency in the Economic Enterprise*, London: Routledge, pp. 116-45.

Pagano, U. (1999), 'The origin of organizational species', in A. Nicita and U. Pagano (eds), *The Evolution of Economic Diversity*,

Popper, K. (1957), *The Poverty of Historicism*, London: Routledge.

Screpanti, E. (1998), *The Fundamental Institutions of Capitalism*, Department of Political Economy, University of Siena.

Simon, H. (1957), *Models of Man*, New York: Wiley.

Simon, H. (1961), *Administrative Behaviour*, New York: Macmillan.

Simon, H. (1997), *An Empirically Based Microeconomics*, Cambridge: Cambridge University Press.

Stigler, G. J. (1961), 'The economics of information', *Journal of Political Economy*, N. 69, pp. 213-25

Veblen, T. (1898), 'Why is economics not an evolutionary science?', *Quarterly Journal of Economics*, V. XIII, pp. 371-97.

Veblen, T. (1899) *The Theory of the Leisure Class*, New York: Viking Press (1953).

Veblen, T. (1914), *The Instinct of Workmanship and the State of Industrial Arts*, New York: W.W. Norton (1964).

Veblen, T. (1918), *The Higher Learning in America*, New York: Sagamore Press (1957).

Williamson, O. E. (1985), *The Economic Institutions of Capitalism*, New York: The Free Press.

Williamson, O.E. (1996), *The Mechanisms of Governance*, Oxford: Oxford University Press.

9.   Is Economics an Evolutionary Science?

Frank Hahn

The above is the title of a paper by Veblen published in 1898. Ugo Pagano suggested that I take it as my *leitmotif*. As will soon become clear, I do not think that economics is a science, let alone an evolutionary science, so sticking closely to Veblen would be a handicap.

In any case, I have found Veblen's essay hard to understand. He writes, for instance, of differences amongst economists as being differences in spiritual attitude. He argues that scientists 'reduce all problems to terms of conservation of energy and persistence of quantity'. Thus Darwin would appear not to be a scientist. Veblen also writes that scientists are after absolute truth, which he holds to be a spiritual fact. And so on. At the end of this essay I shall devote a short section to the meaning I have, after some re-reading, been able to squeeze out of Veblen's paper. However, in his book on the leisure class he is more easily understood, and I shall take note of that. But for now I shall simply plunge into the maelstrom.

I

One way of interpreting the question is this: can one detect a process in the development of economics as a body of theory which could be described as an evolutionary process? One could give an affirmative answer by pointing to the response of economic theory to the changing environment of economic life over the centuries and arguing that, to survive as a subject it had to maximise its usefulness. This clearly is both laboured and imprecise. In a splendid essay, Bernard Williams noted the dangers of the use of the evolutionary analogy in general. He argues that very often it turns out to be vacuous. Among philosophers, Popper is perhaps the most radical evolutionist, arguing that scientific theories are exposed to the selection pressure of possible falsification. Many maintain that Popper's description of this development of science is historically incorrect. But however that may be, it cannot easily be applied to economics. There is no theory, it would seem, which all reasonable people regard as conclusively falsified. Just as in many cases of science, falsification in economics demands statistical inference which in turn, given that there is only a finite amount of evidence and that one can only test a *ceteris paribus* theory, evades the Popperian pressures of falsification.

That of course is the objection to Friedman's 'as if' approach to economic theory. Not only can we not rely on the predictive powers of our theories (none of them predict very precisely since there are always ceteris paribus elements which are hard to verify so that we must resort to statistical inference), but, as Popper argued, prediction can never settle the truth or falsity of a theory. This does not necessarily rule out an evolutionary view of the subject. The driving force here may not be the proven falsehood of a proposition, but simply a suspicion that it is false. What it does rule out is Friedman's epistemological proposal, since lack of suspicion of the verisimilitude of a theory can hardly be claimed to justify it.

One can now ask what exactly would have been achieved if one could show that indeed economics developed in an evolutionary way. Evidently this would be a very imprecise claim. One would have to commit oneself to a view of what constitutes 'fitness' in this case and the mechanism by which changes have increased fitness. This may be a fertile field for theorising, for it may be argued that economics develops under the pressure of justifying the status quo, and so improvements here count as increased fitness. This, for instance, might give a coherence to the history of economic theory. However, this is again a theory which needs some justification.

It seems to me that the question of why are there giraffes is different in kind from the question of why we subscribe to a theory. This is so because teleological explanations are much more acceptable in the latter case. For instance, we may accept a theory because we know that powerful superiors accept it or we may reject it, in order to stand out amongst our fellows. However, we know that we must not say that a giraffe has a long neck in order to get at high-growing vegetation.

In the situations just envisaged we may argue that 'social survival' depends on 'social accommodation', so that subjects can only survive if they do not violate, in one way or another, social norms. It is of the essence of an argument by selection here, that those wishing to pursue a subject know this and predominantly accommodate. There are economists who believe this to be the 'explanation' of the dominance of neo-classical economics.

But do we need to invoke evolution, which is, after all, a technical subject, to make points like this? If one does, one immediately comes up against the problem of heredity of characteristics. No doubt something could be produced to deal with this, but I doubt that it will be worth having.

There are, of course, quite elaborate sociological accounts of theories. For instance, it has been argued that the marginal productivity theory of wages is espoused by those who wish to maintain that the share going to wages in a capitalist society is just. (Let me note that I regard this way of rewarding effort very *unjust*). But this ignores the question of whether it is 'true', which is an alternative for the acceptance of the theory and for many people an overriding criterion for acceptance of *any* theory. Of course, this begs the question of how we know that some economic theory is true. In fact, we don't know, but we also often do not know whether it is false. It is concern with this question which, to some extent, drives the development of the theory, and it is rather easy to make this case.

Consider the situation in the thirties when theory seemed incapable of explaining events, let alone suggesting a plausible policy to deal with them. This no doubt gave the impetus to Keynes and Keynesian theories. One would like to be able to say that the received theories could not survive, and at the time that would have been a sensible judgement. But forty years on, the supposedly discarded theory has many adherents. Typically no convincing account of the world, e.g. the appearance of inflation, can account for this cyclical theorising. (While Keynes was by no means a rigorous theorist, it certainly is not the case that there is no way to make his approach at least as logically acceptable as, say, that of Chicago). One needs to look more precisely and in greater detail at the way in which theorising changes with circumstances. I shall not attempt that. But the situation in economics is not too dissimilar from that which would arise if a large body of professional biologists repudiated Darwin in favour of creationism. Of course this is not the only instance. There are now a fair number of economists who would like to return to the 'Classics', for instance to Ricardo. All of this documents two assertions: (a) economics is not a science in the normal usage of this term, and (b) its development is not evolutionary.

II

It is not at all clear to me that it is best to interpret the question of the title of this essay in the way I have just done. So let us move on to the second interpretation: is the proper subject matter of economics the unravelling of processes which are akin to evolutionary processes? Indeed, on one interpretation Veblen could be taken as criticising economics for being too much concerned with stationary equilibrium and of taking its dynamics from physics. Not surprisingly, economists towards the last quarter of the nineteenth century, e.g. Marshall, began to favour biological analogies over those taken from physics. After all, we are told that Darwin himself was inspired by Malthus, so a two way traffic was already under way. I have already quoted a Veblen passage showing his dissatisfaction with the approach via physics, although to modern ears it is strangely expressed. So one can safely take it that the interpretation now proposed is not far-fetched.

As we all know, evolutionary approaches are now much in fashion. Certainly this is true in game theory but also in the somewhat older approaches to competition, both of the traditional kind as well as in politics. For instance, here is a very old argument: Firms maximise profits not because that is intrinsically desirable for them, but because it increases the chance of survival. Even more drastic is not to give any motive to firms at all - for instance, they may behave almost randomly but only those that accidentally pursue maximum profit survive. Except for a few papers this rather attractive idea has not been implemented formally with any generality. But notice that, if this approach works, it relieves us of the necessity of ascribing to a firm the super rationality and omniscience of the textbook.

Let us for the moment continue with the evolutionary approach to profit. Recall that animals are passive participants in the evolutionary process and it is clear that the same is true for firms in the above approach. However, I believe it is safe to assume that survival is valued by most firms even if they do not know how to maximise profits. It is not fanciful to suppose that they will take some steps to counter the threat of elimination. Indeed, some of the most successful fruits of the New Industrial Organisation theory are games of entry prevention, although of course profit maximisation is taken to be the guiding motivation in these theories. Nonetheless, the question remains: How far is one justified to think of human agents as passive participants in an evolutionary process? This assumption would certainly go against much of economic theory in which the agent is usually assumed to know everything that he needs to know.

This of course is not a decisive objection to the evolutionary approach in economics, but it does suggest that we should not take Darwinian theory without due caution. Comparatively speaking, humans have rather powerful brains and some of them are apt to use them.

It seems to me that conscious motives must enter into any theory of human development, which of course they do not in biology. This does not mean that there are no unintended consequences of actions as a whole. But it does mean that one must not, without argument, proceed to a formalism of the evolutionary process in our subject in which motives are neglected - there is always a prima facie case for including them in most cases. Nor is it a live issue in economics. Some of the more interesting applications of evolutionary theory have been in the theory of games, where it is thought of as a theory of learning the most profitable strategy given that other players are also choosing strategies. The process of learning follows a sort of 'gradient process' and in many cases converges to a Nash equilibrium which can be understood in the light of motives of the agents involved. For instance in certain cases convergence to a Nash or Risk-Dominant Equilibrium can be established where evolution finds a resting place, that is, it no longer induces change.

It is now worthwhile noting that evolution is not a predictive theory in biology; it is an understanding theory. It is unlikely to be more powerful in economics. Moreover, it is a long run theory, and so it is not clear that it is capable of yielding policy fruits in economics. Of course, both in biology and in economics, competition is a central mechanism and this has nourished the hopes of economists that evolutionary approaches are feasible and profitable. They certainly are feasible as far as language is concerned, for instance, there was no way for horse drawn transport to 'survive' the invention of the internal combustion engine. But one needs to be convinced that, in these cases, anything has been gained by an appeal to evolution. Indeed, it seems to me to entail either that inventions are a feature of a random environment or constitute a random mutation in some agents. But many inventions are the result of deliberate search, so the propensity to search must be taken to have evolved. This in turn may be explained by the recognition that an evolutionary weeding-out process is a reality and one is well advised to protect oneself. This then seems to appeal to 'cultural' evolution, which is one of the dubious uses of the vocabulary of biological evolution. Dawson's 'memes' seem to me to replace one vague notion by another.

Ask yourself which 'meme' is responsible for the rise of protestantism. Historians have given us many complex accounts of the event. Sociologists like Weber have claimed that this religious reform was eventually responsible for the rise of capitalism and instrumental rationality. It seems doubtful that evolutionary theory would help our understanding here. In England, Henry VIII wanted a divorce which the Roman church would not grant him. So he decided to do without Rome. The fact that this caused neither a revolution nor significant unrest suggests that the 'time was ripe'. But what does that mean?

It is instructive to consider briefly the use of evolutionary ideas in game theory. The main application is at the population level, that is to say of a sufficiently large group so that one can treat frequencies as probabilities. In particular, evolution is conceived as taking place though changes in a group's strategy profile. Roughly speaking, the proportions in which strategies are chosen by players change under the evolutionary pressure being modelled. For instance, the frequency with which a strategy is chosen by players is affected by its relative profitability in an obvious way. If this process converges to one strategy being chosen by almost every one, the outcome is a convention. But there are many possibilities depending both on the game and the exact process chosen to represent evolutionary pressure.

Before I proceed, some more or less technical remarks are in order.

In almost all cases one will be dealing with a Markov process. One will want to make assumptions that ensure that the transition matrix is irreducible so that standard convergence results can be invoked. As in much of game theory, allowance has to be made for errors in responses which are small, so the final outcome can be found as a limit as the error goes to zero. There are also investigations into best response dynamics (each agent at each date and in each state defined by the strategy profiles of all the other agents, chooses a best myopic response). Here, for a number of cases convergence to a Nash equilibrium or a risk-dominant equilibrium of the process can be proved. (I am assuming that I need not provide proofs on this occasion.)

One notices that, in specifying the processes there is a good deal of latitude as there was, until recently, in Darwinian theory, (although a fair amount remains to be studied). In economics, I do not know of an instance of an empirical study of a proposed plausible selection process. One of the purely theoretical problems is whether to judge plausibility in terms of motives or of survival. For instance, if there is a fraction of firms using a strategy different from the profit maximising one, do we argue that that fraction must decline because some of these firms cannot survive, or is the decline due to the learning from more clever competitors? In economics, there is no straightforward account of either fitness or the survival of the fittest, which in biology give evolutionary theory coherence. Nor is it clear what the counterpart of random mutation is in our subject. It may be that the process of discovering new knowledge qualifies, but we do not need an elaborate theory of evolution to understand the resulting adaptations of skills and possibly of industrial structure. It is true that much of what economists have to say in these situations has a Darwinian ring. But we notice that new knowledge is not automatically utilised, nor as many have reminded us in recent years, does it come out of the blue. R&D is itself a fairly recent development, one in need of explanation not by an appeal to profit maximisation but to the process which made R&D an instrument of such maximisation and the latter a motive.

In biology, teleological arguments are scrupulously avoided; in our case matters are more subtle: we explain actions of agents as goal directed, that is teleologically, but we are often arguing that the consequences of action of a group of teleologically acting agents may not be intended by any one agent. The orderliness of resource allocation, which may be the consequence of a market economy, is not the intended outcome of any of the market participants. If this happens one may argue that it is a struggle for survival which leads to the unintended outcome. While this is closer to what we regard as evolutionary theory, the appeal to the latter does not seem to do more than bring about a change in language. It may indeed encourage pseudo science. This leads me to a small detour.

One is tempted to think of competition amongst economic agents as justifying our appeal to evolution, or at least as being an important element in claiming affinity with the latter. However, in evolutionary biology, one often argues that competition leads to less fierce competition. For instance, competition for food has led to the evolution of a variety of herbivores, each one grazing differently. An evolutionary economist might thus venture the Marxian prediction of increasing monopolisation. For all I know, that is the right prediction, but one notices that the evolutionary analogy allows others. As an example, an equilibrium 'predator prey' situation may be the outcome, a possibility studied in a non-evolutionary model by Goodwin. But the result may also be established by evolutionary arguments. One has here an example relating to an earlier remark that evolutionary theorising does not lead to predictions but possibly to understanding.

However, this is not always so. If a state of affairs is not 'evolutionary stable', then almost tautologically it will not persist with probability one. The difficulty here is that the economic 'game' is not easy to describe precisely. One of the reasons is that the 'pay offs' to strategy profiles will themselves be the result of evolutionary pressure. So, of course, will be the set of strategies. As a simple example one need only consider the choice of strategies open to women today compared with only fifty years ago, and note the changed value women now put on careers. My view at present is this: there are many economic questions and problems which have a family resemblance to those facing the evolutionary biologist. Attempts to restate them in the language of evolution does not seem to have helped very much. Take the application to game theory. It became clear some time ago that the 'eductive' approach was not only unconvincing but yielded unique outcomes only in special cases. It was clear that one needed some dynamics to make a choice of outcomes. Certainly evolutionary ideas were very suggestive in guiding the choice of dynamics. That seems to be its main contribution. But unlike in the case of animals and plants, we have no evidence for the choice. For instance, biologists have some evidence of the time taken for evolutionary effects to manifest themselves; we, by contrast, have neither evidence nor theory to tell us about lags, which are rather important for the behaviour of the dynamics. So, while evolutionary theory may inspire us in the formulation of our theories, these are not *evolutionary* theories.

This undoubtedly is a controversial conclusion and possibly will be shown in the future to be wrong. But let me give an example where the boot is on the other foot. Recently I corresponded with an Oxford evolutionary population biologist. The subject was a signalling game amongst animals in the choice of mate. The Oxford conclusion was that, for these signals to work in demonstrating better genes in a potential partner, the cost of a signal must be monotonic in the reliability of the signal. This of course is no news to economists - it had occurred to Mirrlees and Spence, who as far as I know were innocent of attempting an evolutionary theory. But notice that the Oxford biologists naturally invoked the increase in 'fitness', while we would invoke the notion of rational pursuit of profit. This does make a difference, since the idea of fitness driven evolution seems empirically well established, while profit maximisation is not. It is, I believe, not an accident that recent research in human mating choices supports the Oxford findings for animals, although it is stressed that the choices are not consciously motivated by genetic considerations. It is in the area of human behaviour, in which it is plausible to expect a large biological-determined component, that one is least surprised that straightforward evolutionary theory yields fruits.

So far I have, in a way, been arguing with myself. This is probably inevitable when the subject lacks a firm empirical basis. However I want to sum up what I now think. It seems to me that any dynamics depending on some feedback mechanism from actions to outcome, or (probable outcomes) can be given an evolutionary interpretation. This is so, provided outcomes can be ranked on a scale of unsuccessful to successful, and that actions are not impervious to feedbacks. My objection to this interpretation is that, mostly, it does not add anything to what we already have. But more importantly, it may be very misleading, since it suggests that the system being studied is in some important sense 'natural' and that one has to live with it. It also now seems to me that, inevitably, the invocation of evolutionary theory in areas other than biology sells it short. For instance, the detailed analysis of heredity in biology is missing in economics and I suspect also in sociology and anthropology. Moreover there is a temptation to work backwards from a desired conclusion to an 'evolutionary' process which will deliver it.

The very interesting contributions by Young (1998) seem open to this criticism as indeed are many others. Young removes an important economic assumption of rationality by allowing only myopic calculation of best response. While this is of course necessary for his results, it means that his conclusions are unlikely to apply to economics. I have already made disparaging remarks concerning 'memes'. Here I want to draw attention to a kind of intellectual imperialism. Just as Becker seeks to bring all human behaviour under the sway of neoclassical economics so evolutionists like Dawkins want to bring some of the social sciences under the sway of evolutionary theory. In both cases there are plausible arguments: but that is also all.

What I have just said applies not only to the social sciences. A number of evolutionary theories have been proposed in, for instance, cosmology. Thus it has been argued (Lee Smolin) that, at the singularity of black holes, a universe is created. Black holes arise, it is believed, only when a star collapses. Star formation is only possible when the constants of physics are in a relatively small subset of the space of possible constants. It follows (with a further assumption) that universes with constants in the admissible range for star formation will be the most numerous. It is supposed that any one variation in the values of 'constants' is 'small'. The analogy with evolutionary theory in this case is more exact, for fitness lies in the number of offspring universes any universe with given constants has. This then provides an endogenous theory on why constants which characterise our universe are what they are, even though they are in a small subset of admissible ones. One notices that this story has an account of heredity which is persuasive. Yet even here one cannot help wondering whether evolutionary theory adds anything to the basic science. Here too the role of evolutionary theory, as in the social sciences, is to stimulate ideas and models; it is not to be understood as an application, at least not a direct one.

III

Before closing I return briefly to Veblen. After several re-readings of his paper, I reached the conclusion that it was not about evolution at all but was an argument in favour of abandoning equilibrium economics for a study of processes. It is only in this way that his remarks on 'cumulative' causation as well as his remarks critical of economic practice can be understood. If this is right, then I for one am almost entirely on his side. But considerable care is needed in embracing this position. Firstly, we find it much easier to examine properties of equilibria than of dynamic models. Secondly it is not true that equilibrium means no 'change'. One need only consider the stochastic equilibria of growth theory as evidence. What I believe an equilibrium in economics means is that no one has an incentive to deviate from his or her plan of action. In a sense this implies rational expectations and this in turn suggests that equilibrium states are unlikely. So I am sympathetic to Veblen's views as I have interpreted them. It is also true that some of his remarks were prophetic of the development of our subject. Since these prophecies are not justified by arguments, I do not know how he arrived at them but we must give credit to his intuition.

There is, however, one Veblen contribution on the matter of evolution which deserves to be mentioned. This concerns his classification of humans into two types, the aggressive and predatory and the non-aggressive. (This is not the actual terminology used by Veblen.) The aggressive and predatory have retained a large part of primitive urges, which find expression in selfish and aggressive economic behaviour. Their largest concentration, Veblen appears to argue, is now in finance. The less aggressive adapt and work. It is by the 'mutation' of one of the latter to the aggressive type that the latter type is maintained. This is not so different from the view I heard expressed thirty-five years ago that, since the intelligent also become richer and so join the upper class, any of the less intelligent of the latter drop to the lower classes. This process of 'selection' will see to it that the average I.Q. is strongly correlated with income, due allowance being made to old fashioned aristocrats. Moreover, tastes in goods, etc. are fashioned by the 'elite' and 'rational choice' turns out to be emulation. In all of this, he claims to detect the adaptation of ancient traits which he believes himself to know. He writes: 'Social evolution is a process of selective adaptation of temperament and habits of thought under the stress of the circumstances and associated life' (Veblen 1898, p. 213).

Once again one is bound to say that no careful analysis of selective adaptation is offered. Some plausible remarks on the effects of interaction of his two types do not constitute a theory. Thus Veblen's account is far inferior to that of Marx who was, after all, not striving for a biological analogy and who produced 'a free-standing' theory.

However, it is interesting to observe that Veblen's analysis is profoundly non-Darwinian and indeed Lamarkian. Traits which are useful in social life, as well as arrangements of the latter, are inherited just as the Soviet agriculturists believed plants to 'evolve'. Since there is no objective 'correlative' like DNA, anything goes. But as usual, at least in my view, nothing is gained by the evolutionary analogy, always excepting its role in stimulating observations and ideas.

After this exercise, my conviction remains that evolutionary theory offers no shortcuts to an integrated social science nor advances in economics. It does, however, facilitate the clothing of many rather commonplace ideas in 'scientific dress'.

REFERENCES

Veblen, Thorstein (1898), 'Why is economics not an evolutionary science?', *Quarterly Journal of Economics*, Volume XIII.

Williams, Bernard (1995), 'Evolutionary theory and epistemology', reprinted in *Making sense of humanity*, Cambridge University Press.

Williams, Bernard (1995), 'Evolution, ethics, and the representation problem', reprinted in *Making sense of humanity*, Cambridge University Press

Young, H. Peyton (1998), *Individual Strategy and Social Structure*, Princeton University Press, Princeton, NJ.

PART II

The Challenge Reconsidered

10. The Travelling Salesman Returns from the War: Tjalling Koopmans and Wartime Studies for Peacetime Applications

Albert Jolink

1. INTRODUCTION

In the late 1930s *The Banker*, a journal of the *Financial Times*, published a sequence of articles on the possibility of organising the economy during wartime, with or without the aid of government intervention. In the September 1939 issue, Professor F.A. von Hayek perseveringly argued in favour of the guidance of the free market in the allocation of scarce resources in a war-economy. In 'Pricing versus Rationing', Hayek argued that the efficiency of the market could by no means be surpassed: the market mechanism, or better still, the prices themselves, would serve to achieve an equality of the marginal rates of substitution between the scarce factors of production across all industries, including those affected by the national defence requirements.

The alternative method, forcefully refuted by Hayek, was a method of central regulation imposing a scheme of rationing on the economy. A scheme of rationing, however, would require central planning in every little detail, as every change in scarce resources would induce changes in the substitutes of these resources. 'Thus', Hayek concluded, 'it may be said with fair certainty, so far as its effect on industry is concerned, rationing and price fixing will inevitably cause inefficiency and waste of resources. It deprives industry of all basis of rational calculation. It throws the burden of securing economy on a bureaucracy which is neither equipped nor adequate in number for the task. Even worse, such a system would deprive even those in control of the whole economic machine of essential guides for their plans and reduce major decisions of policy and even strategy to little more than guesswork.'[1] For

Hayek, warfare had become, first and foremost, an economic problem, as ' it is a common fallacy that in the conduct of war everything is needed so urgently that cost does not matter.'[2]

In the October 1939 issue of The Banker, Hayek's 'The Economy of Capital' expressed a similar point of view: capital resources should be applied in their most efficient usage, and the interest rate should express the true scarcity of capital. Hence, capital should be used so as to give the highest possible rate of return for the duration of the war. (A third article by Hayek that was announced never made it to publication.)

In the mid-1950s Tjalling Koopmans reacted to Hayek's unsuccessful appeal to economic 'calculation' in warfare as 'an outstanding example of the overextended belief of the liberalist school of economic thought in the efficiency of competitive markets as a means of allocating resources in a world full of uncertainty.'[3] This reaction, though in a footnote, came after Koopmans's own wartime experience, his wartime efforts as an economist, and his work on 'activity analysis'. As I will illustrate below, Koopmans's objection did not address the application of the marginal cost analysis, but rather the ill-founded beliefs about the world on the basis of a few postulates.

In this paper I will explore Koopmans's economic contribution to the planning of war activities during Word War II which led to the development of linear programming. Furthermore, I discuss the 'transportation problems' of an economic planning instrument to a free market to analyse production decisions. In several post-war publications, Koopmans attempted to introduce linear programming as a tool for a post-war economy. The transition of the instrument from a war economy to a recovering economy can be analysed in a sequence of publications: from linear programming to activity analysis. The element of 'redistribution' from wartime terminology re-emerges in 'redistribution' in welfare economics, as linear programming becomes a fashionable instrument in economic practice. At the same time, the new terminology is adjusted to the needs of the time, as planning falls out of favour and programming appears to be neutral. In the end, the terminology of the market, i.e. efficiency, is the main advocate of the fate of linear programming. Finally, I will develop an argument, an extension of these wartime efforts led to a reformulation of the Calculation Debate.

2. THE TRANSPORTATION PROBLEM

In his 1939 book, *Tanker Freight Rates and Tankship Building*, Tjalling Koopmans analysed the influence of business cycles on tanker freight rates. In his conclusion he alluded to the effects of the eventuality of a large-scale war on the research results: none of the findings would apply, as the demand for naval and mercantile tanker building would be unprecedented. This was confirmed by the outbreak of World War II.

In 1942 Koopmans joined the Combined Shipping Adjustment Board as an assistant economic analyst responsible for the preparation of statistical documents and for arranging shipping information between the US War Shipping Administration and the British Ministry of War Transport. During his stay at the Combined Board, Koopmans developed a line of research on the economics of ship cargo routing. The essence of his work was a linear programming problem, a concept at the time unknown to the economic/academic profession. The problem Koopmans confronted was, given fixed supplies at certain ports and demands at other ports, to construct a shipping plan which would minimise costs. This problem is now known as the transportation problem. The result of his work was written in a 1942 memorandum 'Exchange Ratios between Cargoes on Various Routes', but was published much later.

The memorandum was written in the context of a centralised decision structure, as military effectiveness required a high degree of centralisation. The memorandum was also written in a situation in which the British war economy was heavily dependent on a continual flow of imports and the British merchant fleet was suffering serious losses. In 1942 the US and Britain agreed to collaborate in the joint use of merchant shipping, a strategy which proved to be crucial in keeping the UK in the war.

Koopmans's memorandum was discussed during one of the meetings of the Combined Shipping Adjustment Board, as Koopmans reported, 'as an explanation of the 'paradoxes of shipping' which were always difficult to explain to higher authority.' The Americans and the British presumably never seriously utilised the linear programming technique for cargo routing in World War II.

The paradigm of cargo routing stayed with Koopmans for a long time after the war, when he engaged in research on the efficient allocation of resources leading to his activity analysis of production and allocation, which yielded him the Nobel Prize for Economics in 1975.

3. WAR AND PEACE

Tjalling Koopmans's wartime study for the Combined Shipping Adjustment Board consisted of a table with information on global shipping routes expressed as relative to one particular route. This table offered the possibility of finding either the most economic (cheapest) route to ship cargo, and, more importantly, it allowed for some type of programming. The study was essentially an explanation of the table and only hinted at the instrumental value of it. It also emphasised that it would be of limited value in the case of strategic decisions that would alter the entire pattern of routing.[4] The table also hinged on an efficient allocating authority, a concept which was, even here, only a theoretical one, as Koopmans's own experiences during the War illustrated. The Combined Shipping Adjustment Board, governing joint activity by the British and the American merchant fleets, proved to be in practice two parallel operations carefully not exchanging information. From Koopmans's diary, written during this period, it becomes obvious that he witnessed quite some inefficiencies in the allocating authority. Referring to the inefficient, empty vessels ('ballasting') of the US and UK fleet, Koopmans commented:

> I happened to be the first one who put the two documents side by side and made a close comparison. This confirmed my suspicion (...) that the Americans and the British were ballasting about 20 vessels a month in opposite directions through the Red Sea.... This could only have happened because the allocation machinery of the two organizations had been insufficiently coordinated. (Koopmans diary)

After the war, Koopmans took up his calculating tool again and tried to apply it to the optimum allocation of resources in transportation.[5] The focus at this stage remained a dual one: on the one hand, a focus on marginal costs and, on the other, a focus on the computational method. The 1947 application was an obvious extension of his wartime study, including the assumptions which applied to merchant shipping in World War II. In this case it was argued that the same problems could be observed in peacetime transportation as far as the marginal cost part:

> In a war economy in which shipping is the essential bottle neck, the usefulness of marginal cost estimates as described is obvious. Such estimates are needed to guide decisions of programming authorities, for instance, in balancing competing claims for shipping services or in determining the best source of a raw material on shipping grounds.... What relevance does the foregoing analysis have to peacetime transport problems where there is a market instead of an allocating authority...? I believe that the main part of marginal cost will still be arrived at along the lines described. (Koopmans [1947] 1970, p. 143)

With respect to the computational method, Koopmans extended the seemingly neutral approach to the domain of peacetime economics. But where once 'military importance' was the objective, it now demanded a new, economic purpose. This new objective became 'efficiency'.

3. THE EFFICIENCY OF PRODUCTION

Koopmans's study during World War II had made it obvious that the number of ships available had created a bottleneck which led to shipping problems. The study also claimed that marginal cost estimates could be useful indicators for decisions of an allocating authority. The questions posed by Koopmans after the war were exactly on the relevance of these studies for peacetime transportation problems, where there is a market rather than an allocating authority.[6]

With this type of question, Koopmans touched upon a much larger issue which had aroused the emotions of most of the economists involved in the so-called, 'socialist calculation debate': the relative merits of private enterprise versus a centrally-directed economy. From Enrico Barone's 'Ministry of Production in the Collectivist State' to Hayek's and Robbins's free market economy there was an enormous pile of arguments, pro and con, to be digested. Although there was a general agreement that the conditions of a competitive society would also have to rule in a 'collectivist state', the idea of a centralised authority that could impose these conditions led to a clear division of minds. Some, such as Lange and Lerner, argued that the objectives of a socialist economy would not hinge on a centralised calculating administration; rather, if production were based on minimum costs and a price-equals-marginal cost-rule, efficiency would equally be achieved.

In these early post-war years, Koopmans argued that this literature focused too much on alternative institutional settings, whereas the real world offered a less black-and-white picture.

> Even in the capitalistic enterprise economy there are many sectors where the guideposts of a competitive market are lacking and explicit analysis of the allocation problem is needed. (Koopmans [1951] 1970, p. 213)

The sectors Koopmans had in mind were mainly shipping and railroad, or transportation in general. The issue Koopmans focused on was 'the efficiency of allocation in the economy'.

It was obvious that the market-economy that Koopmans witnessed in the 1930s and 1940s had been anything but 'efficient'. On the other hand, Koopmans did convince himself of the necessity of the centralised decision making process in the case of a maximisation of military effectiveness, which amounted to requiring a level of security obtained by a reallocation of resources. In this respect, Koopmans was supported after the war by studies by Wood and Dantzig of the US Department of the Air Force. In these studies, the development of computers was seen as the panacea for the once reputed centralised calculations of an allocation programme, which reopened for Koopmans the discussion on 'the efficiency of the economy' or 'efficiency of allocation', and hence on 'welfare economics'.

As a large share of the discussion in welfare economics had concentrated on the most desirable distribution of commodities or income, and consequently involved the question of the institutional arrangement, Koopmans attempted to gear the attention to the other side of the coin: the efficient use of resources. The 'activity analysis' that followed from all this would either abstract from certain institutional arrangements, or, as Koopmans would prefer, would allow for certain flexibility in evaluating alternative forms of organisation.

Activity analysis, then, was above all concerned with 'the construction of conceptual models to study and appraise criteria, rules, and practices for the allocation of resources', in other words, linear programming. It was guided by, on the one hand, the function of the price system as a means of allocating resources, and on the other, the desire to develop computational methods and equipment that could be used to deal with complicated allocation problems. Koopmans' activity analysis departed to a certain degree from conventional production theory by stressing discrete, rather than continuous, alternative processes. It also departed from the von Neumann-type of General Equilibrium Theory by stressing the efficiency of allocation, which was defined in the terminology of commodity flows and activity levels.[7]

Activity analysis, and the efficient production therein, also led to a corresponding set of efficiency prices which, according to Koopmans, did in no way presuppose the existence of a market or of exchanges of commodities. These accounting prices were primarily founded on a choice of an efficient level of activity and, hence, on 'technological data'.[8]

This approach in welfare economics was therefore either indiscriminate for decentralised or centralised decision-making, or it specified more precisely the conditions for the one or the other. The approach did make it clear that the allocation of commodities or incomes and the allocation of resources were two sides of the same coin. Koopmans's activity analysis made them equivalent:

> The basic idea underlying this technique [activity analysis] is that the relation between prices on the one hand and choices of production or of rates of output on the other is essentially the same, whether this relation is secured by a competitive market or is adhered to by optimizing decisions within the establishment. Koopmans (1954).

4. CALCULATIONS AND COMPUTATIONS

The experience of, and expectations for, programming merchant shipping during World War II, and of post-war studies on the routing of railroad cars and other types of transportation, led Koopmans to conclude that a) the presumable efficiency of allocation through competitive markets has too often been taken for granted, and b) computational methods and (electronic) computers could be used to deal with complicated allocation problems.

These conclusions can be seen in the light of the (Socialist) Calculation Debate, but have hardly been considered as such. In Koopmans's (1951) article, 'Efficient allocation of resources', the contribution to the Debate is explicit; in other papers, such as the 1954 article 'Uses of prices', this is less so. In both articles, however, the approach is the same: formal and mathematical analysis demonstrates the limitations, and hence the reliability, of economic theory. This formal approach somehow pulled the sting out of the Calculation Debate, as I will try to argue.

The Calculation Debate is usually presented in terms of the feasibility of rational economic planning, a debate which developed from 'logically impossible' to 'practically impossible'. As mentioned above, the study by Wood and Dantzig[9] was presented by Koopmans as an exemplar case in which the 'practical' impossibility of economic planning is solved:

> As they [Wood and Dantzig] report in two articles in ECONOMETRICA, they revert to the method discarded by all participants in the debate who came after Barone: the actual collection of relevant technical information in one center and the calculation of an allocation program to serve as the basis of a large number of detailed directives. They see in the development of electronic computers a new possibility for this method that was unforeseen in earlier phases of the discussion. (Koopmans [1951] 1970, p. 457.)

As the main branch of the Calculations Debate slowly entered into a phase of seemingly entrenched positions, one minor branch evolved into what may be phrased, analogously, the Computations Debate.

> One may also turn around, and look upon the processes of price formation in the market through bidding and selling between business firms as the equivalent of a vast computing machine on a national or even international scale, on which the utilization of our resources is being 'computed'. It may be surmised that, from the point of view of productive and allocative efficiency, this machine works all right if the markets in question are in fact competitive, and provided distributive objectives are pursued by means other than the regulation of prices. (Koopmans [1954] 1970, p. 256.)

But once that had been agreed upon, more importantly than the mechanism of computation is the method that is used to compute. It is this method which

Koopmans emphasised and further developed to find the limiting assumptions of competitive markets. The use of (electronic) computational methods very much hinged, for Koopmans, on the activity analysis he proposed. The competitive market process was gradually replaced by a model of production in which allocative efficiency was the rule.

This approach was geared directly toward what some economists believed was the function of the market: as a kind of information system. Hence, with Mises, prices were considered as the carriers of information about numerous transactions, which would be dispersed among an even greater number of individuals. In Hayek's hands, the market became the process behind the transfer of information which made it possible for individuals to utilise this information more effectively than they would have been able to do without a market.

For Koopmans the issue was not whether this belief in the allocative efficiency of the market, through a transfer of information, would be possible. In fact, this was even acknowledged in Koopmans's analysis:

> the classical belief of economists in competitive markets as an allocative device to attain or at least maintain efficiency is confirmed by rigorous mathematical analysis, although for a rather narrow model of production. (Koopmans [1953] 1970, p. 223)

Koopmans's argument would lie in his perception that economists neglected a focus on the production-side of the economy:

> Economists are sometimes insufficiently aware of the narrow basis of technological assumptions on which their traditional belief in the allocative efficiency of competitive markets has so far been substantiated by analysis. (Koopmans [1953] 1970, p. 229)

The question, then, turned to the kind of information that would be relevant for an efficient allocative device in a market. As we have argued above, Koopmans not only equated the relation between prices in a market-mechanism and the choices of methods of production to conclude that the traditional model of production employed competitive market-model was a very narrow one. He also argued that in several instances, 'activity analysis' could be usefully applied when the conditions that guarantee a competitive market situation could not be fulfilled. Hence, the information contained by market prices was replaced by the knowledge required in a production setting.

The 1951 article, 'Efficient allocation of resources', answered the question of the sort of knowledge required in Koopmans's activity analysis:

In the essential part of our analysis, all that was presumed known to the individual manager or (where so assumed) to a central authority are the technical input-output coefficients characteristic of individual activities. It is perhaps indicative of the nature of our technology that the information supplied by engineers is most often of his type. The economist's concepts of a production function, marginal rates of substitution, and marginal cost, where applicable, are derived from these underlying data . . . (Koopmans [1951] 1970, p. 465)

Turning from information supplied by engineers back to prices, Koopmans argued that the notion of prices still played a crucial role as a guide to the allocation of resources. But rather than using the 'market prices', Koopmans reverted to prices that represented the actual scarcity of resources. Although the former may be equivalent to the latter in a peacetime economy, this would simply illustrate the equivalence of the bidding and selling of business firms and the 'computed' utilisation of resources. But this condition could probably only apply in a peace-time economy, as

it has not been and probably could not have been met in war economies of recent experience, because any price change large enough to induce drastic shifts in the use of resources needed by war would have had extremely unequal distributive effects, unwanted particularly in war. For this reason, direct allocation by such bodies as the War Production Board was substituted for price-guided allocation. (Koopmans [1954] 1970, p. 257)

5. CONCLUSION

In the above, I have presented a) Koopmans's contribution to the World War II economy and its peacetime applications, and b) his attempt to intervene in the Calculation Debate. What can be concluded from this?

First, the experience of economists in general, and Tjalling Koopmans in particular, during World War II was an experience of a centrally planned war economy. This setting was obviously a deviation from the theoretical heritage of (neo)classical economists.[10] It was also a challenge to the economists' belief in the efficiency of the competitive market as an allocative device. Obviously, in the case of Koopmans this led to new insights into the limitations of this device, and to suggestions for improvement. As such, the war experience led to a successful period of peacetime applications.

Second, Koopmans's contribution to the Calculation Debate was one of many, and is not recorded as such in the annals of the Debate. Partly this may be due to the fact that Koopmans's discussion of the Calculation Debate was never a substantial part of his further writings. Also it may be due to the fact that he changed the setting of the Debate into what I have referred to as the Computation Debate. Although this change diverted the attention away from the institutional organisation of the economy, the above has made it obvious that Koopmans's activity analysis was never independent of the institutional environment.

Finally, the war experience and Koopmans's wartime study have contributed to a turn in the Calculation Debate.

NOTES

1. Hayek (1939a), p. 248.
2. Ibid, p.243.
3. Koopmans ([1957] 1979), p.146.
4. In retrospect, historians of World War II have indicated that the emergency of the British merchant fleet was such that it was exactly this limiting condition that made Koopmans' stool obsolete in 1943.
5. Koopmans ([1947] 1970).
6. See for instance Koopmans ([1947] 1970).
7. 'An attainable set of commodity flows, as well as any set of activity levels giving rise to it, is called *efficient*, if there is no other attainable set of commodity flows in which all flows are at least as large as the corresponding flows in the original set, while at least one is actually larger.' Koopmans ([1951] 1970), p. 460.
8. That is, input-output coefficients of the activities.
9. Wood and Dantzig (1949).
10. This is not to say that the theoretical heritage was ever for real.

REFERENCES

Hayek, F.A. von (1939a), 'Pricing versus rationing', *The Banker*, September, pp. 242-9.

Hayek, F.A. von (1939b), 'The economy of capital', *The Banker*, October, pp. 38-41.

Koopmans, T.C. (1939), *Tanker Freight Rates and Tankship Building*, Haarlem: De erven Bohn.

Koopmans, T.C. (1942), 'Exchange ratios between cargoes on various routes', Memorandum for the Combined Shipping Adjustment Board, reprinted in *Scientific Papers of Tjalling C. Koopmans*, MIT Press (1985).

Koopmans, T.C. (n.d.), diary 1942-1946, manuscript at Yale University Library.

Koopmans, T.C. (1947), 'Optimum utilization of the transportation system', Proceedings of the International Statistical Conferences, vol. 5, Washington, 1949, reprinted in *Scientific Papers of Tjalling C. Koopmans*, Springer Verlag, (1970).

Koopmans, T.C. (1951), 'Efficient allocation of resources', Econometrica, vol. 19, pp. 455-65, reprinted in *Scientific Papers of Tjalling C. Koopmans*, Springer Verlag, (1970).

Koopmans, T.C. (1953), 'Activity analysis and its application', The American Economic Review, 43, pp. 406-14, reprinted in *ScientificPpapers of Tjalling C. Koopmans*, Springer Verlag, (1970).

Koopmans, T.C. (1954), 'Uses of prices', Proceedings of the Conference on Operations Research in Production and Inventory Control, Cleveland, reprinted in *Scientific Papers of Tjalling C. Koopmans*, Springer Verlag, (1970).

Koopmans, T.C. (1957), *Three Essays on the State of Economic Science*, New York: McGraw-Hill.

Wood, M. and G. Dantzig (1949), 'Programming of interdependent activities', Econometrica, 17, pp. 193-99.

11. Is Capitalism Doomed?
A Nobel Discussion

Francisco Louçã

INTRODUCTION

Three future Nobel Prize winners - although they had to wait for some decades, since by the time of this discussion it was not even awarded to economists - debated in 1935 nothing less than the future of capitalism. The paper investigates a simple nonlinear dynamic model set forth by Ragnar Frisch in order to settle that discussion and never published until now. Although Frisch neither solved nor simulated the behaviour of the system, he eventually understood that at least some very complicated dynamics emerged from it.

Although this is not the only instance of his concern with the wild side of the street, all through his life Frisch carefully avoided publishing any nonlinear model and argued that linear specifications were satisfactory. Yet, evidence shows that he looked around for something else. The current model is the proof that he found complexity, although he could not deepen the study of the problem.

Section one presents the model and the issue, section two summarises some of the findings about the numerical simulation, and section three presents an extension of the model. Finally some conclusions and implications are indicated.

1. WILL CAPITALISM COLLAPSE OR EQUILIBRATE?

Ragnar Frisch (1895-1973) was one of the more brilliant mathematical economists of this century: he was the founder of econometrics - he also coined the name - and gave it the institution, the *Econometric Society*, the journal, *Econometrica*, methods, programmes of research and the inspiration. He was also deeply involved in statistical theory, in political advice and in planning, and he made major contributions to business cycle research, to the economics of development, as well as to other topics. In recognition of this life work, Frisch was awarded the first Nobel Prize in economics, in 1969, ex-aequo with his close friend Jan Tinbergen.

The paper which gave him the Nobel Prize is a landmark in the history of economics: it was written and published in 1933, presenting an ingenuous three dimensional mixed system of difference and differential equations to account for several modes of oscillation (Frisch 1933). Random shocks were also introduced in the model, which introduced the probabilistic approach into economics and represented a major achievement, defining for a long time the dominance of linear systems and decomposition methods in the early econometric programme (Louçã 1997).

The model investigated in this paper is rather different. It was included in a three-page typewritten document, dated October 1935, under the suggestive title *The Non-Curative Power of the Capitalistic Economy – a Non-Linear Equation System Describing how Buying Activity Depends on Previous Deliveries*. The first and part of the second of these pages are entirely dedicated to the explanation of the purpose of the exercise:

> During the Namur meeting of the Econometric Society [1935] a discussion arose between Tinbergen, Koopmans and Frisch (...). Koopmans maintained that in reality the flexibility of prices would come in as an important element, which would probably counteract the tendency to contraction of activity that was displayed by Frisch's system [1934]. (...) This is of course nothing but a mathematical formulation of the liberalistic argument. Frisch took the position that, even though flexibility of prices were introduced, it would be quite possible to have a system showing exactly the same general features as the system 1.1 [Frisch's 1934]. Indeed, he maintained that the flexibility of prices may even *aggravate the situation*. (Frisch 1935, p. 1, original emphasis)

In order to settle the question, the three scientists adopted quite a singular procedure: Koopmans would formulate the assumptions and Frisch would represent the mathematical form of the model and discuss its solutions. Indeed, Koopmans did his part of the job, since he indicated the economic relations to be embodied in the model. Frisch defined it, although he did not explore the behaviour of the system: 'This I plan to do on a later occasion', which never occurred.

From all points of view, this is an exceptional document. Here we have three founders of modern mathematical economics and econometrics - all to be rewarded with the prestigious Nobel Prize for their decisive contributions - discussing the structure of capitalism and exploring new mathematical insights. Furthermore, in order to define a more realistic model of a simple economy of production and exchange, they constructed a nonlinear model, a quite uncommon feature at that time and most unlike their previous and future work. In this framework, Frisch and eventually Koopmans understood they were forced to turn to numerical simulations in order to uncover its dynamics. Although there is no evidence that Frisch took the issue again with his challenger after the formulation of the model, the paper confirms that at least the author suspected the emerging properties of the model:

> even if flexibility of prices were introduced, it would be possible to find such a set of values of the constants in the equation (the influencing parameters), that would entail a contraction. (ibid.)

This discussion followed the publication of a simpler model by Frisch in one of the earlier issues of *Econometrica*: 'Circulation planning: proposal for a national organization of a commodity and service exchange' (1934). In that paper, Frisch reacted with indignation to the most outstanding feature of the crisis of the thirties: poverty amidst plenty, that 'monstrosity' which follows from the specific mode of organisation of the modern industrial societies, as he wrote. Frisch concluded in a rather gloomy way: 'Under the present system, the blind 'economic laws' will, under certain circumstances, create a situation where these groups [of producers] are forced mutually to undermine each other's position' (Frisch 1934, p. 259).

Frisch illustrated his argument with a simple model of an economy with one shoemaker and one farmer, each one producing to the other's consumption, and assuming that the decision on production was taken on the basis of the sales in the previous period. Accordingly, each one's sales determined his level of expense. Considering the level of prices to be fixed, the sales of the two agents, would be (symbols are changed accordingly to those of the 1935 model):

$$s_t^1 = \alpha \, s_{t-1}^2 \tag{1}$$
$$s_t^2 = \beta \, s_{t-1}^1 \tag{2}$$

What ruled the dynamics of this very simple interrelationship was α and β, what Frisch called the 'coefficients of optimism': if the agents were in an expanding mood, trade would increase; otherwise, if they were in a saving mood, 'the whole system would gradually dwindle down to nothing' (Frisch 1934, p. 263) - a Keynesian argument for the expansion of consumption. This is easily verifiable, since if t is even the general solution takes the form:

$$s_t^1 = A_1 \, \mu^t + (-1)^t \, A_2 \, \mu^t \tag{3}$$
$$s_t^2 = B_1 \, \mu^t + (-1)^t \, B_2 \, \mu^t \tag{4}$$

where $\mu = (\alpha \, \beta)^{1/2}$. In (3) and (4), the first element in the right-hand side of the equation is obviously an exponential trend, whereas the second is a cycle with two phases. If $\mu > 1$, we have the cycle superimposed on a rising trend, but if $\mu < 1$, then trade vanishes. Therefore, cycles and the eventual collapse of the economic system were related to its mode of trading – the concrete form of organisation of the 'liberalistic' society – and not specifically to the existence of the market as a social institution (ibid., p. 272). As a consequence, Frisch suggested the urgent implementation of a national system of planned exchange using credit control, and later on argued that the following events, such as the breakout of protectionism and then of the world war, confirmed the insights and the importance of the action proposed according to his model.

As we saw, Koopmans strongly disagreed and argued that the introduction of flexible prices would modify the behaviour of the modelled economy and allow for the continuation of trade. That is how the 1935 model came about: the new version of the 1934 model should replace the interpretation of the formation of prices, and include a specific form of flexibility: prices could be changed according to a parameter of action of the agents.

The model (equations 5 to 10) defines two agents ('primus' and 'secundus'), producing and exchanging much in the same way as in the 1934 model. The very simple nonlinearity is introduced with the definition of sale for each one of them: price times quantity (there are no stocks). This defines the two first equations, where the superscripts identify *primus* or *secundus*:

$$s_t^1 = p_t^1 q_t^1 \qquad (5)$$
$$s_t^2 = p_t^2 q_t^2 \qquad (6)$$

Afterwards, Frisch assumed that the supply of *primus*'s good was a (negative) function of the price of his own good and a (positive) function of the previous growth of sales of *secundus*. A minimum quantity is always traded, â and ê. Therefore, quantity is fixed by the market conditions and the demand equations are:

$$q_t^1 = \hat{a} - \alpha p_t^1 + \gamma (s_{t-1}^2 - s_{t-2}^2) \qquad (7)$$
$$q_t^2 = \hat{e} - \beta p_t^2 + \lambda (s_{t-1}^1 - s_{t-2}^1) \qquad (8)$$

Finally, Frisch hypothesised that growth of prices, the parameter of which was fixed by the seller, was a proportion of the previous growth in sold quantities:

$$p_t^1 - p_{t-1}^1 = \psi (q_{t-1}^1 - q_{t-2}^1) \qquad (9)$$
$$p_t^2 - p_{t-1}^2 = \xi (q_{t-1}^2 - q_{t-2}^2) \qquad (10)$$

This quite elementary nonlinear six-dimensional system of difference equations encapsulated Koopmans and Frisch's argument about the nature of the evolution of a liberalistic economy.

2. HEROD'S JUDGEMENT

In order to check the model, the following values of the parameters and initial conditions are assumed:

Table 11.1   Initial conditions and values of the parameters

Initial conditions	t-1	t-2	Parameters	
S1	0.21784	0.09	ê	1.1
S2	0.10926	0.09	â	2
Q1	2.1784	1	α	0.2
Q2	1.214	1	β	0.4
P1	0.1	0.09	γ	1.1
P2	0.09	0.09	λ	3
			ξ	0.3
			ψ	0.2

Note that the system is not bounded and therefore the variables may eventually have negative values: the interpretation is that, under some circumstances, the agent does not sell and is forced to buy necessary inputs in order to survive, and that part of the market is perfectly exogenous. Assuming that p_1 remains the same in t-2 and t-1 (0.09), the model generates large cycles at first and both *primus* and *secundus* eventually dominate the market for a short time, but then it stabilises with *primus*'s dominance.

Figure 11.1A   *The behaviour of the model: The evolution of sales*

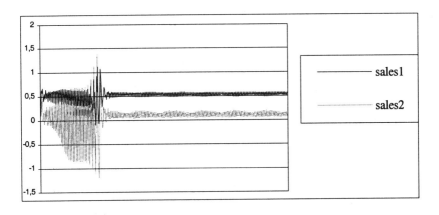

Figure 11.1B   *The behaviour of the model: Phase portrait of the sales of* primus

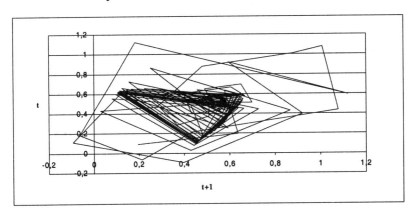

Now, if the initial conditions are modified as stated in Table 11.1, with *primus* taking the initiative of increasing his price 11% from t-2 to t-1, the emergent behaviour is dominated by cycles, with alternating dominance by both agents:

Figure 11.2   *An aggressive intervention by* primus *at t-1*

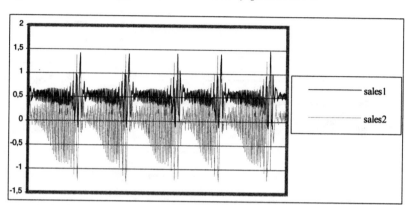

Let's suppose now that *primus* still sharpens his strategy and adopts an inflationary policy, so that the parameter ψ (measuring the impact of previous growth of sales in the following growth of price) is slightly increased. Notice that the cycles in the sales of *secundus* are always larger than those of *primus*, given the chosen set of parameters and the action followed in this story. Surprisingly, this results in the destruction of the structured market relation, since after irregular but shorter cycles the system collapses (after $\psi > 0.204455702$).[1]

Figure 11.3A   A further increase in prices of primus: *An irregular cyclical regime ($\psi = 0.202102994$)*

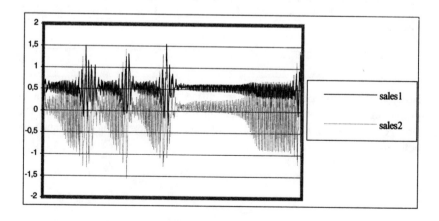

Figure 11.3B $\psi = 0.204455702$

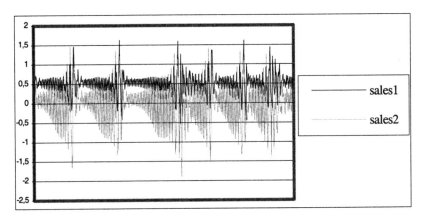

This behaviour evokes that of the 'Circulation Planning' model (equations 1 to 4), although we have also here a larger scope of possibilities. The stabilisation of trade at a very low level is possible, although regimes of regular and then irregular cycles may also happen, and then collapse follows, if the same parameters are increased. The crucial difference is therefore that, in the 1934 model, collapse occurred because of scepticism about the possibilities of trade, and here collapse is the consequence of aggressive action at the market.

The substantial difference between the models is obviously the introduction of nonlinearities. This allows for different and richer patterns of behaviour, as figure 11.4 shows. In this case, the increase of ψ establishes a route to chaos.

Suppose now that *secundus* reacts to the original change in initial conditions, taking a parallel inflationary measure, so that ξ is increased with $\psi = 0.2$. Notice that increases in ψ and in ξ are the most accessible interventions by the agents in order to change their relative position, since they settle prices whereas quantities are defined by market conditions. *Secundus* gets a larger part of the market sometimes, but *primus* still dominates for most of the time. Further, as ψ is increased, both parts are harmed, since large cycles are generated and eventually the market collapses (after $\xi = 0.310531146$). Aggressive competitive strategies based on inflationary action lead to the destruction of the market.

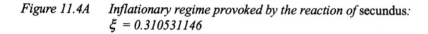

Figure 11.4A   Inflationary regime provoked by the reaction of secundus*:*
                 $\xi = 0.310531146$

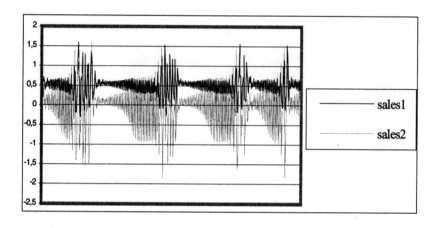

Figure 11.4B $\xi = 0.3105311467$

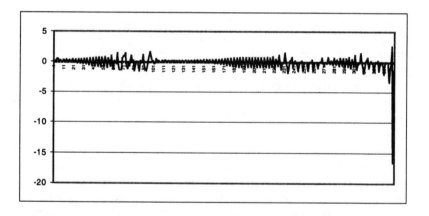

Note: the sales of *secundus* are indicated until t = 339. The system collapses after t = 352.

Finally, under the initial conditions, it is supposed that there is an exogenous change in demand addressed to *primus*, and that γ (measuring the impact of the growth of sales of *secundus* in *primus's* sales) slightly increases. In this case, although generally the sales of *primus* are superior to those of *secundus*, the reverse situation may occur for short periods. But, if γ is still increasing, the market will collapse after 1.1425530.

Figure 11.5 $\gamma = 1.1425530$

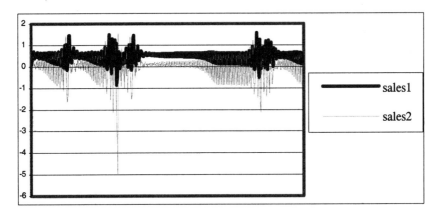

After that value of the parameter, collapse will follow.

3. AN EXTENSION: THE VIRTUE OF COORDINATION

This section provides a simple extension of the model, which was not considered by those involved in the discussion at Namur and afterwards. This extension proves that the model becomes much more robust if some restrictions are introduced. In this case, the possibilities of chaotic outcomes, of exploding oscillations and therefore collapse still exist, but they are severely diminished in the phase space.

Let's consider that the space of the variables is restricted to positive values, meaning that the agents cannot assume debts in order to pay for the continuation of production, and that if they don't sell they don't produce until a new demand is created. In this case, even an inflationary policy by *primus* and a response by *secundus* will allow for the continuation of trade. Figures 11.6 and 11.7 portray that situation.

Figure 11.6 $\psi = 0.202102994$

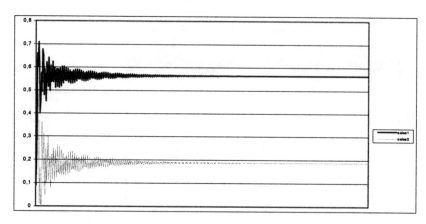

With the increase of 11% in the price of *primus*, which represents the same situation as before (see Figure 11.3A), a stable market is rapidly obtained under these new conditions. Consider now an aggressive response by *secundus*, similar to that portrayed for the previous case in Figures 11.4A and 11.4B:

Figure 11.7A   *Aggressive responses by secundus:* $\xi = 0.3105311467$

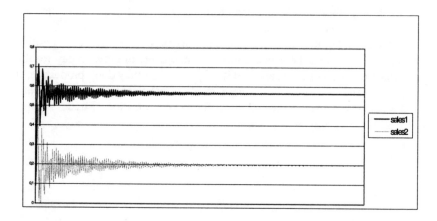

In the previous case, collapse would occur after this value of the parameter is realised. Now, an aggressive policy can be pursued for a much longer period, generating regular several forms of irregular cycles with the clear dominance of *primus* (Figure 11.7B) or at least a very disputed situation (Figures 11.7C and 11.7D).

Figure 11.7B $\xi = 0.35$

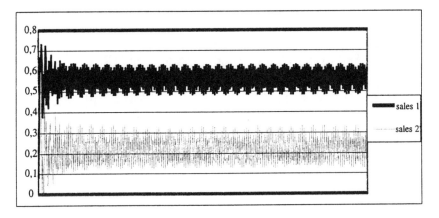

Figure 11.7C $\xi = 0.5$

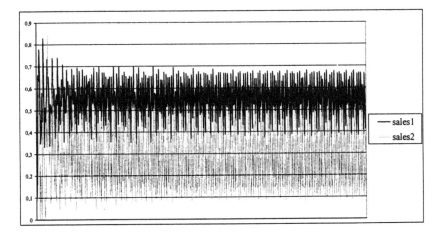

Figure 11.7D $\xi = 0.7$

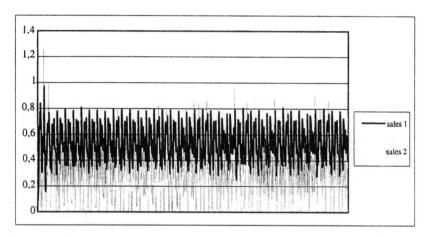

In summary, in the previous case, an increase of 1.05% and then a complementary increase of 1.17% were studied, and it was proved that they led to collapse, under those initial conditions and values. In the new context of the bounded version of the model - and here a specific restriction was chosen to simulate the system under a very simple form of rule, representing an institutional form of coordination - the same parameters can be increased 300% before the collapse occurs. The range of possibilities is therefore much larger, and the model is more robust. This suggests that, under all the provisos of modelling as a representation of complex societies, social forms of coordination may reduce the instability inherent in the dense interaction in systems with large number of different agents making judgements and taking strategic decisions.

It is quite obvious that evidence provides a shared judgement about the Frisch-Koopmans argument. In the framework of the model - and that does not allow for any meaningful claim about reality itself - it is true that, for some values of the parameters, we may have a stable equilibrium in the market (Figure 11.1), vindicating Koopmans' sopinion. But it is also true that, for other values of the parameters, cycles dominate (Figures 11.3, 11.4 and 11.5). Moreover, if the agents are profit maximising, their action may eventually lead to the collapse of trade, vindicating Frisch (e.g., Figure 11.4B). Still, collapse is brought about not by the lack of sales - not by contraction, as Frisch expected - but by the too severe oscillations that imply at some point the bankruptcy of one or both agents. Private vices are not compatible with public virtues, in the case of pure competition, but, in a managed economy, public virtue can impose itself through rules and other forms of coordination and consequently increase the fitness and chances of survival of the system.

4. CONCLUSIONS

For these and other reasons, this 1935 paper is very important to the history of economics. It provided the framework for an investigation about emerging behaviour in a very simple model, namely of the conditions for equilibrium, for cycles, for chaos and for a catastrophe. Last but not least, it also proves that Frisch, the apostle of linear, computable and parsimonious models, also dared to travel along the edge of chaos.

Some contemporary correspondence proves also that Frisch was aware of the nature of the technical and analytical difficulty, and that he had some idea about the need to turn to alternative methods of iterative computation for the case of nonlinear systems (letter to Sam de Wolff,[2] December 14, 1935). Furthermore, Frisch considered the theme as 'exceedingly important from the economic point of view', since he suspected these nonlinearities to be quite general in economics (letter to De Wolff, October 15, 1935), at least because of the existence of several degrees of freedom in the determination of prices and quantities.

Yet this intuition was not developed any further. Two major reasons may have contributed to this. First, the participants in this debate did not have the means to study the behaviour of this system without an enormous amount of painstaking computation. And second, and this may have been the essential reason, Frisch and Tinbergen were deeply convinced that Koopmans's objections and the 'liberalistic' argument were irrelevant. The market economies, given their organisation, could not avoid or prevent major crises – and in the early thirties there was quite a lot of evidence for that point of view – and therefore the Walrasian dreamland was just a figment of the imagination. This is how Tinbergen put it, even before Frisch prepared his short memorandum:

> In the first place the identification of the optimum situation with a Walras situation is, in my view, very questionable. Since it seems that Koopmans himself recognizes this it may be left out of the discussion. My main objection is, then, that the realization of the Walrasian situation is impossible when we have a permanently changing situation in addition to some elements that make absolutely impossible and immediate reaction of all variables to any change in data. Therefore, the Walrasian situation can only accidentally be realized. This is the reason why it seems better to discuss the desirability of a given stabilization policy without any connection with the Walrasian system. (Tinbergen, 1935: 308)

The consequence is straightforward: as Frisch had argued in his previous paper in *Econometrica*, 'Circulation planning', economics should aim at producing the tools for economic intervention and monitoring. Economics is, according to this view, political economy.

NOTES

1. Collapse means here the very large cyclical fluctuations, with enormous sales in one period and enormous losses in the next. The adopted criterion for declaring collapse is the breakdown of the Excel software. It is hypothesised that, under these circumstances, the agents would be expelled from business.
2. Frisch was at that time planning to prepare a book with De Wolff and wanted him to prepare a chapter on nonlinear difference and differential equations, given their importance for economics. In that letter, of October 15, he refers to the Namur debate as an example of the application of nonlinear concepts.

REFERENCES

Frisch, Ragnar (1933), 'Propagation problems and impulse problems in dynamic economics', in Koch, K. (ed.), *Economic Essays in Honour of Gustav Cassel*, London: Unwin, pp. 171-205.

Frisch, Ragnar (1934), 'Circulation planning – proposal for a national organization of a commodity and service exchange', *Econometrica*, 2, July, pp. 258-336 (with a mathematical appendix in *Econometrica*, vol. 2, October, 422-35).

Frisch, Ragnar (1935), *The Non-Curative Power of the Liberalistic Economy – A Non-Linear Equation System Describing how Buying Activity Depends on Previous Deliveries*, manuscript at Oslo University, Frisch's Archive.

Louçã, Francisco (1997), *Turbulence in Economics – An Evolutionary Appraisal of Cycles and Complexity in Historical Processes*, Lyme, US, Cheltenham, UK: Edward Elgar.

Tinbergen, Jan (1935), 'Annual survey: suggestions on quantitative business cycle .theory', *Econometrica*, vol. 3 n. 3, pp. 241-308

12. An Institutionalist Foundation for Development Studies: Re-thinking Polanyi and Veblen on the *Sonderweg*

Eyüp Özveren

1. INTRODUCTION

The rapid proliferation of literature on institutional economics has inevitably led to recent forays into the study of economic development from an institutionalist perspective. This is no surprise as, because of their emphasis on change and evolution, institutional economic approaches were bound to strike a chord where neoclassical economics under the disguise of modernisation theory had long failed. Analytical tools such as the conceptions of 'cumulative causation' (Myrdal 1964) 'path dependence', (David 1985; Arthur 1994) and 'irreversibility' (Dosi and Metcalfe 1991) prove themselves to be particularly useful for the study of economic development (North 1990). What is far more surprising is the fact that it took so long for the institutional approach to venture into the domain of development studies. In fact, one can reasonably identify a paradox here. Until recently, institutional economics has performed rather poorly as far as development studies is concerned. Whereas institutional economics has remained the constant rival of mainstream economics since the turn of the century, it has so far failed to confront the neoclassical approach in the area of development studies, where this latter has proven itself to be particularly vulnerable to an institutionalist critique. After the Second World War, even during the heyday of the so-called neoclassical synthesis promoted under the protective umbrella of the global US hegemony, modernisation theory (that is, the Third World-oriented version of the mainstream approach) suffered serious setbacks when confronting the realities of the less in order to defend the logical consistency of the neoclassical theory, modernisation theorists retreated to enumerating the negative institutional factors prevalent in the Third World as the prime cause for the failure of their approach. In so doing they felt a need to include the institutional factors that they had systematically purged from their approach as it became identified as a pure theory.

Development studies during the very same period became the single domain in which the Third World made its voice heard in the form of the Dependencia (Kay 1989; Love 1996). Latin American theories of, first, structuralism and, subsequently, dependency were indigenous attempts to emphasise the essentially different nature of the historical institutional set-up of Latin America as a point of departure for the so-called development of underdevelopment. As such, these authentic responses to mainstream economics displayed symptoms of an institutionalism by necessity (Özveren 1998).[1] Paradoxically, therefore, the domain of development studies was by its very nature particularly conducive to the spread of institutional analysis, and yet did not experience the influx of the self-proclaimed institutional economists.

When recently the institutional approach made its entry into the field of development studies, it took the virtually exclusive form of New Institutional Economics (Harriss, Hunter and Lewis 1995). As an offshoot of neoclassical economics, New Institutional Economics has confined itself to the deployment of a narrowly defined box of tools. Its foray into development studies has so far been characterised by its partial application of specific concepts, such as transaction costs, without taking into account the broader institutional matrix that determines the general course of the economic processes at work. Furthermore, emboldened by both the seeming momentary success of New Institutional Economics and the lessons of institutional analysis within the domain of industrial organisation, institutional prescriptions for Third World development have taken a form rather reminiscent of the former modernisation recipes. Where modernisation theory has prescribed more of the market, institutionalists now propose the right mix of institutions, the market, and the techno-industrial structure as the key to success. The fact that institutionalist prescription is far more sophisticated than its mainstream predecessor is beside the point. Both approaches share an unfounded optimism that remains ignorant of the major constraints in the way of the would-be developing countries, even when the ingredients of the magic formula obtain.

The above defect has much to do with the fact that the institutional economists long lost track of a whole tradition of development literature, extending from classical institutionalist contributions such as found in the works of Thorstein Veblen and Karl Polanyi, to the original Dependencia theories. The supporting evidence for this argument is best found in the case of Gunnar Myrdal. Originally a 'theoretical' economist in the mainstream sense of the term, Myrdal was converted to institutional economics as he attempted to study first the American South and then the Third World from a development economics perspective. As such, the very realities of the development process itself imposed upon Myrdal an institutionalist perspective. Coming from within the mainstream, and being increasingly aware of its inherent limitations, Myrdal broadened his perspective so as to transcend the confines of the modernisation approach without fully parting ways with it. Even with a limited interior re-decoration of the conceptual framework, Myrdal could outperform his modernisation-minded rivals. It is a pity that Myrdal remained unaware of the development-centred works of Thorstein Veblen and Karl Polanyi that would have helped him put his work in the field of development studies on an entirely new track.

In this paper, I intend to demonstrate that a broader conception of institutional economics that emerges from the history of economic thought has much to offer for the study of development in general. Specifically, I will attempt to assess and synthesise the works of Thorstein Veblen and Karl Polanyi. Whereas Polanyi in his *Great Transformation* (1944) explored the specificity of English development in the nineteenth century, Veblen in his *Imperial Germany and the Industrial Revolution* ([1915] 1990) ventured into the domain of the latecomer's particularity. Both texts concerned themselves with themes of institutional discontinuities and lags, and both entailed a tacit relational conception of their respective subject-matters. To put it differently, inherent in their textual strategies was a logic of the following kind: England could do so-and-so precisely because no country, including Germany, had done it before, and Germany could not do so-and-so, precisely because England had done it already, with the implication that Germany had to do it otherwise. Had they stopped at this stage, their findings would have remained as a replicate of the already-classic representation of the Adam Smith-Friedrich List contrariety.[2]

Polanyi and Veblen went further than their predecessors by venturing into the domain of institutional patterns, institutional tensions, institutional lags, and institutional adjustments and breakdowns in a systematic manner. In this paper, rather than attempting a paradigmatic contrast of the approaches of the two authors, I intend instead to engage myself constructively in a synthesis. I will bring into contact these two different texts and coordinate their elements in a new combination so as to develop a novel conceptual apparatus. Looking back to these now-classic works in the light of the contemporary achievements of institutional economics, I believe, we can cast their findings in a new light so as to lay the groundwork for a comprehensive institutional approach to development studies.

It is no coincidence that the idea of historical difference and therefore *Sonderweg* was already integral to the thinking of the German Historical School, on the basis of which Polanyi and Veblen further elaborated their notions of specificity and development. The entire historiography of addressing the course that German history had taken in modern times is strategically situated *vis-à-vis* the assumption of a normal path, presumably displayed by the forerunner of modernity, namely England/Britain (Blackbourn and Eley 1984). It is argued here that, as far as development studies is concerned, the case of the forerunner was itself the exception to be explained. As such, if anything, one can speak of the English *Sonderweg* with greater historical accuracy and theoretical relevance. Within the Polanyi-Veblen literature, Germany is employed as the counterpoint to the English case as representative of the Continent as a whole. The exemplary nineteenth-century Germany thus allows development studies as a field of inquiry a more promising point of departure.

2. KARL POLANYI'S CASE FOR THE ENGLISH SPECIFICITY

In his *Great Transformation*, Karl Polanyi made a strong case for the exceptionalism of market society within the context of the history of civilisation. He conceived a market society organised in compliance with the logic of a self-regulating market mechanism as substantially different from both what preceded it and what was inevitably likely to succeed it. This exceptional difference was owing to the fact that, within the market system, the economy was disembodied from society, a fact that could not be sustained in the long run as it carried with it the seeds of its own destruction. For Polanyi, such a market system had come about in the aftermath of the Industrial Revolution by way of a rupture, had subordinated labour, land, and money as fictitious commodities to the logic of the market, and, as such, had transformed the market to an organising principle. The market in this context, far from being a spontaneous natural growth, was the product of rigorous institutionalisation on the basis of the separation of the 'political' and the 'economic', where the political served to institute market logic as the foundation of the new economy.[3] Furthermore, Polanyi envisaged an asymmetry: whereas the genesis of the market system was far from spontaneous, its eventual breakdown inevitably would be.

Having characterised the exceptionalism of market society, Polanyi dated it from nineteenth century and mapped it to England. He further established a crucial asymmetry between England and the Continent (best represented by Germany) in terms of the prospects of the market system:

Market society was born in England - yet it was on the Continent that its weaknesses engendered the most tragic complications. In order to comprehend German fascism, we must revert to Ricardian England. The nineteenth century, as cannot be overemphasised, was England's century. The Industrial Revolution was an English event. Market economy, free trade, and the gold standard were English inventions (Polanyi 1944, p. 30; emphasis mine).

The factors that contributed to the specificity of England formed a coherent chain. The experience of the Industrial Revolution - the consequent social dislocations, and the institutional arrangements concerning the re-constitution of labour as a fictitious commodity - served to single out England. According to Polanyi, during the path-breaking stage of the Industrial Revolution (1795-1834) England remained without a competitive labour market, thanks to the Speenhamland Law. During this period, England was in reality 'capitalism without a labour market' (Polanyi 1944, p. 124), a specification that would now sound like oxymoron to many. Only at the end of this critical period were the three tenets of liberal creed instituted as one system:

Thus the Anti-Corn Law Bill of 1846 was the corollary of Peel's Bank Act of 1844, and both assumed a laboring class which, since the Poor Law Amendment Act of 1834, was forced to give their best under the threat of hunger, so that wages were regulated by the price of grain. The three great measures formed a coherent whole. (Polanyi 1944, p. 138)

Within this very period, the English working class was further defined politically by way of the Parliamentary Reform Act of 1832, which excluded them from the political process:

The laboring people themselves were hardly a factor in this great movement the effect of which was, figuratively speaking, to allow them to survive the Middle Passage. They had almost as little to say in the determination of their own fate as the black cargo of Hawkins' ships. Yet it was precisely this lack of participation on the part of the British working class in deciding its own fate that determined the course of English social history and made it, for better or for worse, so different from that of the Continent. (Polanyi 1944, p. 166)

Therefore, the most distinguishing characteristic of the English case was the way in which labour was gradually instituted as a fictitious commodity outside the realm of political society.

In approaching the nineteenth century, Polanyi identified two cases of exceptionalism. At one end of the spectrum was England, which dominated the 'planetary economy', set the institutional rules of the game, and determined its course and pace. At the opposite end of the spectrum, Polanyi identified the United States, the land of the free market and, ergo the mecca of liberal economists. It was by definition what England was not:

> Up to the 1890's the frontier was open and free land existed; up to the Great War the supply of low standard labor flowed freely; and up to the turn of the century there was no commitment to keep foreign exchanges stable. A free supply land, labor, and money continued to be available; consequently no self-regulating market system was in existence. As long as these conditions prevailed, neither man, nor nature, nor business organization needed protection of the kind that only government intervention can provide. (Polanyi 1944, p. 201)

Hence, the nineteenth-century United States represented within the general framework of Polanyi's analysis the preconditions for the emergence of a market society, namely the institution of the fictitious commodities of land, labour, and money.

In contradistinction to the two exceptions discussed above, the wide grey area of Polanyi's spectrum of development was occupied by Continental Europe. As such, it represented the normalcy as opposed to any exceptionality. In particular, after the world-wide Great Depression of 1873-1876, the spontaneous reaction to the self-regulating market took shape in the Continental countries increasingly in the form of an alternative institutional mix. As opposed to the English market-centred particularism, there emerged a 'universal "collectivist" reaction' (Polanyi 1944, p. 150) among the ranks of which, England herself was bound to take place.

The characteristics of the Continental mode of development demand a closer look here. First of all, the Continent witnessed no disruptive Industrial Revolution but rather a gradual process of industrialisation. This had a formative effect on the labour factor:

> The Continental worker needed protection not so much against the impact of the Industrial Revolution - in the social sense there never was such a thing on the Continent - as against the normal action of factory and labour market conditions (Polanyi 1944, p. 176).

Furthermore, the would-be Continental working-class was cushioned in an urban environment, a factor that had helped aggravate the misery of their English counterpart:

> England's rural civilisation was lacking in those urban surroundings out of which the later industrial towns of the continent grew. There was in the new towns no settled urban middle class, no such nucleus of artisans and craftsmen, of respectable petty bourgeois and townspeople as could have served as an assimilating medium for the crude laborer who - attracted by high wages or chased from the land by tricky enclosers - was drudging in the early mills. The industrial

town of the Midlands and the North West was a cultural wasteland; its slums merely reflected its lack of tradition and civic self-respect. (Polanyi 1944, p. 98-9)

According to Polanyi, the Continental worker was spared the ills of the transition to a market society, and, in juxtaposition to his English counterpart, was bestowed with as much political recognition as economic, precisely because he had been an ingredient in the making of a national unity. To use a violent metaphor, the Continental 'working-class in the making' was not derailed socially and politically on the way to economic development, as had been its English counterpart:

Materialistic preconceptions have blurred the outlines of the working-class problem. British writers have found it difficult to comprehend the terrible impression that early capitalistic conditions in Lancashire made on Continental observers. They pointed to the even lower standard of life of many Central European artisans in the textile industries, whose conditions of work were often perhaps just as bad as those of their English comrades. Yet such a comparison obscured the salient point which was precisely the rise in the social and political status of the laborer on the Continent in contrast to a fall in that status in England. The continental laborer had not passed through the degrading pauperization of Speenhamland nor was there any parallel in his experience to the scorching fires of the New Poor Law. From the status of a villein he changed - or rather rose - to that of a factory worker, and very soon to that of an enfranchised and unionized worker. Thus he escaped the cultural catastrophe which followed in the wake of the Industrial Revolution in England. (Polanyi 1944, p. 175)

The comparison of England with the Continent puts the emphasis on a conception of development with a lag. Whereas England was the forerunner, Continental countries were latecomers in industrialisation and the transformation into a market society. There was a lag of half a century in this respect (Polanyi 1944, p. 173). This very idea of a lag implies at first sight the assumption of a 'stage theory' of development. This view gains further support from statements such as the following:

Victorian England and the Prussia of Bismarck were poles apart, and both were very much unlike the France of the Third Republic or the Empire of the Hapsburgs. Yet each of them passed through a period of free trade and laissez-faire, followed by a period of antiliberal legislation in regard to public health, factory conditions, municipal trading, social insurance, shipping subsidies, public utilities, trade associations, and so on. (Polanyi 1944, p. 147)

However we should not allow ourselves to be misled by this superficial resemblance. For Polanyi, the time interval makes a critical difference:

While Germany repeated England's domestic development only after a lag of half a century, external events of world scope would necessarily affect all trading countries alike. (Polanyi 1944, p. 213)

The time lag meant that, on the Continent, the same kind of transformation problem 'brought conflicts to bear on an industrially more modern but socially less unified environment' (Polanyi 1944, p. 223). Precisely because the times and therefore the contexts were different, Continental countries did not replicate the path of England. Furthermore, the Continental countries displayed a new mode to which the once-exceptional England also increasingly approximated:

> In each case the considerable time lag between English, Continental, and American development had important bearings, and yet by the turn of the century the protectionist countermove had created an analogous situation in all Western countries. (Polanyi 1944, p. 162)

Evidently, various countries arrived at the common endpoint by way of different paths. One could speak of the stages of industrialisation, but the way in which they are framed within an institutional matrix depends on the timing.

The overall difference between England and Continental Germany boils down to two factors of critical import. First, with respect to the process of industrialisation, implicit in Polanyi is a distinction between trial-and-error based learning-by-doing and selective imitation. Learning-by-doing can give the learner a momentary lead, but this is achieved at a high price because of the errors involved in the process. At least in one respect, selective imitation is emphasised as an advantage of the latecomer. The Continental countries could avoid the social price England paid by adopting the lessons of English experience:

> Moreover, the Continent was industrialised at a time when adjustment to the new productive techniques had already become possible, thanks, almost exclusively, to the imitation of English methods of social protection. (Polanyi 1944, p. 175)

One could say that, by the very course England had taken to a market society, she rendered important lessons to Germany which thereby inadvertently helped put her on a different path. This does not preclude the possibility that England may have diverted Germany from her own path irrespective of whether or not imitable lessons existed. Furthermore, for Polanyi, there exists an asymmetry between the positioning of different countries *vis-à-vis* alternative institutional sets:

> A nation may be handicapped in its struggle for survival by the fact that its institutions, or some of them, belong to a type that happens to be on the down grade - the gold standard in World War II was an instance of such an antiquated outfit. Countries, on the other hand, which, for reasons of their own, are opposed to the status quo, would be quick to discover the weaknesses of the existing

institutional order and to anticipate the creation of institutions better adapted to their interests. (Polanyi 1944, p. 28)

This second factor had much to do with the different prospects of England and Germany during the so-called great transformation away from the market system. Once a beneficiary of the institutional pattern she had innovated, England comes to represent in the end a case of institutional lock-in:

> While Germany was thus greatly assisted in her conspirative plans by her ability to adjust to the dissolution of the traditional system, Great Britain found herself severely handicapped by her adherence to that system. (Polanyi 1944, p. 245)

One major way in which the forerunner consolidates the likelihood of the expected benefits of her lead is to innovate along institutional lines. By designing new institutions and articulating them in a 'font matrix', the forerunner becomes the incontestable beneficiary of a situational advantage. At the same time, having invested so much in this process, the forerunner eventually becomes overburdened with her responsibilities of keeping the engine going at a time when the returns continue to diminish. As such, the forerunner has so much more at stake than the latecomer(s) should an attempt be made to overhaul the system in a radical manner. Consequently, institutional innovation and the benefits thereof are left to the lot of the contestor(s).

3. THORSTEIN VEBLEN ON ENGLAND VERSUS GERMANY

Thorstein Veblen sought to explore the true meaning of Germany's 'new departure of 1870' by way of which her historical trajectory had come to diverge so notably from that of modern Europe (Veblen [1915] 1990, p. 61). The striking achievements of Germany in this new era were a simultaneous gain in population, in industrial efficiency, and in military force. Germany seemed to match successfully modern industrial advance with a modernised dynastic state. This was paradoxical in that one would expect, given the lessons of past English experience, an erosion of the atavistic dynastic state under the auspices of industrial modernisation. Quite the contrary, no Glorious Revolution (1688) of the English type had taken place on the way from feudalistic particularism to the formation of an imperial state. The German state displayed strong signs of continuity and an ability to modernise itself from within:

This modern state of the industrial arts that so has led to the rehabilitation of a dynastic State in Germany on a scale exceeding what had been practicable in earlier times, - this technological advance was not made in Germany but was borrowed, directly or at the second remove, from the English-speaking peoples; primarily, and in the last resort almost wholly, from England. What has been insisted above is that British use and wont in other than the technological respect was not taken over by the German community at the same time. The result being that what is by contrast with England an anomaly, in that it shows the working of the modern state of the industrial arts as worked out by the English, but without the characteristic range of institutions and convictions that have grown up among English-speaking peoples concomitantly with the growth of this modern state of the industrial arts. Germany combines the results of English experience in the development of modern technology with a state of the other arts of life more nearly equivalent to what prevailed in England before the modern industrial régime came on; so that the German people have been enabled to take up the technological heritage of the English without having paid for it in the habits of thought, the use and wont, induced in the English community by the experience involved in achieving it. (Veblen [1915] 1990, pp. 85-6)

Veblen insisted that this path was far from unique to Germany, but instead represented the general course for Western countries. As such, the only thing unique about the English precedent was that it could not be repeated exactly. On the other hand, the specificity of the German experience provided the clear-cut features of a model otherwise applicable to the study of the many:

The case of Germany is unexampled among Western nations both as regards the abruptness, thoroughness and amplitude of its appropriation of this technology, and as regards the archaism of its cultural furniture at the date of this appropriation (Veblen [1915] 1990, p. 86).

Veblen's great contribution to development studies with an institutional bent is his awareness of the importance of borrowing amidst an otherwise equally important background of the cultural embeddedness of technology and industry. He was a forerunner of the thesis of latecomer's advantage (Gerschenkron 1962). Whereas Germany was put on a different track because of the implications of the English precedent and, once on that track, Germany could benefit from various opportunities that had not existed along the original English trajectory.

Veblen emphasised two kinds of cumulative processes that eventually locked-in a country on the way to development. One had to do with the cultural consequences of the very process of technological and industrial renewal. In this context, the spread of the inhibitive habits of business practice,[4] individualism and wasteful conspicuous consumption can be cited. The dichotomy between the slow-changing and relatively inflexible ceremonial-institutional aspect on the one hand, and the dynamic technological-industrial aspect on the other is of critical importance.

According to Veblen, 'standing conventions out of the past unavoidably act to retard, deflect or defeat adaptation to new exigencies that arise in the further course' (Veblen [1915] 1990, p. 30). The other cumulative process was due to strictly technological and economic reasons, and has been overlooked so far, yet offers a vital link with the more recent literature:

> But this work of retardation is also backed by the like character attaching to the material equipment by use of which the technological proficiency of the community takes effect. The equipment is also out of the past, and it too lies under the dead hand. In a general way, any minor innovation in processes or in the extension of available resources, or in the scale of organisation, is taken care of as far as may be by a patchwork improvement and amplification of the items of equipment already in hand; the fashion of plant and appliances already in use is adhered to, with concessions in new installations, but it is adhered to more decisively so in any endeavor to bring the equipment in hand up to scale and grade. Changes so made are in part of a concessive nature, in sufficiently large part, indeed, to tell materially on the aggregate; and the fact of such changes being habitually made in a concessive spirit so lessens the thrust in the direction of innovation that even the concessions do not carry as far as might be. (Veblen [1915] 1990, pp. 30-1)

The above two cumulative processes gradually led the system to a deadlock and constituted what might be dubbed the forerunner's disadvantage.

According to Veblen, the historical specificity of England was not due to her being the first; in fact, England had also been a borrower at the threshold of the Elizabethan era (Veblen [1915] 1990, p. 95). If anything, the most important single cause of English specificity was its geographic isolation from the Continent (Veblen [1915] 1990, p. 98). Thanks to her insularity, England had emerged from a weak warlike dynastic state as early as the seventeenth century (Veblen [1915] 1990, pp. 91, 111). So, what we may refer to as chronic low protection-costs, or, to put it differently, high protection-rents (Lane 1979) that systematically accrued to the English enterprise must have been of critical import. Consequently, in England the notion of a commonwealth had gained ground, whereas in Germany one spoke of the State with a capital 'S' (Veblen [1915] 1990, p. 160).

Intrinsic to Veblen's analysis is a probable two-stage specification of the development process. In comparing England's and Germany's passage through these stages, Veblen identified a gap and a lag:

> The earlier of these two periods [Elizabethan era] is the high tide of English borrowing and assimilation in the industrial arts, and so corresponds in some sense with the Imperial era of Germany; the latter period [Industrial Revolution] is to be remarked as in a special sense a creative era in English life, which has engendered the current technological system, characterised and dominated by the machine industry; and which has no counterpart in the life-history of the German people hitherto. There would accordingly appear to be an interval of, loosely, some three

or four hundred years' experience included in the life-history of the English community, but omitted from the experience that has gone to make the national genius of the German people. (Veblen [1915] 1990, p. 93)

Quite clearly, there is some replication involved in the developmental process, but it is replication with a difference, and whether or not the second stage will also have a counterpart remains to be seen. Furthermore, whatever there is of replication is condensed in time, and because of the borrowing factor, it brings together a strange coincidence of archaic institutions with modern industry:

> It is at least conceivable that in the course of time the protracting disintegrating impact of the discipline exercised by modern industrial habits would have brought this dynastic State and its coercive organisation to much the same state of decay as that which once overtook its smaller and feebler counterpart in Elizabethan England. But the course of time has not had a chance to run in this Prussian case. (Veblen [1915] 1990, pp. 172-3)

Even if the endpoint of the trajectory is far from being pre-determined, for Veblen, Germany is in 'an eminently unstable, transitional phase' (Veblen [1915] 1990, p. 236), and the warlike-dynastic character it displays is 'presumably of a transient nature' (Veblen [1915] 1990, pp. 269-70). This is so because of an inherent dynamic contradiction built into the odd couple of modernised archaic state and borrowed modern technology. The dynastic state needs the best of machinery and technology to carry out its warlike ambitions, yet the very deepening of the machine process cultivates a mentality at odds with the ideological foundations of the state:

> The Imperial State, therefore, may be said to be unable to get along without machine industry, and also, in the long run, unable to get along with it; since this industrial system in the long run undermines the foundations of the State. (Veblen [1915] 1990, pp. 270-1)

Veblen's analysis brought to the fore the role of an active state as responsible for perpetuating Germany's difference. In juxtaposition to liberal theories that tend to play down the role of the state, Veblen bestowed on the state a problematic centrality. For the Imperial State, Veblen identified a positive and a negative function. The negative function was to detract the country from the peaceful international free-trade oriented specialisation, a 'historical alternative' that Veblen deployed as a yardstick for economic performance (Veblen [1915] 1990, p. 180). The positive function was that, once within the given trajectory, the state played a major role in perpetuating further economic development in conformity with its dynastic ends. However,

Veblen identified the transitional nature of this positive role of the then-efficient German bureaucracy:

> It is apparently unavoidable that such a system should gradually achieve a certain consistency of procedure, a binding texture of routine and precedent. So long as the routine is still in process of adaptation to the exigencies to meet which it is being elaborated, it will have but a slight if any retarding or hindering effect in the work to be done. It is flexible so long as it is engaged in establishing precedents; but so soon or so far as the precedents have once been established, and in the measure in which the exigencies gradually change their character, so as to be less well served by routine embodying precedents already established, in the same measure the bureaucratic system working under such routine will grow inflexible and inhibitive, the amount of lost motion and waste energy will increase, and the margin of perquisites and sinecures will widen. (Veblen [1915] 1990, p. 234)

Irrespective of whether or not the overall balance is negative or positive, the fact that the state occupies the central place of analysis points to a continuity with later heterodox development literature on which institutional analysis has to count.

A further continuity with contemporary development literature can be identified in the placement of emphasis on investment in the human factor. Veblen agreed that modern warfare was capital-destructive, yet noted the quick recuperation of losers as far as their material prosperity was concerned. This he linked to the indestructibility of know-how and human capital:

> The material equipment in such a case of devastation will have been greatly damaged, and that is always a handicap; but the immaterial equipment of technological proficiency - the state of the industrial arts considered as a system of habits of thought -will have suffered relatively slight damage, provided the season of hostilities is not protracted beyond reasonable expectation; and what damage it may have suffered in the way of a loss of specially trained personnel is relatively easy to remedy under the current technological system. This immaterial equipment is, far and away, the more important productive agency in the case; although, it is true, economists have not been in the habit of making much of it, since it is in the main not capable of being stated in terms of price, and so does not appear in the statistical schedules of accumulated wealth. (Veblen [1915] 1990, p. 272)

Last but not least, for Veblen the challenge of development was a race against time, a race against all others involved. The advantage of Germany was that modern machinery in the service of the dynastic state had provided the latter with the ability to extract a greater surplus and divert it to strategic ends until the German people could internalise modern habits of wasteful consumption and 'the disposable margin between the industrial output and the current consumption might be expected shortly to disappear' (Veblen [1915] 1990, p. 210). This was indeed Germany's race against herself. But, in the meantime, Germany was engaged in an equally important race against all others on the European scene:

> Other European countries, as, e.g., France, Italy, Russia, and the minor and outlying nations, have also increasingly come in for the usufruct of the same British machine technology to which Imperial Germany owes its dominant place in the industrial world; and while none of them may have made, or even prospectively will be expected to make, gains of the same absolute importance as those recently made by Germany, they still have already begun to narrow the lead of Germany in the industrial field. Their larger resources, more commodious emplacement, and greater aggregate mass will make their competition sufficiently serious even without the same efficiency per capita. So, e.g., even on a smaller coefficient, Russia, with its large mass and unlimited resources, might be counted on presently to overtake Germany in point of aggregate industrial strength, and therefore presumably in point of warlike capacity; and Russia has of late been making disquieting advances in modern industry. (Veblen [1915] 1990, p. 261)

Because he worked with the image of a race, there is something of a 'zero-sum-game' metaphor in Veblen's conception of development. By definition, there can not be all winners at the end, but there must be winners and losers. Moreover, winners early on in the race would turn out to be relative, - but not necessarily absolute - losers at the end, precisely because, for their early lead, they were drawn into 'paying the penalty for having been thrown into the lead and so having shown the way' (Veblen [1915] 1990, p. 132). As for the latecomers, they could take advantage of the lessons provided by their predecessors and compensate for their original handicap.

4. CONCLUSION

The tacit image of a race with winners and losers links well with the heritage of pre-classical mercantilist literature as well as with the post-World War II Dependencia theory. As such, it contrasts sharply with the orthodox neoclassical modernisation approach, where each country traces its private path of development (Rostow 1960). On the whole, the struggle for development is indeed a race, but not necessarily a 'zero-sum-game'. However, the imagery of a 'zero-sum-game', inaccurate as it may be, serves better to demonstrate the competitive nature of the developmental process than does a monadic conception of countries moving along separate paths.

The affinity of the legacy of the Polanyi-Veblen tradition in institutional analysis with both the mercantilist literature that preceded it and the Dependencia that succeeded it requires further qualification. The mercantilist literature, obsessed with the metaphor of a 'zero-sum-game', took off from the premise that the stock of precious metals such as gold was given at any time, and therefore international trade was a struggle for redistribution among the contestors. Put this way, the argument was logically consistent so long as its fundamental assumption was not challenged. The mercantilist conception, particularly in its re-constructed nineteenth-century version identified with Gustav von Schmoller ([1884] 1967) and the German Historical School, conceived the object of the race as a simultaneous motivation for power as well as for plenty. In doing so, it resisted the temptation to shift the focus from political economic to purely economic consideration, and foreshadowed political economic approaches of which the Polanyi-Veblen perspective is an offshoot.

This being so, later links in the chain, such as the Dependencia and its world-systemist successors, increasingly suffered from a dilemma. On the one hand, they insisted on the competitive nature of the struggle for development. On the other, they had difficulty in identifying the object of the race. Fully aware that the stock of wealth in the world was not given, as the mercantilists had originally assumed, these novel approaches met with difficulty in defining what the object of the race was. One way out has been the endorsement of an archaic and controversial labour theory of value on the basis of which unequal exchange and value-transfers could take place. It goes without saying that this relatively easy way out nevertheless leaves much to be desired.

The Polanyi-Veblen synthesis presented above entails an important line of argument that could serve to surmount this difficulty of post-mercantilist political economy. It is all the better that this line of argument is fully congruent with the findings of contemporary institutional analysis. Within the Polanyi-Veblen framework, the paths are interdependent and so are the fortunes of individual countries. This is because the development process of the forerunner inevitably generates a series of obstacles that then make it increasingly difficult and costly for the latecomer(s) to emulate. Having found the path ahead of them obstructed, either the latecomer(s) have to make big jumps - for example, by way of innovative substitutions in the sense of Gerschenkron - that move them along an alternative path, or they remain locked-in to a self-reinforcing circle of underdevelopment. This argument puts important weight on the time factor. There may well be a difference between the latecomers and the 'late latecomers'. While latecomer(s) early on could have been forced to an alternative path of development along which they could benefit from the advantages usually associated with a latecomer-status, 'late latecomers' can find it increasingly difficult to make the necessary jump because of the accumulation of practically insurmountable obstacles on their way. As such, historically speaking, there can in fact be a critical threshold beyond which seeking to develop as a latecomer may prove to involve dramatic costs, human and otherwise.[5]

The exploration of the intellectual origins of the Latin American Dependencia has led the way to the re-discovery of the Eastern Europe of the inter-war period as the first arena of dependency conceptualisation (Love 1996). Somewhat pessimistically, Dependencia approaches place the emphasis on the relative insurmountability of the obstacles on the way to development. Somewhat more optimistically, the study of nineteenth-century transformations in the aftermath of the Industrial Revolution led to the conception of development as a historical process unfolding along a variety of paths (Senghaas 1985). It may well be that the critical threshold referred to above was reached when development ceased to be a European phenomenon and increasingly became a global problem. Hence, the time-space coordinates of the debates in question may in fact reflect a changing environment.

The re-constructed legacy of Veblen and Polanyi not only casts doubt on the orthodox modernisation approaches, but also highlights the path towards a new conceptualisation in which the latecomer takes the place of the forerunner and becomes the quintessential model of normalcy.[6] The richness of this tradition has much to praise in comparison with the lessons of contemporary new institutional economic forays into the study of the Third World. However, this should not be taken to mean that the Polanyi-Veblen approach can be applied as it stands to the study of development in the contemporary world. This is so because the world itself has changed drastically from the nineteenth to the brink of the twenty-first century.

Both Polanyi and Veblen took as given some attributes of the nineteenth-century order and carried out their analyses on that basis. The very fact that these 'givens' may no longer hold invites a revision of the analytical framework. First and foremost among such parametric shifts is the assumption of 'national economy'. This concept is itself a reflection of the historic moment when German scholarship confronted the problem of differences with England. The idea of a 'national economy' presupposed the territorial congruity of economic and political borders, hence a one-to-one correspondence between a state and an economy. It was in this sense that the race for development could be personified as a contest between states. Within this conceptual framework, even the British state was a nation-state, albeit an awkward one with multiple nations at home and with pretensions to cosmopolitanism abroad. On the verge of the twenty-first century we observe that the world has significantly changed. We now encounter perhaps more than ever before a globalised economy that escapes the jurisdiction of any singular state or a consortium of all states as a whole. Consequently, the relative power of the state *vis-à-vis* the economy has been drastically reduced. This means that we can no longer assume that the state is the effective policy instrument. Furthermore, we can no longer conceptualise the struggle for the riches of the world exclusively in terms of nation-state units, as Polanyi and Veblen once could.

The above shift has already made a major impact on the state-of-the-art literature. The proliferation of conceptual devices, such as transnational enterprise systems, techno-industrial systemic units, and national innovation systems, attests to developments in this direction. Questions that were formerly posited in terms of the perspective of national economic development now need further coordination. Consequently, the analytical category of the national economy has to be supplemented - but not replaced - by additional units of analysis, the referential scope of which will help problematise the national economy itself as a category. In the foreseeable future, either the world-economy as a whole, or its specific segments headed by technologically leading and organisationally innovative enterprises, extending backwards into a vast geography (less than the whole world, as there will likely be a number of such competing chains), will constitute the legitimate alternative units of inquiry to the once-privileged concept of national economy. Fortunately, this domain is not new to institutional or evolutionary economics. Ever since Veblen ([1904] 1988), institutional economics has been intricately linked with the study of the business enterprise. New Institutional Economics, inspired by Ronald Coase (1937) and the transaction costs approach, has further reinvigorated the interest in the study of the firm. As for the brand of evolutionary economics, a Schumpeterian perspective that emphasises cycles of technological and organisational innovation as the key to the realisation of entrepreneurial profits ([1934] 1989) has motivated deeper probes into industrial dynamics.

Unfortunately, because the shift in focus has come about from within the study of the firm and industrial organisation, it has concentrated exclusively on the commanding heights of enterprise systems where technological and organisational innovations concentrate. The dynamism encountered in this area captures scholarly attention rather easily at the expense of other opaque fields where equally, if not more, vital questions wait to be answered. This has dire consequences from the perspective of development studies. It seems that the once Third World that has constituted the privileged domain of development studies is rapidly dropping out of the picture. In this respect, a corrective intervention from within development studies is badly needed.

What looks like a cost factor from the point of view of business enterprise and industrial organisation is essentially a human phenomenon, with major social dimensions. It is no coincidence that Polanyi gave great weight to the constitution of the labour market in England and its formative effects on the working-class. What was at issue was the determination of the quality of life of the bulk of the population. In the case of England, because of its exclusion from the political realm, deterioration in the quality of life was the price paid by the working-class for the Industrial Revolution. The Continent escaped this abyss precisely because, amidst slower change, the working-class came to form an integral part of the political life of the nation. As such, growing political strength could offset weaknesses in the marketplace for labour.

In the light of the above orientation, what remains as conspicuously missing from the industrial restructuring literature already referred to is the study of the nature of capital-labour relations in the periphery. This is all the more important as the ongoing rapid erosion of 'traditional' social structures, such as rural community life, undermines the 'embeddedness' of labour that has so far cushioned social discontent. This process towards proletarianisation takes place at a time when the state itself is subjected to increasing constraints that deprive it of the partial role it has historically played as a second-best substitute for containing labour unrest. The political-economic scope of the Polanyi-Veblen frame of analysis is essential in bringing such pressing problems back to the development agenda. It goes without saying that this is far from being the only plausible corrective effect of this approach. Among other likely contributions, we enlist the following two: first, the relational conception of the developmental race highlights the asymmetric distribution of initial endowments, defined in the broadest possible sense. The accumulation of obstacles in the way of latecomers dictates their prospects as likely candidates to specialise in the lesser links of business enterprise systems. Secondly, the relative stability of the distribution of gains among the different links of the very same chain deserves as much scholarly attention as the technological and organisational dynamism of the leading nodes.

In summary, to enrich an alternative approach to the study of development, a blend of institutional approaches - both old and new - together with their distant relations, such as the Dependencia theory, is a necessary but not a sufficient condition. As a matter of fact, it is not only a blend we need, but a genuine reconstruction that can lead the way to a new developmental perspective, one that is trans-disciplinary in scope, and fair to all parties involved in the ongoing developmental experience.

NOTES

1. Professor Dieter Senghaas of Bremen University, who has kindly agreed to read an earlier draft of this paper, has called my attention to the fact that W.W. Rostow's *How It All Began* (1975) also qualifies as an example of institutionalism by necessity, despite his dramatic impact on the modernisation approach.
2. Whereas Smith and List are often represented as polar opposites in the development literature, List in fact made a case for protection of infant industry as a transitional strategy

for development, at a later stage of which the economy would open up to further competition (List 1885; Senghaas 1991). As such, List gave a corrective touch to the otherwise Smithian approach.

3. The emphasis Polanyi put on the fact that the market itself is an institution is of major importance in combating the trappings of still fashionable neoliberal critiques of structuralism and transcending the limits of conventional development economics. Not the market as such, but the efficient mix of cooperation within with competition abroad characterises the economic success stories in today's world (Öniþ 1995).

4. For Veblen, the way in which technology and industry were instituted under business concerns fell under the heading of the ceremonial institutions. As such, there was no strict economic/noneconomic division at work in the commonplace sense: 'At the same time, as fast as commercial considerations, considerations of investment, come to rule the industry, the investor's interest comes also to exercise an inhibitory surveillance over technological efficiency, both by the well-known channel of limiting the output and holding-up the price to what the traffic will bear, - that is to say what it will bear in the pecuniary sense of yielding the largest net gain to the business men in interest, - and also by the less notorious reluctance of investors and business concerns to replace obsolete methods and plant with new and more efficient equipment.' (Veblen [1915] 1990, p. 32). On the conflicting viewpoints concerning outdated technology, see also (Veblen [1915] 1990, p. 131).

5. The miraculous development of South Korea during the last third of this century is a case in point (Amsden 1989). Under a special set of circumstances that insulated South Korea from the negative effects of the global political economic conjuncture (namely, military protection at zero-cost and US economic assistance), South Korea could replicate the classic path of development by way of industrialisation. However, an against-the-grain reading of this economic miracle brings to light three important facts. First, an enormous human and social cost has been endured, namely the repressive regime. Second, all the economic and social sacrifice has at best created a Hyundai, an industrial achievement that remains a faint copy of its Japanese precursors. Third, the whole house of cards had rested on the artificial insulation of the national economy by way of a highly regulated financial structure that served to allocate resources favourably to indigenous accumulation. Not surprisingly, this enclave of the 'archaic' could not long resist the ebbs and flows of the global financial system and fell apart during the recent crisis.

6. Veblen was well aware of the applicability of his model to the study of latecomers, as he engaged himself in a discussion of Japanese development at a time when scholarship hardly ventured into the domain of development studies outside of Europe (Veblen, [1915] 1990).

REFERENCES

Amsden, A.H. (1989), *Asia's Next Giant: South Korea and Late Industrialization*. New York: Oxford University Press.

Arthur, W.B. (1994), *Increasing Returns and Path Dependence in the Economy*, Ann Arbor: The University of Michigan Press.

Blackbourn, D. and E. Eley (1984), *The Peculiarities of German History: Bourgeois Society and Politics in Nineteenth Century Germany*, Oxford: Oxford University Press.

Coase, R. (1937), 'The nature of the firm', *Economica*, vol. IV, n. 15, 386-405.

David, P. (1985), 'Clio and the economics of QWERTY', *American Economic Review*, Proceedings, 75, pp. 332-7.

Dosi, G. and J.S. Metcalfe (1991), 'On some notions of irreversibility in economics', in P.P. Saviotti and J.S. Metcalfe (eds), *Evolutionary Theories of Economical and Technological Change*, Chur, Switzerland: Harwood Academic Press, pp. 133-59.

Gerschenkron, A. (1962), *Economic Backwardness in Historical Perspective*, Cambridge: Belknap Press of Harvard University Press.

Harriss, J., J. Hunter and C.M. Lewis (eds) (1995), *The New Institutional Economics and Third World Development*, London: Routledge.

Kay, C. (1989), *Latin American Theories of Development and Underdevelopment*, London: Routledge.

Lane, F.C. (1979), *Profits from Power: Readings in Protection Rent and Violence-Controlling Enterprises*, Albany: State University of New York Press.

List, F. (1885), *The National System of Political Economy*, New York: A. M. Kelley (1966).

Love, J.L. (1996), *Crafting the Third World: Theorizing Underdevelopment in Romania and Brazil*, Stanford: Stanford University Press.

Myrdal, G. (1964), *An American Dilemma*, New York: McGraw Hill.

North, D.C. (1990), *Institutions, Institutional Change and Economic Performance*, Cambridge: Cambridge University Press.

Öniþ, Z. (1995), 'The limits of neoliberalism: toward a reformulation of development theory', *Journal of Economic Issues*, vol. 29, n. 1, pp. 97-119.

Özveren, E. (1998), 'An institutionalist alternative to neoclassical economics?', *Review of the Fernand Braudel Center*, vol. XXI, n. 4, pp. 469-530.

Polanyi, K. (1944), *The Great Transformation: The Political and Economic Origins of our Time*, Boston: Beacon Press.

Rostow, W.W. (1960), *The Stages of Economic Growth: A Non-Communist Manifesto*, Cambridge: Cambridge University Press.

Rostow, W.W. (1975), *How It All Began: Origins of the Modern Economy*, New York: McGraw-Hill.

Schmoller, G. von (1884), *The Mercantile System and its Historical Significance*, New York: Augustus M. Kelley (1967).

Schumpeter, J.A. (1934), *The Theory of Economic Development: An Inquiry into Profits, Capital, Credit, Interest, and the Business Cycle*, New Brunswick, New Jersey: Transaction Publishers (1989).

Senghaas, D. (1985), *The European Experience: A Historical Critique of Development Theory*, Leamington Spa/Dover: Berg Publishers.

Senghaas, D. (1991), 'Friedrich List and the basic problems of modern development', *Review*, XIV, 3, pp. 451-67.

Veblen, T. (1904), *The Theory of Business Enterprise*, New Brunswick, New Jersey: Transaction Books (1988).

Veblen, T. (1915), *Imperial Germany and the Industrial Revolution*, New Brunswick, New Jersey: Transaction Publishers, (1990).

Veblen, T. (1915), 'The opportunity of Japan', *The Journal of Race Development*, vol. 6, pp. 23-38.

13. The Future's Unknowability: Keynes's Probability, Probable Knowledge and the Decision to Innovate

Marco Crocco[1]

INTRODUCTION

The aim of this paper is to show that Keynes's concept of probability can enrich the understanding of the process of innovation offered by the neo-Schumpeterian approach. The latter has a peculiar understanding of the technical change process, which includes concepts such as knowledge base, cumulativeness, technological paradigm, technological trajectory, and uncertainty. To deal with uncertainty, in particular, neo-Schumpeterians introduce the concept of routines. What is suggested here is that the concepts of Probable Knowledge and Weight of Argument, draw from Keynes's theory of probability, when used together with the concept of routines, can clarify the rationality of the decision-making process in the introduction of an innovation.

In section 1, the main features of Keynes's approach to probability and the concept of probable knowledge are presented. In section 2, I describe those aspects of the neo-Schumpeterian approach to technology that are important for our discussion. The possible links between these approaches are discussed in section 3. Finally, section 4 concludes with suggestions for further development.

1. KEYNESIAN UNCERTAINTY

The concept of uncertainty in Keynes has been a subject of debate since the publication of the *General Theory*. Initially, the main feature of this discussion was the distinction between 'risk' and 'uncertainty'.[2] While the Neoclassical approach, e.g. Lucas, argued that only situations of risk were analytically tractable in economic analysis heterodox schools maintained that economic analysis should not neglect 'true' uncertainty. However, since the early years of the 1980s the debate has changed. Despite the fact that the previous distinction still remains, within the heterodox field a discussion regarding Keynes's concept of uncertainty in the Treatise on Probability and its link to the *General Theory* has emerged (Carabelli 1985, 1988, 1992 and 1995; O'Donnell 1989, 1990; Lawson 1985, 1988; Runde 1990, 1991, among others). Thus, we think that it is important to look at the Treatise on Probability before we define what is understood here as Keynesian uncertainty.[3]

For Keynes, probability is about logical relations between sets of propositions, premises and conclusions. Let the conclusions be the set of propositions a, and the set of premises, h. If a knowledge of h justifies a rational belief in a of some degree, one can say that there is a probability relation between a and h. This relation can be written as: a/h.

The probability relation or the degree α of rational belief that it entails ranges from a situation of certainty ($a/h = 1$), meaning that the relationship between a and h is tautologic, to a situation of impossibility ($a/h = 0$), where a and h are contradictory. A situation where $0 < a/h < 1$, means that the probability relation warrants a degree of belief between 0 and 1. Moreover, the probability relation is defined solely in terms of the relation between the conclusion and the premises. If, after establishing a probability relation of type a/h, new evidence h_1 appears, this does not invalidate the previous probability relation, but gives rise to a new one, a/hh_1. An important feature of Keynes's theory of probability is that not all probability relations can be numerically measurable.

What is important is that, in Keynes's approach, probability is a branch of logic. As pointed out by Carabelli (1988, p. 18), 'Keynes's logic of probability appealed to those categories traditionally associated with the theory of belief, opinion, limited knowledge, logical doubt and ignorance, i.e. uncertainty and probability.' Logic in this sense is not restricted to demonstrative knowledge or truth relations. According to Keynes, probability arguments, in general, are non-demonstrative and non-conclusive and thereby generally opposed to the Cartesian/Euclidean mode of thought. Moreover, this logic is 'non-demonstrative because it referred to organic relations would not be amenable to formal representation' (Dow 1996, p. 7).[4]

An interesting way to represent Keynes's theory of probability is suggested by Koopman (1940). In this article, he defines the axioms and the algebra of intuitive probability, and he identifies Keynes's theory of probability as a case of intuitive probability. The intuitive thesis in probability holds that probability derives directly from the intuition, both in its meaning and in the majority of laws it obeys. Contrary to the common use of the term probability, the intuitive approach claims that experience should be interpreted in terms of probability and not the inverse. Thus, intuition comes prior to objective experience. The main aphorism of this thesis is that '*knowledge is possible, while certainty is not*' (Koopman 1940, p. 269, italics added).

The importance of intuitive probability to our discussion is that it simplifies the conditions for the comparability between probabilities, without discrediting the main aspects of Keynes's interpretation. According to Koopman (1940, p. 270), 'the fundamental view point of the [intuitive probability] is the primal intuition of probability expresses itself in a (partial) ordering of eventualities'.

Let a_1, h_1, a_2, and h_2 be propositions, where the meaning is perceived by an individual who does not know whether this apprehension is true or false.

Then the phrase '$[a_1]$ on the presumption that $[h_1]$ is true is equally or less probable than $[a_2]$ on the presumption that $[h_2]$ is true', conveys a precise meaning to his intuition . . . That is, . . . , a first essential in the thesis of intuitive probability, and contains the ultimate answer to the question of the meaning of the notion of probability (Koopman 1940, p. 270).

This can be represented in symbolic form:[5]

$$a_1/h_1 \geq * a_2/h_2$$

This is precisely the kind of comparison that Keynes discusses in the Treatise on Probability. So, hereafter we will use the above symbolic form to describe Keynes's approach.

Another important element on the Keynes approach is the concept of weight of argument. Keynes's main concern in discussing probability is to show that one can act rationally in situations in which complete certainty about the future is absent. In these situations, one should look not only at the probability relation itself, but also at the size of the evidence - evidential spread - that support this probability. Here Keynes brings in to the discussion the concept of the weight of argument.

According to Runde (1991), it is possible to find in the Treatise a relative definition of weight, the degree of completeness of the information set on which a probability is based. It is the balance between the amount of relevant knowledge in relation to the relevant knowledge plus relevant ignorance possessed. This is expressed, according to Runde (1991, p. 281), as

$$V(a/h) = K/(K_r + I_r)$$

Where: K_r is the relevant knowledge and I_r is the relevant ignorance. Two aspects deserve more attention. The first is related to the meaning of 'relevant ignorance'. As insightfully pointed out by Runde (1991), it is always possible to know, or at least to identify, the factors that affect our probability relation, and about which one is ignorant. Secondly, more information does not necessarily mean an increase of the weight of argument. New evidence could decrease the weight if it implies the increase of relevant ignorance. A new piece of evidence can show that our previous relevant knowledge was wrong - decreasing the weight - albeit, simultaneously, the apprehension of relevant ignorance is increasing.

Finally, it is well known that Keynes assumes a direct relationship between weight and confidence in using the probability estimate as a guide to conduct. The definition of weight as a degree of completeness of information is helpful to the understanding of this relationship. Confidence can either decrease or increase with new information, in that new evidence can increase the relevant ignorance or knowledge.

It is important to note that the Keynes approach to probability and the concept of weight allow a definition of a different kind of knowledge, that is probable knowledge. It is this kind of knowledge that is obtained from the establishment of a probability relation and from the information set that grounds it. It is a knowledge that emerges in situations of true uncertainty and so is different from probabilistic knowledge where the latter is that knowledge that arises in situations in which the use of probability distributions is possible, in other words, situations of risk.

These two main aspects of the *Treatise* - probability relation and weight of argument - have been used by some scholars (Runde 1990; Dow 1996) to define uncertainty in a Keynesian sense and, in addition, to demonstrate that Keynesian uncertainty admits degrees. Runde (1991, 1990) argues that uncertainty, according to Keynes's approach, could be related to the size, in some sense, of the information set upon which the probability relation is based. In other words, uncertainty can be related to the weight of argument if the latter is defined as a degree of completeness of information on which a probability is based. Despite the fact that this notion is not fully explored in the Treatise, Runde gives two quotations from *The General Theory* that support this claim:

> The state of long-term expectations, upon which our decisions are based, does not solely depend, therefore, on the most probable forecast we can make. It also depends on the confidence with which we make this forecast - on how highly we rate the likelihood of our forecast turning out quite wrong. (Keynes 1973c, p. 148)

And:

> The liquidity-premium, it will be observed, is partly similar to the risk-premium, but partly different; - the difference corresponding to the difference between the best estimates we can make of probabilities and the confidence with which we make them. (Keynes 1973c, p. 240)

It is clear from the previous quotations that confidence is the essential factor in this interpretation of uncertainty. As was shown above, the concept of weight, as a degree of completeness of information, appears to capture the role of ignorance in the assessment of the confidence in the probability relation. As a consequence of this approach, the complete absence of probable knowledge should be interpreted as the extreme case of uncertainty. If it is impossible to establish the probability relation, whatever the reason - no existence of probability or a lack of skill to determine or identify it - it is also impossible to have any confidence. Thus, this situation could be interpreted as an extreme case not only for uncertainty, but also for confidence.

From this extreme position, one can move to situations in which uncertainty prevails due to low weight of argument, which implies low confidence. Thus, there is a qualitative change in the uncertainty, from a situation in which a probability relation does not exist to another in which the probability relation exists but the weight is low. Moreover, as the weight of argument increases, the confidence follows in the same direction and uncertainty decreases. In this approach, probable knowledge is taken into account as a guide to conduct, and the degree of reliability of this probable knowledge - the confidence it merits - determines the degree of uncertainty that exists in a specific situation. Therefore, the concept of weight allows the understanding of uncertainty as a relative concept.

Dow (1995) goes further in the development of the concept of degrees of uncertainty. She argues that to take weight into account in defining uncertainty, one must bring to consideration the knowledge of what constitutes relevance. To do this, it is necessary to have a 'degree of belief in a hypothesised structure on which to base an estimate weight' (Dow 1995, p. 124), in other words, a degree of belief that there is a logical relation between the hypothesis (a) and the evidence that supports it (h). This is important since, to identify relevance, it is necessary to believe that the relationship between (a) and (h) is known. The main point here is to note that there is a difference between the acknowledgement that it is possible to establish a logical relation between a and h, and to define what extent the size and quality of h allows the conclusion a. One has now two orders of uncertainty that work together. First, there is uncertainty about the probability relation: it is a case of 'uncertainty about uncertainty'. Uncertainty now is inversely related to a lower order of knowledge of the probability relation relative to evidence and ignorance. Second, there is uncertainty about the degree of completeness of information on which a probability is based. From this perspective, the limit situation is that one in which knowledge about the probability relation is absent and ignorance is complete.[6]

Summing up this section, we can define Keynesian uncertainty as arising in those situations in which decision-makers do not have access to numerically definite probabilities.[7] Under this definition, it is possible to explain situations that are qualitatively different: both the extreme situation of uncertainty - complete absence of probable knowledge - and the situation of probable knowledge - where weight is interpreted as a measure of gradability of uncertainty fit the definition above.

Qualitative degrees of uncertainty can be visualised in Table 13.1.

Table 13.1   Scale of qualitative degrees of uncertainty

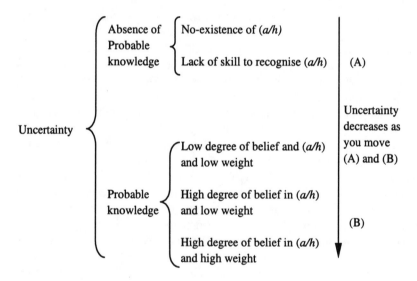

2. TECHNICAL CHANGE AND UNCERTAINTY

Until the second half of the 1970s, the majority of the economic literature relating to technical change was divided into two groups according to their understanding of the nature of an innovation: the so-called demand pull and technology push approaches. The basic difference between them depends on what is viewed as the main source of innovation: the former attributes to market mechanisms the unique determinant of technical change, while the latter postulates the state of science as the main source of innovation.[8] However, by the end of the 1970s a number of authors (Rosenberg 1976; Nelson and Winter, 1977 among others) argued that an intermediate approach could be found. In other words, neither the demand-pull nor the technology push approach could alone provide the elements for the full comprehension of the technological change process. This group will be named here neo-Schumpeterian (hereafter NS), as they find in Schumpeter's writings the inspiration for their analyses.[9]

An important feature of the innovative activity, according to the NS approach is uncertainty, which plays an essential role in the understanding of technical change. According to Freeman and Soete (1997, pp. 242-5), there are three kinds of uncertainty that affect innovative activity: business, technical and market uncertainties. The first is related to environmental variables (political, economic, legal, etc.) and affects all decisions related to the future. This kind of uncertainty is not specific to the innovative activity, but to economic decisions as a whole. The other two kinds of uncertainty are project-specific. Technical uncertainty refers to realised standards of performance under various operating conditions for a given expenditure on R&D, while market uncertainty refers to the extent to which the innovation will be commercially successful for a given product specification (Kay 1979, p. 18).

Despite the fact that these categories of uncertainty appear in every innovation, the degree varies according to the type of innovation. Freeman and Soete (1997, p. 244) show that there is a qualitative difference between the uncertainty associated with a radical product innovation, which is of a very high degree, and that related to the introduction of a product differentiation, which is of a much lower degree (Table 13.2). This difference in the degree of uncertainty is related to the development of technological paradigm and technological trajectories (hereafter TP and TT respectively), in the sense that they focus the direction of research and give better grounds for the formation of technological and market expectations (cf. Dosi 1988 p. 1134).[10]

Notwithstanding the fact that these degrees of uncertainty are related to different aspects of the innovative activity, they have the same basic source. According to Dosi & Egidi (1991, p. 145), the sources of uncertainty are,

> incompleteness of the information set, which means the lack of all the information which would be necessary to make decisions with certain outcomes and knowledge incompleteness, which means the inability of the agents to recognise and interpret the relevant information (limitations on the computational and cognitive capabilities of the agents).

Table 13.2 Degree of uncertainty associated with various types of innovation

1. True Uncertainty	Fundamental research
	Fundamental invention
2. Very high degree of uncertainty	Radical product innovations
	Radical process innovations outside firm
3. High degree of uncertainty	Major product innovations
	Radical process innovations in own establishment or system
4. Moderate uncertainty	New 'generations' of established products
5. Little uncertainty	Licensed innovation
	Imitation of product innovations
	Modifications of products and processes
	Early adoption of established process
6. Very little uncertainty	New 'model'
	Product differentiation
	Agency for established innovation
	Late adoption of established process innovation and franchised operations in own establishment
	Minor technical improvements

Source: Freeman and Soete, 1997, p. 244.

When related to the introduction of an innovation, the first source (incompleteness of the information set) means that when someone starts to search for a solution for a technological problem, he lacks some fundamental information, and this lack of information makes the innovative activity completely uncertain. This information might include, for example, the length of time it will take for the innovation to be found; the cost of this innovation; and its acceptance by the market. One is, therefore, faced with strong uncertainty, which means the impossibility, even in principle, of defining the probability distribution of future events (cf. Dosi and Egidi 1991). Thus, the innovative activity is not an activity subject to risk but rather to true uncertainty.

The second source (knowledge incompleteness) is based on the concept of procedural uncertainty. There is here a clear distinction between knowledge and information, since access to the latter does not guarantee the acquisition of the former. The acquisition of knowledge lies in the ability to process information, which depends on the computational and cognitive capabilities of the agents. Therefore, uncertainty here has its source on the lack of knowledge, despite the fact that information could be available. To deal with this uncertainty, the agents develop a 'rational behaviour', which implies the search for stable rules and procedures (routines) which give them security.

The use of routines in innovative activity may sound a little odd, as innovation represents something new. However, there is no contradiction in this approach. What should be clear is the difference between the 'search' for an innovation and the 'outcomes' of this 'search'.[11] Uncertainty relates to the outcomes of the research activity and not to the activity itself. One could correctly argue that, at initial stages of the research activity, uncertainty is strong. Nevertheless, as knowledge becomes consolidated or, in other words, as some heuristics have been established, one could assume strong patterns (routines) of a high predictability in the research activity. Nelson and Winter (1982, p. 133) synthesise the point:

> We propose to assimilate to our concept of routine all of the patterning of organizational activity that the observance of heuristics produces, including the patterning of particular ways of attempting to innovate . . . But we emphasize . . . that viewing innovative activity as 'routine' in this sense does not entail treating its results as predictable.[12] By placing the discussion in the terms discussed before, one can say that the research routines codify the procedures and knowledge involved in the solution of a particular problem, and are conditioned by the technological paradigm.[13]

To sum up, the NS approach to technical change assumes that substantive and procedural uncertainties are essential features of the innovative activity and, in order to deal with them, routines are developed. These routines, in turn, are contingent on the competencies and heuristics of the technological paradigm, which allows the emergence of the concepts of appropriability, opportunity and cumulativeness, making the understanding of the technical change unique. Moreover, it was shown that uncertainty varies according to different types of innovation, decreasing from a situation in which there is a high degree of uncertainty - usually in research activities - to situations with a low degree of uncertainty - development activities.

The question to be raised here is whether routines are sufficient to understand the decision to introduce and/or to develop an innovation. My claim is that they are not. Routinised behaviour is not only a characteristic of the innovative activity, but is also present in every situation of human life. Indeed, some authors (Farmer 1996; Giddens 1984; Lawson 1997) argue that it is an important element of human action. It is related not only to situations of uncertainty but is essential in facilitating interactions between individuals and in giving 'ontological security' (sense of stability and sameness) to human beings.

Thus, as a part of today's situations, routines cannot by themselves explain the behaviour of the innovator faced with uncertainty. They are part of this behaviour and must be taken into consideration, but they are insufficient to provide a full understanding of it. As pointed out by Fransman,

> [w]hile the routine-based approach does not assume certainty, it does not deal adequately with the way in which uncertainty is confronted in decision making in the firm (1998, p. 175).

In the case of technical change, routines and technological trajectories reduce but do not eliminate uncertainty. They are fundamental in a problem-solving activity since they help in

> The identification of relevant information, the application of pre-existing competences or the development of new ones to the problem solution and, finally the identification of the alternative courses of action (Dosi and Egidi 1991, p. 150).

However, the last act of a problem-solving activity (choice) under uncertainty remains to be made. That is to say, which course of action should be taken by the agent? What is it that makes an investor decide between the immediate introduction of an innovation or in postponing it? To answer these questions, we think that the use of Keynes's theory of probability can be helpful, as it is related to the decision-making process under uncertainty.

3. ANALYSING THE INTRODUCTION OF INNOVATION USING KEYNES'S PROBABILITY

The discussion made in sections 1 and 2 above shows that there is an important element linking the NS approach to innovation and Keynes's theory of probability, that is, the decision making under uncertainty. As shown, uncertainty is an irreducible element in innovative activity: it is always present when some technological solution is sought. Moreover, Keynes's theory of probability tries to explain the way in which rational behaviour can emerge within an uncertain environment. Thus, in this section we attempt to interpret the introduction of innovations using the concepts of technological paradigm, technological trajectories and probable knowledge.

The first aspect to be analysed is uncertainty. To make the argument clearer, we first analyse the effects of technological and market uncertainty on the innovative decision, assuming that business uncertainty is very low at this point. By the end of the essay, business uncertainty is incorporated into the argument.

As shown in section 2, for the NS, innovative activity involves two sources of uncertainty: the incompleteness of the information set and incompleteness of knowledge. However, it is worth noting that these two sources of uncertainty fit well within the definition of Keynesian uncertainty. The incompleteness of the information set is nothing more than a problem of low weight. What is missing in the information set is the relevant knowledge about the innovation. Moreover, the acknowledgement of the existence of relevant ignorance creates uncertainty. The lack of information is not a problem of imperfect information, but rather reflects the fact that the future is unknown and unknowable. The impossibility of knowing *a priori* the length of time it will take for the innovation to be found, the cost of this innovation and its acceptance by the market, all have the same nature, as e.g. the impossibility of knowing *a priori* 'the price of copper and the rate of interest twenty years hence, or the obsolescence of a new invention' as Keynes pointed out (1973b). Moreover, knowledge incompleteness can also be interpreted as a lack of skill in recognising the main probability relation (a/h). The specification of the sources of uncertainty by the NS approach only helps us to understand the different degrees of uncertainty associated with different innovations. However, from a theoretical point of view, the Keynesian approach, being more comprehensive, is capable of encompassing the NS approach to uncertainty. Thus, as a starting point to the discussion here proposed, we think that the use of Keynesian uncertainty can provide new insights to the analysis of technical change.

The second aspect to be analysed is the knowledge used in an innovative activity. There are important contributions from the NS that help us understand this aspect. First of all, one has to keep in mind that there are different types of innovation with different degrees of uncertainty (Freeman and Soete 1997; Kay 1979). Roughly speaking, the most important difference is between radical and incremental innovations, where the former is based on completely new knowledge and the latter on pre-existing knowledge.

The decision-making process related to radical or incremental innovation will differ according to the role of previous knowledge. Here the concepts of technological paradigm and technological trajectory are very helpful. One can, in a simplified manner, identify the introduction of a new TP as a radical innovation, and the development of one of many possible TTs as a process of incremental innovation. Therefore, in the case of radical innovation, the knowledge (premiss) that will be used as a ground for the innovation decision is limited and extremely weak, and the future response of the market is very uncertain. In other words, there is a low reliability of the evidence that is used to decide whether to introduce an innovation. On the other hand, the incremental innovation is based on existing knowledge, defined by the TP. Moreover, as one develops along a TT, the introduction of successive incremental innovations result in the accumulation of knowledge and so the premise for the decision becomes better founded.

One of the most important kinds of knowledge is tacit knowledge - that knowledge that comes from experience but is not codified in manuals or books. Tacitness is a fundamental factor in the cumulative aspect of the innovative activity. As one moves along a TT, one's knowledge increases for two reasons: (i) the innovator improves his/her understanding of the technology that he/she is using,[14] and (ii) also, he/she improves his knowledge about market behaviour in relation to this previous innovation. Thus, there is a learning process, which is similar to the learning process implicit in Keynes's theory of probability. What is changing in this process is the weight, defined as the degree of completeness of the information set. A successful move through the TT increases the relevant knowledge about the technology and market behaviour in relation to this specific technology and, simultaneously, decreases the relevant ignorance. As a consequence, the state of confidence in the success of the introduction of a new innovation becomes greater.

Moreover, at each improvement of the product/equipment, the set of premisses increases, and as past innovations have been successfully introduced, the new premises work to increase the probable knowledge about the success of a new innovation. This approach helps us to understand the different degrees of uncertainty associated with different kinds of innovation.

As said before, probable knowledge can be seen as a guide in situations where uncertainty prevails, and the degree of reliability in this probable knowledge - confidence - determines the degree of uncertainty that exists in a specific situation. In the case of the development of a technological trajectory, one can see that the probable knowledge about the success of the introduction of an innovation is increasing and so the reliability of this probable knowledge as a guide to conduct increases as well. Thus, confidence is increasing and the degree of uncertainty decreasing.

However, there are situations in which either the introduction of an innovation is not successful or the search for technological solutions leads to a creation of new knowledge that increases the uncertainty about the future.[15] In these cases, the relevant ignorance is increasing due to ignorance about market conditions (meaning the acceptance of the innovation) or due to ignorance about the technology itself. In both cases, the weight is decreasing and so is confidence. Thus, the degree of uncertainty increases and may either determine a change on the technological trajectory or show the need for more research in the same trajectory. In any case, these situations imply a decrease in confidence in the introduction of the next innovation.

What has so far been discussed can be formalised in the following way. The main question faced by the innovator when deciding whether or not to develop and to introduce an innovation is the profitability of the innovation. In Keynes's probability terms the question is: What is the reliability of the success of an innovation (conclusion *a*) given the features of the TP and TT (premisses *h*)? Formally, we have:

ag_j = conclusion: 'the innovation *gj* will be profitable', where:
j = technological age of the innovation;
if g_j is a radical innovation, then $j = 1$;
if g_j is an incremental innovation, then $j > 1$;
h_j = set of premisses when the innovator is deciding whether or not to develop and introduce an innovation *j*.

Basically *hj* is the knowledge about the variables that affect the investment decision, including the knowledge about the technical characteristics of the new innovation, the knowledge of the outcome (successful or not) of the introduction of the innovation g_{j-1} (in other words, the knowledge about TP and TT).

$V_j (ag/h_j)$ is the weight of argument related to the development and introduction of an innovation *j*;
V_j is the relevant knowledge and relevant ignorance about the technological trajectory in relation to its potential frontier.

Thus, what one wants to know is whether the existing probable knowledge is a reliable guide; in other words, the probable knowledge about '*a*' (success) for the innovation *g*, which has a technological age of *j*.

Now, one has to try to analyse the question put above in such a way as to incorporate the concepts of technological paradigm and technological trajectory. Table 13.3 below can help us to understand this process. It incorporates Tables 13.1 and 13.2 and introduces some elements of Keynes's theory of probability. Following Dow's approach, let us call the probability relation *ag/h* the 'structure'. At the beginning of the development of the trajectory, probable knowledge does not exist due either to the absence of the probability relation or the lack of skill in recognising it. This is the extreme case of uncertainty, and animal spirits or institutional factors will determine the decision of developing the trajectory.

A qualitative change occurs when one moves from stage 1 to stage 2. A previous fundamental discovery has been made and, thus, it is possible now

Table 13.3 Types of innovation and degrees of uncertainty

Type of Innovation (Technological Trajectory)	Order of Knowledge about the Structure	Weight of Argument $V_j = K_j / (K_j + I_j)$	Probable Knowledge ag_j/h_j	Degree of Uncertainty (U_j)
Fundamental research Fundamental invention $J = 1$	Non-existent	Non-existent	Absent or lack of skill to recognise ag_1/h_1	U_1: True uncertainty (extreme case)
Radical product innovations Radical process innovations outside firm $J = 2$	Low order of knowledge of structure	V_2: Very low weight $K_2 < K_2$	ag_2/h_2	U_2: Very high degree of uncertainty $U_2 < U_1$
Major product innovations Major process innovations in own establishment or system $J = 3$	High order of knowledge of structure		$Ag_3/h_3 > ag_2/h_2$	U_3: High degree of uncertainty $U_3 < U_2$

Table continued over leaf.

New 'generations' established products $J=4$	High order of knowledge of structure	V_4: Medium Weight $K_3 < K_4 \approx I_4$	$Ag_4/h_4 > ag_3/h_3$	U_4: Moderate uncertainty $U_4 < U_3$
Licensed innovation Imitation of product innovations Modifications of products and process Early adoption of established process $J=5$	High order of knowledge of structure	V_5: High Weight $V_3 > V_2$ $K_2 < K_3 < I_3$	$Ag_5/h_5 > ag_4/h_4$	U_5: Little uncertainty $U_5 < U_4$
New 'model' Product differentiation Agency for established innovation Minor technical improvements Late adoption of established process $J=6$	High order of knowledge of structure	V_6: Very High Weight $V_6 > V_5$ $K_5 < K_6 < I_6$	$Ag_6/h_6 > ag_5/h_5$	

to recognise the probability relation, despite the fact that some degree of uncertainty about it exists (this explains the low order of knowledge of the structure *agj/hj*). In this case, the weight of argument is very low due the acknowledgement of the relevant ignorance in this phase. Both the technological knowledge and the market responses to the innovation are very weak and, so, the degree of uncertainty is very high.

When the major innovations starts, knowledge on the structure has already been established, but the relevant ignorance is still greater than the relevant knowledge and, so, a high degree of uncertainty prevails.

What is important here is to understand the occurrence of three processes:

4. after introducing the innovation g_2, the investor goes through a process of learning, which creates tacit knowledge about the innovation. This allows him/her to increase his understanding of the possible future improvements in the innovation;
5. as this knowledge is in some extent tacit, the technological asymmetries between the investor and his/her competitors increase, increasing thus confidence that he/she will be not superseded by another competitor with a better innovation;
6. as the innovation g_2 is introduced with success - it has been accepted by the market - the investor becomes more confident about the possibility of success of the incremental innovation g_3.

These processes operate to increase the weight for the next innovation, decreasing the degree of uncertainty attached to each innovation. At the end of the trajectory (product differentiation), the relevant knowledge - technological and economic viability - is very well established and there is a very low degree of uncertainty. A good example of this situation is the computer industry. For the firms that are well established in the market, the uncertainty inherent in the decision to introduce a new generation of personal computer is very low due to the relevant knowledge these firms possess.

The process of development of a technological trajectory discussed above represents a case of a successful trajectory. However, as said before, an innovator can also be surprised either by the introduction of a product with better technology, or if the research process shows that the relevant ignorance is bigger than was initially supposed. The innovator's response in this situation will depend on whether the new technology introduced by the competitor and/or the outcome of the research process represents a change on the technological paradigm. A change of the TP will affect not only the weight, but also the knowledge about the structure. There is no alternative for the investor other than to change his/her trajectory. If there is no change, there is no modification of the knowledge about the structure, but the weight decreases nonetheless. In this case, two things can happen: either the innovator allocates more effort on the research process to improve the innovator allocates more effort on the research process to improve the performance of his/her innovation or he/she changes his/her trajectory. One important aspect to determine what decision should be made is the position of the innovator inside the trajectory: the further he/she is on the technological trajectory (or the nearer he is phase 6) the more difficult it is to change trajectory.

The question to be raised here is the following: to what extent does the use of probable knowledge improve the description of the decision-process related to the introduction of an innovation? Part of the answer has been given before, as it was argued that routines are insufficient to deal with the last act of a problem-solving activity, that is, the final choice in each problem-solving process. However, what remains to be considered is the role of probable knowledge (and weight of argument) in dealing with all aspects of uncertainty inherent the innovative activity.

Although the discussion has mainly been concerned with technical and market uncertainties, a full account of the decision to introduce an innovation warrants the analysis of business uncertainty as well. As an investment decision, the introduction of an innovation has to deal with *all* aspects of this decision, not those only affected by technological and market factors, but also by the investors' perception of the economic environment as a whole.

The weight of argument in this case should not be viewed as incorporating only the relevant knowledge and ignorance related to technological and market problems, but also the relevant knowledge and ignorance on all aspects that affect the investment decision. In this sense, the increase of technological knowledge on a technological trajectory does not necessarily increase the probable knowledge on the success of the introduction of an innovation if the business ignorance was increased for some other reason. In this case, even when walking along a successful technological trajectory, a decision about the introduction of an innovation may be postponed.

4. CONCLUSION

We think that the ideas outlined above could represent a possible link between the NS approach to technical change and Keynes's theory of probability. First, the NS approach to innovation stresses the importance of uncertainty as a feature always present in the innovative activity. To deal with this uncertainty NS theorists have developed the concept of routines.

Moreover, the concept of technology used by this approach sheds light on features such as cumulativeness, appropriability and knowledge base, which are incorporated in the technological paradigm and technological trajectory. These factors shape the routines that are used by the firms.

However, as uncertainty is never eliminated, routines themselves are not sufficient to explain the decision-making process during the introduction of an innovation. They explain the use of the premisses used in this process, but they do not explain the logical development of this choice. A decision remains to be made: whether to introduce an innovation or not?

At this point, we have tried to show that Keynes's theory of probability can complete the set of tools required to understand that process. From the use of Keynes's probability it is clear that this process can be seen as rational, despite the fact that one may never know for certain whether the innovation will be a success. The concepts of probable knowledge and weight of argument are the key factors in the understanding of the rationality that is behind the development of a technological trajectory. Routines embody the knowledge accumulated, and they are constrained by the *Treatise on Probability*. The learning process that occurs during the continuous innovative activity weakens the influence of some sources of the uncertainty related to the investment process. The basis on which successive decisions to introduce innovation is found becomes more sound as both weight of argument (state of confidence) and the probable knowledge increase, driving the formation of the expectation in the same direction.

Thus, one can say that routines form the premisses (h) upon which the decision is taken. Based on these routines, a probable knowledge of the success of the introduction of the innovation can be established, and as new routines are developed, as a result of the innovative process, the weight of argument changes.

NOTES

1. The author is grateful to Professor Victoria Chick, Dr. Jochen Runde, and Fabiana Santos for their useful comments on earlier versions of this paper. Needless to say, the usual disclaimers apply. Scholarship from CNPq (Brazilian Government) is also gratefully acknowledged.
2. This distinction first arises in Knight's works: 'It will appear that a measurable uncertainty, or 'risk' proper, as we shall use the term, is so far different from an unmeasurable one that it is not in effect an uncertainty at all. We shall accordingly restrict the term 'uncertainty' to the cases of the non-quantitative type' (1921, p. 20).
3. We will not discuss Keynes's theory of probability in its details as this discussion has already been done by other scholars. For the present we will only make a brief presentation of the general ideas.
4. According to Dow (1996, p. 15), 'An organic system involves interdependencies which preclude the selection of one set of axioms as universally causal; it also involves interdependencies which are complex and evolutionary, and thus not amenable to formulisation with respect to separable elements within a single system of reasoning.'

5. Where '≥ * is the qualitative probability relation "at least as probable as"' (Runde 1997, p. 223).
6. However, this situation is admitted as not feasible: 'As uncertainty is compounded at higher recursive levels, our necessary conceptual structures become complex, counterintuitive and involuted to the point that they collapse under their own weight. Put in another way, absolute ignorance is incompatible with knowledge of absolute uncertainty.' (Dow 1995, p. 124)
7. As pointed out by Runde (1998, p. 3), this definition follows along the lines of Knight's definition.
8. For a review about the critics to these approaches, see Dosi 1982.
9. This group is also called evolutionary or institutionalist. However, as these labels have been used to classify theoretical approaches which cover more than technological aspects of the economic system, we prefer to use the label neo-Schumpeterian, as the main concern of the essay is technical change.
10. It is important to note that although uncertainty can be reduced, it is never eliminated. According to Mansfield *et al* (1977, quoted from Dosi 1988, p. 1134), 'even when the fundamental knowledge base and the expected directions of advance are fairly well known, it is still often the case that one must first engage in exploratory research, development, and design before knowing what the outcome will be [...] and what some manageable results will cost, or, indeed, whether very useful results will emerge.' (Mansfield *et al.*, 1977).
11. In Nelson and Winter's words: 'the relationship of routine behaviour to innovation is centered on a simple distinction between organisational activity directed to innovation (or problem-solving more generally) and the results of such activity. (1982, p. 132)
12. Nelson and Winter give an illustrative example: 'the case of systematic sequential search of a well-defined population for an element with attributes that makes it the solution to a well-defined problem. When and whether a solution will be found may be quite uncertain, but the search itself follows a routine with a simple structure: select element, test for desired attributes, terminate with success if attributes are present, select next element if they are not. (1982, p. 132)
13. The concept of path-dependency is very useful in grasping why these routines are conditioned by the technological paradigm. For a discussion of this point, see David (1985) and Rosenberg (1994).
14. Remember that technology is never a free good. The technological solution for one specific problem is always constrained by the technical characteristics of the technological paradigm, and these characteristics are not known *ex ante*.
15. This is very common in those situations where the new knowledge contradicts previous knowledge taken for granted.

REFERENCES

Carabelli, A. (1985), 'Cause, chance and possibility', in T. Lawson and H. Pesaran (eds), *Keynes's Economics: Methodological Issues*, London: Croom Helm.

Carabelli, A. (1988), *On Keyne's Method*, London: Macmillan Press.

Carabelli, A. (1992), 'Organic interdependence and the choice of units in the General Theory', in B. Gerard and J. Hillard (eds), *The Philosophy and Economics of J. M. Keynes*, Aldershot, UK and Broomfield, US: Edward Elgar.

Carabelli, A. (1995), 'Uncertainty and measurement in Keynes: probability and organicness', in S. Dow and J. Hillard (eds), *The Philosophy and Economics of J. M. Keynes*, Aldershot, UK and Broomfield, US: Edward Elgar, pp. 137-160.

David, P. (1985), 'Clio and the economics of QWERTY', *American Economic Review*, 75, pp. 332-7, reprinted in C. Freeman (ed.) (1990), *The Economics of Innovation*, Aldershot, UK and Broomfield, US: Edward Elgar.

Dosi, G. (1982), 'Technological paradigms and technological trajectories', *Research Policy*, vol. II, pp.147-162.

Dosi, G. (1988a), 'The nature of the innovative process', in G. Dosi, C. Freeman, N. R., G. Silverberg and L. Soete (eds) *Technical Change and Economic Theory*, London: Pinter Publishers.

Dosi, G. (1988b), 'Sources, procedures and microeconomic effects of innovation', *Journal of Economic Literature*, XXVI:1120-71, reprinted in C. Freeman (ed.) (1990), *The Economics of Innovation*.

Dosi, G. and M. Egidi (1991), 'Substantive and procedural uncertainty', *Journal of Evolutionary Economics*, 1, pp.145-68.

Dosi, G. and L. Orsenigo (1988), 'Coordination and transformation: an overview of structures, behaviours and change in evolutionary environments', in G. Dosi, C. Freeman, N. R., G. Silverberg and L. Soete (eds), *Technical Change and Economic Theory*, London: Pinter Publishers, pp. 13-37.

Dosi, G., D. Teece, and J. Chytry (1998), *Technology, Organization and Competitiveness: Perspectives on Industrial and Corporate Change*, Oxford: Oxford University Press.

Dow, S. (1995), 'Uncertainty about uncertainty', in S. Dow and J. Hillard (eds), *Keynes, Knowledge and Uncertainty*, Aldershot: Edward Elgar.

Dow, S. (1996), *The Methodology of Macroeconomic Thought: a Conceptual Analysis of Schools of Thought in Economics*, Cheltenham, UK: Edward Elgar.

Dow, S. and J Hillard (eds) (1995), *Keynes, Knowledge and Uncertainty*, Aldershot: Edward Elgar.

Farmer, M. (1995), 'Knowledgeability, actors and uncertain worlds', in S. Dow and J. Hillard (eds), *Keynes, Knowledge and Uncertainty*, Aldershot: Edward Elgar.

Fransman, M. (1998), 'Information, knowledge, vision, and theories of the firm', in G. Dosi, D. Teece, and J. Chytry (eds), *Technology, Organization and Competitiveness*, Oxford: Oxford University Press.

Freeman, C. and L. Soete (1997), *The Economics of Industrial Innovation*, London: Penguin Books.

Giddens, A. (1982), *Profiles and Critiques*, London: Macmillan.

Giddens, A. (1984), *The Constitution of Social Theory*, London: Macmillan.

Harcourt, G. and P. Riach (1997), *A Second Edition of The General Theory*, vols. 1 and 2. London and New York: Routledge.

Kay, N. (1979), *The Innovating Firm*, London: The Macmillan Press.

Keynes, J.M. (1973a), 'Essays in Biography', in D. Moggridge (ed.), *The Collected Writings of John Maynard Keynes*, vol. X, London: Macmillan Press and Cambridge University Pres.

Keynes, J.M. (1973b), 'The General Theory and after: Part II. Defence and development' in D. Moggridge (ed.), *The Collected Writings of John Maynard Keynes*, vol. XIV, London: Macmillan Press, p. 583.

Keynes, J.M. (1973c), 'The general theory of employment, interest and money', in D.M.A.E. Johnson (ed.), *The Collected Writings of John Maynard Keynes*, vol. VII, London: Macmillan, St Martin's Press and Cambridge University Press, p. 428

Keynes, J.M. (1973), 'A Treatise on Probability', in D. Moggridge (ed.), *The Collected Writings of John Maynard Keynes*, vol. VIII, London: Macmillan Press.

Koopman, B. (1940), 'The axioms and algebra of intuitive probability', *Annals of Mathematics*, vol. 41, pp. 269-92.

Lawson, T. (1985) 'Uncertainty and economic analysis', *Economic Journal*, vol. 95, pp. 909-27.

Lawson, T. (1988), 'Probability and uncertainty in economic analysis.' *Journal of Post Keynesian Economics*, vol. 11, pp. 38-65.

Lawson, T. (1997), *Economics & Reality*, London: Routledge.

Nelson, R. and S. Winter (1977), 'In search of useful theory of innovation', *Research Policy*, vol. 6, pp. 37-76.

Nelson R. and S. Winter (1982), An Evolutionary Theory of Economic Change, Belknap, Harvard.

O'Donnell, R. (1989), *Keynes: Philosophy, Economics and Politics*, London: Macmillan.

O'Donnell, R. (1990), 'An overview of probability, expectations, uncertainty and rationality in Keynes's Conceptual Framework', *Review of Political Economy*, vol. 2, pp. 253-66.

Rosenberg, N. (1976), *Perspectives on Technology*, Cambridge: Cambridge University Press.

Runde, J. (1990), 'Keynesian uncertainty and weight of argument', *Economics and Philosophy*, vol. 6, pp. 275-92.

Runde, J. (1991) 'Keynesian uncertainty and stability of beliefs', *Review of Political Economy*, vol. 3, pp. 125-45.

Runde, J. (1997), 'Keynesian methodology', in G. Harcourt and P. Riach (eds) *A 'Second Edition' of The General Theory*, vol. 2, London and New York: Routledge, pp. 222-43.

Runde, J. (1998) 'Some links between Keynes's "A Treatise on Probability" and "General Theory"', mimeo.

PART III

Perspectives

14. Instituted Economic Processes, Increasing Returns and Endogenous Growth

J.S. Metcalfe[1]

INTRODUCTION

The way in which economies grow in scale and change in structure has been a central concern of economists and economic historians since the earliest days of these disciplines. The diversity of growth experience according to place and time, the changing ranking of firms, sectors and countries by their growth records, create together several of the major intellectual puzzles of our age. In this essay I propose to explore economic change from an evolutionary perspective and to use this approach as a framework to emphasise the interacting roles of firms, institutions and markets in economic growth. In particular, I shall suggest that the interaction between markets and innovation systems plays a central role in generating technical progress and in translating new knowledge into economic growth. The case for this evolutionary perspective rests ultimately on two claims: that it can give an explanatory role to the enormous range of differences in behaviour of individuals, firms and other organisations; and that this explanatory role hinges on the co-ordinating role of markets and other institutions. The most important consequence to follow from this view is that modern capitalist economies are inherently restless. In Schumpeter's terms, they are incessantly being transformed by the acquisition of new knowledge, which arises as a joint product with 'real' economic activities. Such knowledge-based economies enjoy various degrees of coordination but they are never in equilibrium, if we mean by that a state of rest or a balanced growth in which all activities expand at a common rate.

This approach is quite different from the modern development of macroeconomic models of endogenous growth, which also place a strong emphasis on knowledge generation. Although we can certainly measure growth at the macro level, it cannot be understood there; the comprehension must arise from the understanding of micro forces and their coordination. Thus the wellsprings of economic growth must be found in the many sources of microeconomic creativity which interact to produce economic growth at firm, sector and economy levels. In this regard, the overarching point that I wish to emphasise is that the growth of an economic system is inseparable from the pattern of development of that system.

One consequence of this approach is that we can treat the process of economic growth at a series of interconnected levels. The more we aggregate, the more we average away the diversity of experience, which provides the essential clue to the growth process. For an emphasis on structural change is simply another way of focusing upon the variety of growth rates within and between economies, and the higher the level of aggregation, the less is the observable diversity. On the other hand, as we come closer to the micro level of firms, we risk being overwhelmed by the immense variety of experience and the apparent negligible significance of individual events. I shall argue that we can provide strong links between the micro and the macro by focusing on the processes of coordination and their implications for the rules by which we aggregate micro behaviour into macroeconomic consequences. That coordination plays the central role in this story should not surprise anyone, but equally coordination should not be confused with equilibrium. Economic growth is open-ended: the way in which it is co-ordinated strongly influences from within the manner in which one position evolves into another. Behind this inherently restless nature of capitalist economies lie two important insights. First, that the dynamic properties of the economy depend on its structure and that structure changes endogenously in response to the dynamic process. Secondly, that a key dynamic process relates to innovation, or more generally to the accumulation of practically applicable knowledge and its translation into economic consequences. The foundations of economic growth lie in what is understood but what is understood, the knowledge we possess, is itself deeply dependent on how firms, sectors and economies grow. Growth of knowledge and growth of the economy are simultaneous and interdependent processes.

Now this is nothing new to anyone who has reflected on Schumpeter or Marshall or Marx. Moreover, much recent work in the evolutionary tradition (Nelson and Winter 1982; Saviotti and Mani 1995; Silverberg and Verspagen 1998; Eliasson 1996, 1998; Day 1998) takes these insights and explores them through the medium of simulation models. I want to complement these contributions by working through the insights provided by a different tradition, that associated with Adam Smith, Allyn Young, and Nicholas Kaldor. I shall combine increasing returns and evolutionary processes to explore the way in which micro development leads to the macroeconomics of growth. As we shall see, this involves making a distinction between two kinds of evolutionary process, one in relation to selection, the other in relation to sorting. Needless to say, like any tractable growth theory this remains a partial account. I have chosen to emphasise some features of a dynamic economy and suppress others, but my concern is to illustrate one approach, not to provide an all-encompassing explanation.

Before turning to this task, I should make clear what I consider to be a principle advantage of this micro-to-macro approach. It is that we can connect growth theory with rich literatures on topics such as innovation and its management and organisation, the history of technology, the capabilities of firms, and the nature and development of social and other institutions in which firms are necessarily embedded. These literatures fit naturally with an evolutionary emphasis on variety and development, and we should be able to connect them with what we understand to be an economics of growth. To take an economic approach should not preclude the ability to learn from other disciplinary approaches, and it is implicit in what I am arguing that a macroeconomic approach cannot connect effectively with this wider disciplinary context.

By following this particular line of enquiry, I hope to achieve a number of objectives. Specifically: to deduce some wider consequences of a sectoral innovation perspective; to establish an empirical agenda, both in the narrow statistical sense and in terms of a broader agenda of qualitative case studies of innovation systems; to demonstrate the way in which aggregate growth theory can be written without resort to aggregate production functions or residual productivity measurement; and to develop evolutionary thinking in a general rather than a partial sense. Most of all, I intend this to be an account of growth that is in touch with history. Needless to add, the foundations of this approach are inherently evolutionary in the 'old' sense of the unfolding development of the technical capabilities of firms and sectors, and in the 'new' sense of processes of change driven by variety and selection.

1. EVOLUTIONARY THEORY AS GROWTH THEORY

Our starting point is the claim that evolutionary explanations are directed at understanding why a world consisting of particular entities changes, how rapidly and in which directions. More specifically, they are explanations of the sources of differential growth in the appropriate entities. Evolutionary theory is growth theory in this specific sense, and it is naturally micro growth theory. Broadly speaking, two kinds of change are involved (Metcalfe 1998). There are developmental processes in which the changes are internal to the appropriate entities, in our case firms. Accounts of innovation, imitation or any kind of novel, creative behaviour fall under this heading, and their evolutionary importance lies in the link with the generation of different, co-existing behaviours. Different behaviours are the basis for the second broad category of evolutionary process, namely variational change. This is concerned with the changing relative importance of the various entities in a population, and thus with the explanation of why growth rates differ. Of course the two broad processes of change are interdependent. Selection depends upon prior variation, but variation depends on differences in development processes and these cannot, in turn, be treated as independent of selection. Thus economic evolution, at least, is a three-stage process involving variety, selection and feedback, and this is why increasing returns is such an important part of this story: it shapes the regeneration of variety from within the economic process.

Evolutionary theorists have provided a useful distinction to frame our discussion of differential growth. Any process that creates differences in the growth rates of entities in a population leads to sorting, that is to say, a pattern of structural change in the relative importance or weight of the entities in the population. In this general category, selection processes are of a special kind: they translate variety in the behavioural characteristics of the entities into a pattern of differential growth through the intermediation of a specific coordination mechanism (Gould and Vrba 1986). The growth rate differences that arise are interdependent; they are mutually determined and can be equated with the notion of fitness differences. Nothing remotely tautological is involved in this. Fitness is caused, not causal; it is the outcome, not the explanation of selection.

In the economic and social sphere, it is obvious that the random regeneration of variety cannot carry much weight. The development of variation is a purposive, conjecture-dependent process. It surely meets all the conditions required for bounded rationality, and it is best seen as a process of guided variation. The combinatorial possibilities are too vast for practical knowledge to develop in any other way, so it is accumulated along paths which, at least *ex post*, appear clear (Petroski 1992; Pool 1997). Thus memory as well as expectation constrain the questions that guide the accumulation of knowledge. It is this idea of guided variation which I shall connect with the more economic notion of a technical progress function, specific to a particular pattern of activity and its associated knowledge base and institutional location.

2. COMPETITION, MARKETS AND INNOVATION SYSTEMS

Within the evolutionary economics perspective, a central role is given to institutions in terms of their role in generating and constraining economy variety and in their role in the coordination of decision making. Firms, or rather business units, are the key institutions in this regard. They are the locations for the accumulation of applicable knowledge, they are the principal sources of developmental change and their actions capture a central paradox of capitalism: that it creates coherent patterns of economic order through the market coordination of the vast diversity of uncoordinated creative behaviours. However, firms are much more than the sources of developmental change, determining what is produced and how; they also play key roles in the selection process. It is typically firms which set prices and shape the operation of the market institutions, which simultaneously constrain their price setting behaviour. Markets are essentially constructed devices for disseminating information concerning what is available and demanded and on what terms. Markets cannot do what firms do, and conversely. Now, from the evolutionary perspective, markets coordinate the process, which depends on the rivalry explicit in the differential behaviour of competing firms. In this regard, markets are to be judged not by their static equilibrium properties in relation to the efficiency on which given resources are allocated, but by their role in facilitating innovation and adaptation to new opportunities, new needs and new resources. There is an inevitable Austrian hue to this view of markets as selective institutions and indeed to the view of the market process as a device for discovering and accumulating new knowledge (Vanberg 1994).

Now it is particularly in regard to the opportunities to acquire new knowledge that firms are linked to a wider matrix of innovation supporting institutions (Carlsson 1995). Universities, public laboratories, research and design consultancies, suppliers and customers all play an important role in supporting firms as they innovate.[2] The manner in which a firm is connected with the appropriate set of institutions becomes a central issue in understanding the rate and direction of innovation in different sectors. Hence the importance of understanding that firms are embedded within wider sets of overlapping markets and other institutions that support the generation and exploitation of new knowledge. Indeed, the unique position of the firm is that it is located between different kinds of knowledge generating processes in relation to the scientific and technological knowledge of what is possible and the market knowledge of what is in demand, potential or actual. All of this is part of a wider dimension, one which locates the activities of firms within instituted economic processes (Polanyi et al 1957) and which provides a clear rationale to enquire into the social dimensions of economic growth (Abramovitz 1989; Hodgson 1994).[3]

This supporting matrix of institutions provides a distributed knowledge resource available to any firm, but raises the obvious question of how coordination between different institutions is to be achieved. The problem arises because of the specialised nature of the institutions on opposite sides of the science and technology interface. Science and technological knowledge may have in common a public good dimension but the ways in which the different bodies of knowledge are accumulated is quite different, the incentive structures for accumulation are quite different, and the respective institutional contexts are very different. Putting it broadly (and too broadly at that): science is open, technology is closed; science is judged in relation to accepted standards of 'truth', technology is judged in terms of accepted standards of 'utility'; science is theory driven, technology is trial and error driven. Thus, universities and firms reflect this division of labour and are, as a consequence, institutions with different objectives and different communication structures.

Given these differences, the prospect of knowledge transfer through the emergence of spontaneous order among specialised, differentiated knowledge generating institutions is likely to be limited. Consequently, the last two decades have seen serious attempts by policy makers to improve on this situation through policies aimed at a greater degree of bridging between public knowledge institutions and firms, and policies to develop a greater degree of coordination of their respective knowledge generating programmes. The emphasis in Europe, for example, upon collaborative research, the creation of specific bridging institutions and research programmes, and the development of foresight activity are each indicative of different aspects of the new innovation policies. The point about these bridging and coordination policies is that they seek to expand the problem-solving and problem-generating capacity of firms in regard to their innovative activities. But since innovation depends not only on basic scientific knowledge but also on a detailed practical knowledge of given artefacts, it follows that users and other suppliers often play a crucial role in the innovation systems in specific sectors (Lundvall 1992; Carlsson 1995). Market coordination of production and demand provides the background for coordinating innovation activity by identifying the relevant customers and suppliers.

In the evolutionary approach, institutions operate as loci of developmental change and as frameworks for sorting and selection, and these institutions are themselves subjected to developmental and variational change on different timescales. Consequently, there is much merit in looking at the competitive process at a number of interdependent levels. Competition in the market place with a given range of goods and processes at a moment in time is shaped by competition between different ways to innovate products and processes over time. Just as markets and innovation systems are constituted by interpenetrating networks of actors so the different levels of competition overlap and constrain one another.

3. EVIDENCE FOR ECONOMIC EVOLUTION

At this point it is worth pausing and enquiring as to the kinds of evidence which constitute support of an evolutionary approach. At one level this is provided by evidence on differential development, the infinite variety of innovations, radical and incremental, which figure in economic and technological history, each with its own economic characteristics in terms of resource utilisation and capacity to meet market needs. That these innovations often appear in connected sequences of developments, as trajectories, simply adds weight to the evolutionary dimension. At a different level, the evidence relates to differential growth of entities and thus to structural change. This is seen most sharply within industries in terms of the competitive process between firms promoting rival business conjectures in national and foreign markets. Indeed, changes in trade patterns are as good an index as one can find of economic evolution at work. Naturally, as we aggregate into sectors at higher levels we begin to average away the evidence for structural change and growth rate diversity so that change appears less abrupt, smoother, less a matter of competition in tooth and claw.

To give an illustration of the kinds of evidence that can throw light on economic evolution, we use the NBER-CES/Census Manufacturing Productivity Industry data base for the US economy compiled for 450, four digit manufacturing industries (sectors) over the period 1958-1994. This provides us with a vast amount of detail. To illustrate the main points to be made we have worked with employment data, which show considerable differences in employment generation which we can capture by the sectoral movements of employment shares. Obviously, if a sector is growing faster than average for the manufacturing sector as a whole, its share in total employment is increasing, and conversely. Figures 14.A and 14.B show the movements over time for the three sectors with strongest growth and the three sectors with strongest decline. However, to proliferate evidence of this kind soon runs into diminishing returns. Certainly it is evidence of structural change, but one naturally looks for ways of generating summary statistics.

One candidate is the Herfindahl index of employment shares (e_i), which is exactly the average market share, $H = \sum e_i(e_i) = \sum e_i^2$. Since this index is sensitive to changes in the level of aggregation we have produced a normalised

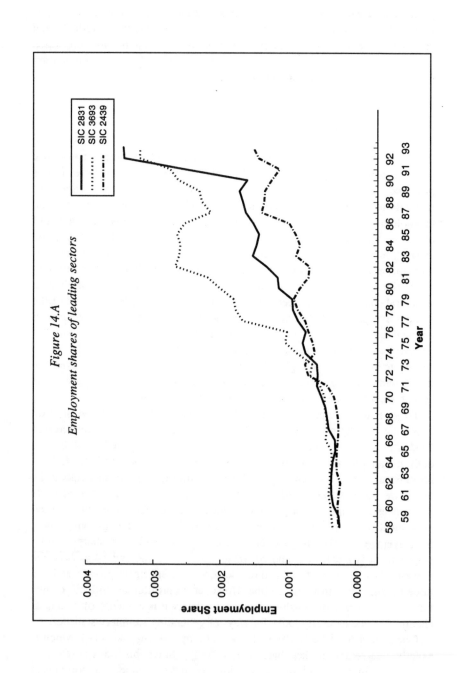

Figure 14.A
Employment shares of leading sectors

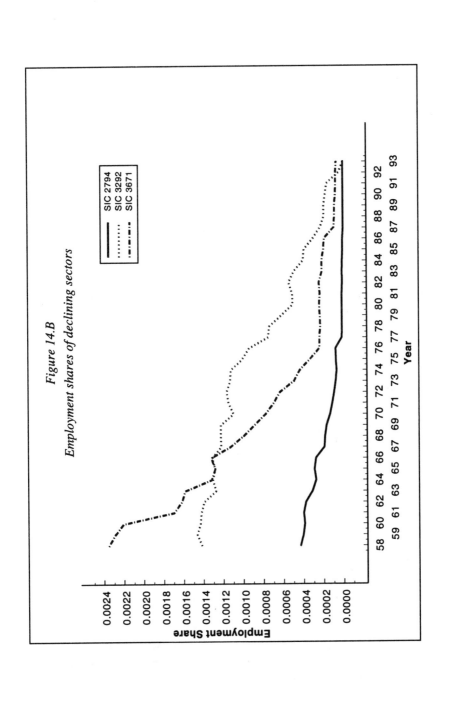

Figure 14.B
Employment shares of declining sectors

version, the adjusted Herfindahl, the movements of which are shown in Figure 14.C for employment and employment hours[4]. Now the interesting property of the Herfindahl is that its rate of change is measured by the covariation between employment shares and employment growth rates (g_i)

$$\frac{dH}{dt} = 2\sum e_i \frac{de_i}{dt} = 2\sum e_i^2 (g_i - g) = 2C_e(e_i, g_i)$$

The attraction of this statistic is that it provides an average measure of the degree of structural change in the system. If the Herfindahl is increasing, it is because the sectors with above-average employment share have above-average employment growth rates, and conversely when the Herfindahl is decreasing. If the Herfindahl is constant there is no statistical association between the two variables, as could happen, for example, if all the growth rates were the same. In Figure 14.C we see two broad phases in US manufacturing. From the late 1950s to the early to mid-1970s, the employment pattern is becoming less concentrated; on average, high growing sectors are low share sectors. After 1975 the pattern in US manufacturing is reversed, employment is becoming more concentrated as the higher than average share sectors grow more quickly. At this stage I have no explanation for this pattern of change but it is, I believe, clear evidence of economic evolution.

Since evolution is inherently connected with growth rate diversity, we can also take the (mean standardised) variance of the employment growth rates as a further index of evolutionary change. This is shown in Figure 14.D, and it is marked by a strong cyclical pattern coinciding with movements in the average growth rate.

The above brief account clearly provides evidence for economic evolution. It is certainly evidence for differential growth and sorting, but whether it is evidence for selection hangs first upon a theoretical articulation of a precise evolutionary process. In short, to go further we need a theory of evolutionary growth.

4. ENDOGENOUS GROWTH THEORY

By endogenous growth I mean a process by which the expansion in the scale and the composition of economic activity has positive feedback effects upon the productivity with which resources, in this context labour, are utilised.[5] Thus I interpret endogeneity in terms of the many ways in which increasing returns impinge upon the development of an economy. As such, endogeneity connects back to Adam Smith and Allyn Young, and, as Frank Knight put it,

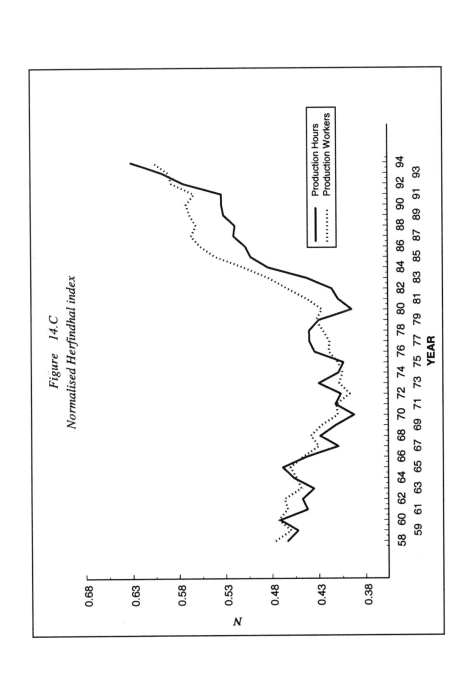

Figure 14.C
Normalised Herfindhal index

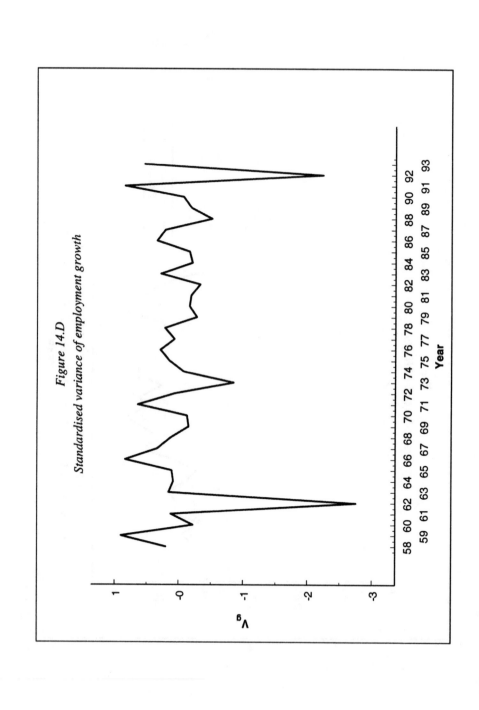

Figure 14.D

Standardised variance of employment growth

the self-exciting nature of the Smithian perspective on growth, in which the division of labour and the extent of the market are mutually determined.[6]

Young's (1928) work is particularly relevant to our evolutionary perspective. His emphasis on reciprocal interrelationship, in which every increase in supply of one commodity is simultaneously an increase in the demand (and thus supply) for other commodities, will provide us with the aggregation rules to construct the macro from the micro. Yet his is not a macroeconomic explanation of economic growth. Quite the contrary, growth depends on the dynamism of firms and sectors, and what matters are the processes of economic coordination that connect firms and sectors together in a reciprocally dynamic fashion. It is these connections which determine why some industries grow faster than others and the way in which progress is generated from within the economic system. Thus Young's account is simultaneously one of growth and structural change.

Modern endogenous growth theory developed as a reaction to Solow's growth model with the explicit aim of generating an economic explanation of the limits to growth. One branch of this theory plays down the role of diminishing returns to accumulation (Manuelli and Jones 1996), of which models with a fixed capital:output ratio, à la Harrod-Domar, are good exemplars.[7] A second branch eliminates the limits to growth by providing an economic explanation of the rate of total factor productivity growth, through externalities of some kind (Romer 1986; Lucas, 1988) or through an explicit 'residual factor' production function (Phelps 1966; Gomulka 1990; Jones 1995a, 1995b; Kremer 1993).

Since the latter attempt to deal with technical progress directly, they deserve serious attention, but my reading of them is that they are seriously flawed. It is not only that they equate the state of knowledge with the level of total factor productivity, or even that they conceive of an aggregate state of knowledge, reducible to a single number, assumptions which are certainly problematic in themselves. Rather it is that they seek to establish a steady state of knowledge accumulation as a characteristic of a growth equilibrium, and that they treat the conditions of knowledge accumulation as independent of the operation of the rest of the economy. Neither proposition is acceptable. The generation of knowledge is inherently open-ended, and much productive knowledge arises inseparably from the conduct of the economic activities of production and trade. Some of these approaches reflect too much the linear model of innovation and its corollary that the accumulation of knowledge about the natural world is the essential prerequisite for technical progress. Not only does this privilege science relative to technology, it also forgets entirely the role which practical knowledge of market application and organisation plays in the innovation process. It is an approach that also fails to recognise the very different conditions of innovation and technical progress in different sectors of the economy. We need, I suggest, a different approach, one approach which allows us to connect with the rich literatures on the history of technology and the conduct of innovation in firms, yet which allows the economic significance of innovations to be placed in the broader context of economic growth and development.[8] The way I propose to do this is to turn to the line of development suggested by Kaldor (1957), in which the 'production function' is replaced by a 'technical progress function' specific to the individual firm.[9] Such a concept is for the moment to be interpreted broadly but it is a core element in our endogenous growth theory, since it draws together the many ways in which increasing returns are built into the process of economic coordination.

I propose to develop the insights of endogenous growth theory by emphasising the following points, which provide a checklist on the rest of the essay:

- that the fundamental source of growth is innovation at the level of the firm, and that it is this which underpins structural change within and between economic sectors;

- that the micro growth perspective requires rules of aggregation to build up changes in the emergent sectoral and macroeconomic pictures, and that these dynamic rules are not always obvious;

- that there are major differences in the technical progress functions of different sectors which shape the overall pattern of growth and which should be a principal focus of empirical investigation;[10]

- that economic growth is open-ended with no necessary tendency to approach a steady state or attractor, and that, as a consequence we should build our understanding of growth around market and institutional coordination, not around equilibrium;

- that endogenous growth can be considered to be neither explosive nor automatic, but it is, in Jones' useful phrase, semi endogenous;

- that the institutions that shape innovation and the diffusion of innovation are central to the process of growth;

- that the evolution of demand and innovations in demand must be given equal weight with the evolution of product and process technology in any treatment of economic growth.

The formal development of the argument now proceeds in two stages. A full picture would allow for the introduction of new sectors and the demise of old ones, and with that the entry and exit of firms within and across sectors. While this can be done, we will ignore these complications by tracing the development of an economy with a given number of sectors and a given number of firms in each sector. We consider first the growth of productivity within a sector, making use of replicator dynamic arguments to discuss the process of competitive selection. We then turn to the determinants of the sectoral growth rates and the reciprocal interdependence of productivity growth rates.[11]

5. INNOVATION AND SELECTION WITHIN A SECTOR

Let us begin by developing the argument within a given sector, characterised by a given number of 'firms' producing a uniform good using different, idiosyncratic, production methods (Nelson 1989, 1991). The chief simplification we allow ourselves is that the capital coefficient, b, is the same for all firms and that all improvements within the sector are Harrod neutral. Measured in terms of wage units, at a common wage rate, unit costs for the ith firm are $h_i = a_i + bR$, R being the real rental on capital employed, and a_i being unit labour requirements. Labour productivity for the firm is, of course, $q_i = 1/a_i$. Let S_i be the share of firm i in the output of the sector and be the corresponding share of employment, so that $e_i a_i = s_i a_i$, $\bar{a}$. being $\sum s_i a_i$, average unit labour requirements in the sector. If $\hat{q}_. = \sum e_i q_i$, it follows that $\hat{a}_. \hat{q}_. = 1$. In what follows, all changes in unit costs will be associated with changes in technology, that is, with changes in production knowledge; there is no substitution within firms independently from innovation. It is, of course, a considerable simplification that product innovations are ruled out of this account, particularly in the light of the arguments below about the evolution of demand. However, the traditional reasons for following this particular pattern of enquiry will be obvious in terms of the literature on economic growth.

With these assumptions and definitions in mind, we can decompose the sectoral rate of productivity growth into two components, one reflecting productivity growth within firms and the other reflecting the changing relative importance of firms with different levels of productivity. The first is the innovation effect and the second is what I shall call the diffusion or selection effect, the differential growth of the rival firms arising out of the competitive process.

To deal with the first note that

$$\frac{d}{dt}\log q_i = -\frac{d}{dt}\log a_i = -\frac{1}{m_i}\frac{d}{dt}\log h_i$$

where m_i is the share of labour in unit costs. Then with $h_s = \sum s_i h_i$ it follows that

$$\frac{d}{dt}\log \overline{h}_s = \sum \frac{s_i h_i}{h_s}\left[m_i \frac{d}{dt}\log a_i + \frac{d}{dt}\log s_i \right] \qquad (1)$$

The first term within the bracket is, when aggregated, the own rate of technical progress for the sector; the second term is the competitive, diffusion effect, an average of the rates of change of market shares within that particular sector. It is this second term which provides the bridge between evolutionary competition and endogenous technical progress via the technical progress functions.

To proceed further, we require a 'technical progress function' for the individual firm, and we let this have an exogenous innovation component, α_i and an endogenous positive feedback component in relation to the growth rate of the firm. This latter could reflect traditional internal economies of scale (Metcalfe 1995), learning by doing, or the effect of investment as a carrier of increasing efficiency (Scott 1989; De Long and Summers 1991). For our purposes, it does not matter which of these sources of positive feedback contributes to the overall rate of efficiency enhancement.[12] The technical progress function, specific to each firm can then be written as

$$\frac{d}{dt}\log a_i = -[\alpha_i + \beta_i g_i] \quad , 0 < \beta_i < 1 \quad (2)$$

g_i being the growth rate of the firm's capacity, which will be also equal to the growth rate of its output as explained below. That the technical progress elasticity, β_i, is assumed to be the same for all the firms within the sector is not material to the argument. It follows from this specification that the average rate of increase in labour productivity across the population of firms in the sector due to technical progress alone is given by

$$\sum \frac{s_i a_i}{h_s}\frac{d}{dt}\log a_i = -\overline{m}_s \left[\frac{C_s(a,\alpha) + \beta_i C_s(a,g)}{\overline{a}_s} + \overline{\alpha}_s + \beta_i g_s \right] \qquad (3)$$

with $\overline{m} = \overline{a}_s / h_s$ being the average share of labour in aggregate unit costs, not aggregate reserve.

For any individual firm, the degree to which its rate of technical progress lies above or below the population average depends upon whether its innovation rate, α_i, is above or below average and upon whether its growth rate is above or below average. The innovation rate for a given firm will depend on its own efforts and abilities at innovation and on the extent to which it is able to catch up with more efficient firms by imitation. One may find an efficient firm, enjoying a high growth rate but a low rate of technical progress because its innovation imitation rate is too small. Conversely, an efficient firm may be growing slowly but rapidly improving its technology because of its intrinsic innovativeness. Feedback matters, but only in relation to the distribution within the population of efficiency and innovativeness.

Equation (3) is a typical evolutionary expression in which the change in average behaviour depends upon various moments of the relevant population distribution of behaviours. Of those, the average rate of innovation $\bar{\alpha}_s$ and the covariance $C_s(a,g)$ between levels of efficiency and rates of innovation depend upon the specifics of which firms innovate and by how much. Clearly it is beneficial to average progress if high efficiency firms also have high rates of innovation.[13] At this stage in our knowledge there is little more that can be said, save to stress the uncertainty that inevitably surrounds individual acts of creativity. Of the remaining terms much more can be said. Consider the covariance between unit labour requirements and rates of growth $C_s(a,g)$, a statistic that is at the heart of the competitive process. To determine this I rely upon arguments familiar in the evolutionary literature that specify an accumulation process for each firm and a separate process for the growth of its market. I have explored this replicator dynamic argument at length elsewhere (Metcalfe 1998), so perhaps I can be permitted a certain brevity at this point. Let the accumulation function be $g_i = f[p_i - h_i]$, p_i being the price set by firm i and f being the propensity to accumulate, which for ease of exposition is the same for each firm within the sector. For each firm, capacity grows in proportion to its unit profit margin. The rate of growth in the firm's particular market is given by $g_{Di} = g_D + \delta[\bar{p}_s - p_i]$, where g_D is the overall rate of market growth, $\bar{p}_s$ is the average price in the sector and δ is a coefficient that determines the speed of the market selection process (Metcalfe 1998; Phelps and Winter 1970; Iwai 1984). Let each firm set its normal price to equate the rate of growth of its capacity with the rate of growth of its market and, with the capital:output ratio the same in each firm, it follows that

$$C_s(a,g) = \sum s_i(g_i - g)h_i = -\Delta \sum s_i(a_i - \bar{a}_s)h_i = -\Delta V_s(a)$$

$$\Delta = \frac{\delta f}{f + \delta} \qquad\qquad (4)$$

In (4), Δ is the coefficient of selection, the parameter which determines how quickly the competitive process works, and which depends upon the operation of the institutions in the capital and product market, and $V_s(a)$ is the variance of unit labour requirements in the population. Having established that $C_s(a,g)$ is necessarily negative in only one term remains to be explained in (3), the sectoral growth rate g_s of capacity and output. Given our assumptions about firm behaviour, this is equal to g_D, the rate of growth of the market, the determination of which must wait until we consider the relationship between different sectors.

Corresponding to the diversity in unit costs and growth rates is a diversity in profit rates. The marginal firms just break even and any more efficient firms earn quasi-rents, which increase with their distance from the marginal firm. The average profit margin increases with the growth rate of the sector and decreases with the propensity to accumulate, while an individual firm's share in the total profit generated in a sector equals the contribution that firm makes to the average growth rate $(s_i g_i / g)$. It is essential to interpret their statements as a reflection not of imperfect competition but as a consequence of competitive selection driven by variety in behaviour. They are a reflection not of market power but of the dispersion of efficiency.

It remains to consider the diffusion term in (1), which follows immediately from the arguments leading to the determination of $C_s(a,g)$. This term reflects the differential growth of the competing firms and the corresponding comparative rates of diffusion of their different methods of production. It is given by

$$\sum \frac{s_i h_i}{h_i} \frac{d}{dt} \log s_i = \sum \frac{s_i h_i}{h_s}(g_i - g_s) = \frac{C_s(a,g)}{h_s}$$

$$= -\Delta \overline{m} \frac{V_s(a)}{\overline{a}_s} \qquad\qquad (5)$$

Again this is a typical evolutionary expression, the rate of change in average unit costs as a result of competitive selection is proportional to the variance in unit labour requirements across the population.[14] Of course, because of feedback, the rates of diffusion across firms influence the distribution of rates of technical progress, which redefines the distribution of labour efficiencies and thus the rates of diffusion. In this sense we have cumulative causation. Efficiency differences generate progress differences, which redefine the efficiency differences and so on. This is precisely what is meant by endogenous growth.

On combining (3), (4) and (5), we have an expression for the overall rate of productivity growth in the sector, namely,

$$\frac{d}{dt}\log \overline{q}_\iota = -\frac{d}{dt}\log \overline{a}_\iota = \overline{m}\left[\frac{C_\iota(a,\alpha) + \Delta(1-\beta_\iota)V_\iota(a)}{\overline{a}_\iota} + \overline{\alpha}_\iota + \beta_\iota g_D\right] \quad (6)$$

Notice how this combines evolutionary propositions with the Kaldor-Verdoorn dependence of efficiency gains upon the growth rate of the sector as expressed in the coefficient $\overline{m}, \beta_\iota$. This is the element of endogenous feedback that we require. Notice also that this feedback reduces but does not reverse the effect of the variance in efficiency upon the rate of growth in efficiency. A higher variance implies a higher rate of productivity growth.

In deriving these results, it is important to recognise that they depend upon the micro behaviour of firms and the coordination of those behaviours in a market context. Indeed, there is a direct link between the market institutions and the rate of productivity growth in the sector. To take one example, if the market in which firms sell is more efficient, the coefficient Δ will be larger, the variance of prices will be lower, and, as a consequence, for any given value of the variance in unit labour requirements, the rate of growth of productivity in the sector will be greater. An increase in the propensity to accumulate, perhaps reflecting a greater flow of funds into the sector, would have exactly the same effect. The way market institutions work matters greatly for competition and, with positive feedback, competition matters greatly for growth.

4. STRUCTURAL CHANGE, SECTORAL AND MACROECONOMIC PRODUCTIVITY GROWTH

We turn now to the patterns of change that arise between sectors and their macroeconomic consequences. The overall rate of productivity growth between two dates is clearly an amalgam of three separate effects: productivity change within sectors as discussed above; changes in the relative economic importance of these sectors; and the addition of new or deletion of old sectors between those dates. In terms of innovation, this is much in line with Mokyr's (1990) distinction between micro innovations incrementally developing the efficiency of an established sector and macro innovations that create new sectors. For the moment we leave aside the latter and focus on the developments within and between established sectors.

Demand, Sorting, and Structural Change

The evolution of average productivity within sectors has depended upon innovation and selection, the mutual determination of the different growth rates of rival firms in relation to their different efficiencies. This competitive process has been shown by Bailey *et al* (1992) to be particularly important in the micro explanation of productivity growth. In contrast to selection, sorting involves non-competitive differential growth and the most commonly postulated source of such intersectoral changes lies in hypotheses about the evolution of demand. Indeed, in pursuing this theme it will be clear that the evolution of demand must occupy a central position, for, as Pasinetti expressed it '. . . any investigation into technical progress must necessarily imply some hypotheses . . . on the evolution of consumer preferences as income increases'. He went further: 'Increases in productivity and increases in income are two facets of the same phenomenon. Since the first implies the second, and the composition of the second determines the relevance of the first, the one cannot be considered if the other is ignored' (my emphasis, 1981, p.69). In dealing with demand, there are three general matters to be considered: shifts in preferences as a direct consequence of technical progress, particularly associated with the emergence of new sectors; changes in average prices between sectors, particularly if the outputs concerned are close substitutes; and, the matter that Pasinetti considered, different income elasticities of demand for the different sectors. Like him, I treat only this latter effect, leaving the other mechanisms for further study.

Of course, in emphasising the role of income elasticities in the intersectoral sorting process, we should not be deluded into thinking that we have said anything terribly profound. What is needed is some empirical and conceptual understanding of the determinants of income elasticities in general, and in relation to innovation, in particular. This we do not yet have.

As is appropriate for this kind of growth analysis, we continue to assume that within each sector the growth of capacity matches the growth of demand, and use the same symbol g_i to denote both.[15]

Let n be the aggregate rate of employment growth (a work force of constant age structure) and ψ_j be the per capita income elasticity of demand for sector j. Then we can write the rate of growth of demand in that sector as

$$g_j = n + \psi_j \hat{q} \qquad (7)$$

where

$$\hat{q} = d \log \hat{q}/d_t$$

is the yet to be constructed aggregate rate of productivity increase. Now clearly $\hat{q}$ is a weighted average of the sectoral productivity growth rates, but what are the appropriate weights? To determine these weights, let n_j be the rate of growth of employment in sector j so that $g_j = n_j + \hat{q}_j$, whence $n_j - n = \psi_j \hat{q} - \hat{q}_j$. Now if we sum this last expression by the employment shares e_j we find that

$$\sum e_j (n_j - n) = (\sum e_j \psi_j) \hat{q} - \sum e_j \hat{q}_j = 0$$

since $\sum e_j n_j = n$ by definition. Thus our weighting scheme is provided by

$$\hat{q} = \frac{1}{\sum e_j \psi_j} \sum e_j \hat{q}_j \qquad (8)$$

Unless $\sum e_j \psi_j = 1$ these weights do not sum to unity.

To elaborate further upon the employment weighted sum of income elasticities, let z_j be the share of sector j in total output and note that $\sum z_j \psi_j = 1$, since aggregate output equals aggregate income. Then it follows immediately that

$$\sum e_j \psi_j = 1 + \frac{C_z(\psi_j \bar{a}_j)}{\bar{a}_z}$$

where $C_z(\psi_j \bar{a}_j)$ is the 'z'-weighted covariance between sectoral income elasticities and average unit labour requirements in each sector. Thus the employment weighted average of the income elasticities is only one if this covariance is zero, which, absent any compelling reason to think otherwise, we assume to be so.

This detour on weights being complete, let us return to the main argument and consider how the sectoral productivity growth rates are mutually determined. In so doing we are following the line of enquiry first emphasised by Young (1928), who saw clearly how increasing returns generates reciprocal interdependence of productivity growth between sectors. To do this, divide the elements in (6) into those whose aggregate contribution, H_j, is independent of the growth rate of output, and those whose contribution depends on the growth rate of output. Then we can write

$$\frac{d}{dt} \log \bar{q}_j = \hat{q}_j = H_j + \beta_j g_j \qquad (9)$$

when H_j contains all of the average, variance and covariance effects explained in the derivation of (6), which arise from the intrasectoral process of innovation, imitation and selection. This expression is the sectoral technical progress function, properly aggregated from the individual firm technical progress functions (2).[16]

Now using (7) and (8) this becomes

$$\hat{q}_j = H_j + \beta_j \left[n + \psi_j \left(\frac{\sum e_j \hat{q}_j}{\sum e_j \psi_j} \right) \right] \qquad (10)$$

Thus productivity growth in any sector increases with productivity growth in all other sectors provided that its output is a normal good. Such goods have complementary effects on each other's productivity growth. Equation (10) constitutes a set of simultaneous productivity growth equations, the solution of which in the two-sector case is sketched in Figure 14.1. The schedules Q_1 and Q_2 are the reciprocal interdependence functions (10), derived by averaging across the firms, and they intersect at 'a' to determine the respective co-ordinated rates of productivity growth. Through point 'a' draw the straight line L-L with slope, e_1/e_2, the relative employment shares, to intersect the 45° line at 'b'. This point measures the rate of aggregate productivity growth $\hat{q}$.[17] As drawn, $\hat{q}_1 > \hat{q} > \hat{q}_2$. Consider now point 'c' and its related point 'd', which depict the pattern of productivity growth if there are no feedback effects in either sector. The differences between point 'b' and 'd' is then a measure of the importance of reciprocal interdependence and increasing returns in the growth process.

To determine the aggregate rate of productivity growth, we simply multiply each equation (10) by the corresponding employment share weights (8) and sum to yield the following

$$\hat{q} = \frac{\overline{H}_e + \overline{\beta}_e n}{(\sum e_j \psi_j)(1 - \overline{\beta}_u)} \qquad (11)$$

In this expression, $\overline{H}_. = \sum e_j H_j$ and $\overline{\beta}_. = \sum e_j \beta_j$. The average progress elasticity, $\overline{\beta}_. = \sum e_j \beta_j$ is derived from the weights $u_j = e_j \psi_j / \sum e_j \psi_j$, the contribution that sector makes to the employment weighted average of income elasticities. Of course, the u_j are proper weights satisfying $\sum u_j = 1$. With $\overline{\beta}_. < 1$ we have semi-endogenous growth, and with $\overline{\beta}_. = 1$, explosive growth of a rather implausible kind.

Figure 14.E The coordination of productivity growth

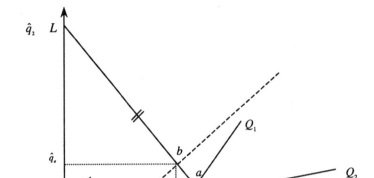

From this we see that endogenous growth amplifies the effects of innovation and selection within sectors and links the productivity dynamics of different sectors together in a transparent way which depends upon demand sorting linkages.[18] As drawn, the sectors are dynamic complements. Notice carefully, however, that Figure 14.1 represents a process of growth coordination at a point in time. It does not represent a growth equilibrium in some more general sense, an attractor towards which productivity patterns converge. Indeed, it is a fundamental assumption of the evolutionary perspective that growth is open-ended; there is no state of dynamic rest in the presence of innovation-driven growth. Thus points 'a' and 'b' are continually on the move, as the relative employment shares and the rates of innovation and diffusion vary over time.

Equation (11) is the properly constructed expression for aggregate productivity growth in this multisectoral economy. Positive endogenous growth with respect to the sectoral rates of technical progress H_j and with respect to the aggregate employment growth into n, arise in two ways. On the one hand, the within sectoral rates of productivity increase, H_j, are multiplied by the factor $e_j/(1-\beta_i)$, and on the other hand, the rate of employment growth is multiplied by the factor, $\beta_i = (1-\beta_i)$. It is a particular feature of the Young perspective that employment growth is associated with productivity growth, and that income elasticities and the technical progress function elasticities interact to boost the aggregate rate of productivity growth above the level which would hold in the presence of zero dynamic returns ($\beta_j = 0$). It is easily seen that the proportional bonus arising from reciprocal interdependence is measured by the ratio $bd/0d$ in Figure 14.1. It will also be clear that the greater the number of sectors in the economy that benefit from dynamic increasing returns, then the greater will be the boost from the forces of cumulative causation.[19]

Thus (11) combines the reasoning underlying the Kaldorian technical progress function with the reasoning behind semi-endogenous growth theory. The point about positive feedback, as Young emphasised, is that it augments growth within and between sectors, amplifying the wellspring of progress created by the within-sectoral innovation and diffusion rates.[20] In this way, we can comprehend Young's insistence that changes in one sector induce changes in other sectors, mutually reinforcing the growth of productivity in all the sectors. As he puts it, 'Every important advance in the organisation of production . . . alters the conditions of industrial activity and initiates responses elsewhere in the industrial structure which in turn have a further unsettling effect' (p.533). The precise form those changes in organisation take is not the issue; it is the reciprocal effects on productivity growth that matter. Could growth be more endogenous than this?

At this point, there is an obvious connection with one of Young's principal themes, namely that the growth of activity results in the progressive development of the division of labour. He focused his case on the adoption of more roundabout methods of mechanisation and capital usage, but we can readily substitute for this the emergence of more roundabout methods of knowledge production. As a sector grows, so one might expect the institutional ways in which new knowledge is acquired to change, new connections to be formed, old ones abandoned, and new specialisations to be created around the growing activity. That Young's analysis should apply to the generation of knowledge and the emergence of specialised knowledge generating activities is perhaps the most important aspect of this perspective on endogenous growth.

CONCLUSION

Three final remarks are appropriate. I have developed this essay entirely in the context of a closed economy, in contradistinction to much of the 'Kaldoran' literature which emphasises the role of foreign demand growth in the determination of domestic output growth. However, I consider it essential to develop first our understanding of growth in a closed economy, out of which can come an understanding of trade arising as a consequence of dynamic differences between national sectors. But that is for another occasion.

Moreover, I have not attempted to connect this picture of open-ended growth with the important growth and development literature developed in the 1950s by, among others, Hirschman (1958). This highly original literature linked growth to structural change within a world of disaggregated economic sectors, demand interlinkages and increasing returns to create exactly the kind of dynamic complementarity highlighted in this paper. In his Ohlin lectures, Krugman (1995) has provided a detailed critique of that literature, advancing the claim that it failed to develop, and is now largely forgotten, because it did not come to terms with the connection between increasing returns and imperfectly competitive markets. I doubt if this is the whole story. For the issue is not a question of increasing returns and the meaning of competitive equilibrium, but rather increasing returns in relation to the competitive process. This is the core of the Smith-Young-Kaldor perspective on which this essay has been built. There are many sources of and kinds of increasing returns, many of which are incompatible with any competitive equilibrium. In contrast, competition as a process takes all forms of increasing returns in its stride; they simply speed up competition, and in no way threaten the wreckage of the economic analysis. Hence growth, technical progress and the competitive process are inseparable. They are genuinely endogenous evolutionary processes driven by microeconomic diversity and coordinated by market and other institutions to generate emerging, ever-changing patterns of economic structure. If the development theorists have been forgotten it is more likely because the idea of equilibrium, competitive or not, was for them anathema.

One final point is to be emphasised, even at the risk of repetition I have made much of the idea that equilibrium capitalism is a contradiction in terms. By this I do not mean that we can dispense with market coordination as the central element in our economic understanding. One can dispense with particular hypotheses about individual behaviour, but one cannot dispense with interaction. How the pieces fit together is what the economics of growth and competition is about. It is not about equilibrium in the sense of the existence of and rapid convergence to independently defined states of rest, or even states in which all change of state is to be explained by extra economic forces. History is open-ended, and so is economic growth.

NOTES

1. A first draft of this paper was presented at the Italian Society of Labour Economists Conference in Messina, May 1997. I am grateful to Giovanni Pegoretti, Luigi Pasinetti, Gilberto Antonelli and Daniele Schilliro for helpful comments. Revised drafts were

presented at seminars at the University of Queensland, the University of New England and the Australian Defence Force Academy, in August 1997, and at CESPRI, Bocconi University in November 1997. I thank Malcolm Treadgold, Peter Hall, John Foster, Clem Tisdell, Franco Malerba, Fabio Montobbio, Francesco Lissoni and their respective colleagues for stimulating discussion. Colleagues in the School of Economic Studies also provided helpful comments at a seminar in February 1998. I am grateful to Ronnie Ramlogan who prepared the statistical material, and to Sharon Dalton and Deborah Woodman who helped greatly in producing the final draft.

2. The innovation systems literature is vast. See in particular, Lundvall 1992; McKelvey 1996; Nelson 1993; Freeman 1987; Carlsson 1995, 1997 and Edquist 1997 for authoritative treatments. Marshall provides a detailed discussion of innovation systems in all but name, three quarters of a century before the idea resurfaced! (Marshall, 1919, p. 100 *et seq.*).

3   See Murmann (1998) for an absorbing account of the coordination of markets and innovation systems in the synthetic dye industry.

4. If n is the number of sectors, the adjusted Herfindahl is given by $h = (nH - I)/(n - I)$. Notice that the square root of the statistic $(nH - I)$ also measures the coefficient of variation of employment levels. We have also used the normalised entropy index $\sum e_i \log e_i / \log n$, but the general picture is the same.

5. Notice that endogeneity would apply just as well with negative feedback but with constricting rather than enhancing effects on growth.

6. 'Thus change becomes progressive and propagates itself in a cumulative way' (Young 1928, p. 533).

7. See Kurz (1996) for an excellent critical view of the literature along the lines that there is nothing new under the sun.

8. For three very different approaches compare Mokyr (1990), Cameron (1989) and Landes (1998).

9. For an excellent account of Kaldor's ideas, see Targetti (1992). Further development of this strand of endogenous growth theory is contained in the work of Eltis (1973) and Scott (1989). The literature on Kaldor's technical progress function is immense. For a useful summary list of references see Setterfield (1997).

10. This is an old problem. Classical economists portrayed manufacturing as dynamic and agriculture as stagnant; for modern economists, the principal issue relates to where services fall in this spectrum of possibilities (Gershuny and Miles, 1983).

11. Entry and exit of firms in a sector are considered at length in Metcalfe (1998). The creation and deletion of sectors is more complicated for reasons which become clear below.

12. The empirical embodiments of the relationship are the Kaldor-Verdoorn Law and the Fabricant Law. For detailed, up to date discussion of the empirical issues see Scott (1989) and Targetti and Foti (1997).

13. Note that (3) can be derived equivalently by weighting each rate of reduction in unit labour requirements by that firm's share in total sectoral employment and summing to give the bracketed part of (3).

14. Elsewhere I have termed this relationship 'Fisher's Principle', after the eminent English statistician and geneticist who first applied it to evolutionary theory. See Metcalfe (1995) and (1998) for further discussion.

15. From now on I suppress intersectoral subscripts. Thus g_j is to be read as the appropriate sectoral average.

16. Empirical results not reported here find that the progress elasticities for 97% of the 450 sectors discussed in section 3 above lie in the range between zero and one. More refined estimation procedures are unlikely to significantly alter this picture.

17. Strictly speaking it determines the value of $(\sum e_j w_j) \dot{q}$, but having set $\sum e_j w_j = I$ the text follows.

18. Another way to generate interdependence would be to assume spillovers between technical progress functions, but that is another story. One way forward might be to make the innovation rate in each firm also depend on the innovation rate in the sector. But clearly there are a wide range of options to explore.

19. In Figure 14.1 it is clear how an increase/decrease in any H_j raises/lowers the aggregate growth rate according to the principle of reciprocal interaction.
20. Of course, it is trivially obvious that without innovation there would be no technical progress functions, no positive feedback and no productivity growth. We haven't yet escaped from Usher's warning that no progress means no growth (1980).

REFERENCES

Abramovitz, M. (1989), *Thinking About Growth*, London: Cambridge University Press.

Bailey, N.M., C. Hulten, and D. Campbell (1992), 'Productivity dynamics in manufacturing plants', *Brookings Papers*, Microeconomics, pp. 187-267.

Cameron, R. (1989), *A Concise Economic History of the World*, London: Oxford University Press.

Carlsson, B. (1995), *Technological Systems and Industrial Dynamics*, Kluwer, Dordrecht.

Day, R. (1998), 'Bounded rationality and firm performance in the experimental economy', in G. Eliasson, C. Green and C.R. McCann, *Micro Foundations of Economic Growth: A Schumpeterian Perspective*, Ann Arbor: University of Michigan Press.

De Long, B. and L.H. Summers (1991), 'Equipment investment and economic growth', *Quarterly Journal of Economics*, Vol. 106, pp. 445-503.

Edquist, C. (1997), *Systems of Innovation: Technologies, Institutions and Organizations*, London: Pinter.

Eliasson, G. (1996), 'Endogenous economic growth through selection', in J. Harding (ed.), *Microsimulation and Public Policy*, Amsterdam: North Holland.

Eliasson, G. (1998), 'On the micro foundations of economic growth', in J. Lesourne and A. Orléan (eds), *Advances in Self Organization and Evolutionary Economics*, London: Economica.

Eltis, W. (1973), *Growth and Distribution*, London: Macmillan.

Freeman, C. (1987), *Technology Policy and Economic Performance*, London: Pinter.

Gershuny, J. and I. Miles (1983), *The New Service Economy*, London: Pinter.

Gomulka, S. (1990), *The Theory of Technological Change and Economic Growth*, Routledge.

Gould, S.J. and E.S. Vrba (1986), 'The hierarchical expansion of sorting and selection: sorting and Selection cannot be equated', *Paleobiology*, vol. 12, pp. 217-28.

Hirschman, A. (1958), *The Strategy of Economic Development*, Yale University Press.

Hodgson, G. (1994), *Economics and Evolution*, Cambridge: Polity Press.

Iwai, K. (1984), 'Schumpeterian dynamics: part II', *Journal of Economic Behaviour and Organization*, vol. 5, pp. 321-51.

Jones, C.I., (1995a), 'RandD-Based models of economic growth', *Journal of Political Economy*, Vol. 103, pp.759-804.

Jones, C.I., (1995b), 'Time series tests of endogenous growth models', *Quarterly Journal of Economics*, vol. 110, pp. 495-525.

Kaldor, N. (1957), 'A model of economic growth', *Economic Journal*, vol. 67.

Kremer, M. (1993), 'Population growth and technological change: one million BC to 1990', *Quarterly Journal of Economics*, vol. 108, pp. 681-717.

Krugman, P. (1995), *Development, Geography and Economic Theory*, MIT Press.

Kurz, H. (1996), 'What could the 'new' growth theory teach Smith or Ricardo', *Economic Issues*, vol. 2, pp. 1-19.

Landes, D. (1998), *The Wealth and Poverty of Nations*, Little Brown, New York.

Lucas, R.E. (1988), 'On the mechanics of economic development', *Journal of Monetary Economics*, vol. 22, pp. 3-42.

Lundvall, B.A. (1992), *National Systems of Innovation: Towards a Theory of Innovation and Interactive Learning*, London: Pinter.

McKelvey, M. (1996), *Evolutionary Innovations: The Business of Biotechnology*, Oxford University Press.

Manuelli, R. and Jones, L. (1996), 'The sources of growth', *Journal of Economic Dynamics and Control*, vol. 21, pp.75-114.

Marshall, A. (1919), *Industry and Trade*, London: Macmillan.

Metcalfe, J.S. (1995), 'The design of order: notes on evolutionary principles and the dynamics of innovation', *Revue Economique*, Vol. 46, pp. 327-46.

Metcalfe, J.S. (1998), *Evolutionary Economics and Creative Destruction*, Routledge.

Mokyr, J. (1990), *The Lever of Riches*, Oxford University Press.

Murman,P.,1998, "Knowledge and Competitive Advantage in the Synthetic Dye Industry:1850-1914, The Coevolution of Firms,Technology and National Institutions in Great Britain, Germany and the United States", Ph.d dissertation, Columbia University.

Nelson, R. (1989), 'Industry growth accounts and production functions when techniques are idiosyncratic', *Journal of Economic Behaviour and Organization*, vol. 11, pp. 323-41.

Nelson, R. (1991), 'Why do firms differ and how does it matter?', *Strategic Management Journal*, vol. 12, pp. 61-74.

Nelson, R. (1993), *National Innovation Systems*, Oxford University Press.

Nelson R. and S. Winter (1982), *An Evolutionary Theory of Economic Change*, Belknap, Harvard.

Pasinetti, L.L. (1981), *Structural Change and Economic Growth*, Cambridge University Press.

Petroski, H. (1992), *The Evolution of Useful Things*, New York:Vintage Books.

Phelps, E. (1966), 'Models of technical progress and the golden rule of research', *Review of Economic Studies*, Vol. 33, pp. 133-45.

Phelps, E. and Winter, S. (1970), 'Optimal price policy under atomistic competition', in Phelps, E. (ed.), *Micro Foundations of Employment and Inflation Theory*, W W Norton.

Polanyi, K., C. Armstrong and H. Pearson (1957), *Trade and Markets in the Early Empires*, New York: Free Press.

Pool, R. (1997), *Beyond Engineering*, London: Oxford University Press.

Romer, P. (1986), 'Increasing returns and long-run growth', *Journal of Political Economy*, vol. 94, no. 5, pp. 1002-37.

Saviotti, P.P. and G.S. Mani (1995), 'Competition, variety and technological evolution: a replicator dynamics model', *Journal of Evolutionary Economics*, Vol. 5, pp. 369-92.

Scott, M. F.G. (1989), *A New View of Economic Growth*, Oxford University Press.

Setterfield, M. (1997), "History versus equilibrium' and the theory of economic growth', *Cambridge Journal of Economics*, Vol. 21, pp.365-78.

Silverberg, G. and B. Verspagen (1998), 'Economic growth as a evolutionary process', in J. Lesourne and A. Orléan (eds), *Advances in Self Organization and Evolutionary Economics*, London: Economica.

Targetti, P. (1992), *Nicholas Kaldor*, Oxford University Press.
Targetti, P. and A. Foti. (1997), 'Growth and productivity: a model of cumulative growth and catching up', *Cambridge Journal of Economics*, vol. 21, pp.27-43.
Usher, D. (1980), *The Measurement of Economic Growth*, London: Blackwell.
Vanberg, V.J. (1994), *Rules and Choice in Economics*, London: Routledge.
Young, A.A. (1928), 'Increasing returns and economic progress', *Economic Journal*, vol. 38, pp. 527-42.

Index